DYLAN THOMAS

a reference guide

A
Guide
to
Literature

Michael Begnal
Editor

DYLAN THOMAS

a reference guide

GEORG M.A. GASTON

G.K. HALL &CO.
70 LINCOLN STREET, BOSTON, MASS.

Library of Congress Cataloging-in-Publication Data

Gaston, Georg, 1938–
  Dylan Thomas : a reference guide.

  (A Reference guide to literature)
  Includes index.
  1. Thomas Dylan, 1914–1953—Bibliography.   I. Title.
II. Series.
Z8870.5.G37   1987   [PR6039.H52]   016.821′912   87-8552
ISBN 0-8161-8779-7

This publication is printed on permanent/durable acid-free paper
MANUFACTURED IN THE UNITED STATES OF AMERICA

Contents

The Author

Georg M.A. Gaston received his B.A. degree from Texas A&M University and his M.A. and Ph.D. degrees from Auburn University. He has taught English at Texas A&I University, North Texas State University, and Appalachian State University, where he is currently professor of English. His writing specialties are modern literature and film. He is the author of The Pursuit of Salvation: A Critical Guide to the Novels of Graham Greene (Troy, N.Y.: Whitson Publishing Co., 1984), Karel Reisz (Boston: Twayne Publishers, 1980), and Jack Clayton (Boston: G.K. Hall & Co., 1981).

Preface

In attempting to provide as comprehensive and accessible a research guide to Dylan Thomas as possible, I have used the following principles. I have included what I consider the most important and useful pieces in the annotated bibliography section. Thomas has been written about more than any other English-language poet of this century. Thus, for practical reasons, I haven't cited each and every item ever written about him. That is, I have left out the passing references, the briefest descriptive review notices, the repetitive encyclopedia entries, and other such pieces that would only add to the bulk of the bibliography without adding any new or significant substance. I have had to be selective, then, but I trust I have included all of the truly important and useful critical and descriptive pieces about the poet written between 1934 and 1985.

The material in the bibliography section is arranged chronologically. Within each year the numbering is sequential and begins with number one. Thus, for example, an item cited as 1945.2 would be the second entry for the year 1945. This code is used within the text for reprints and references, and it is also used in the index.

The annotations are purposefully objective in tone. Each attempts to give the gist of the article as succinctly as possible. If the annotation assumes any unusual length, this is an indication of the article's ambition, complexity, and significance. This is true especially of book-length studies of Thomas. The page numbers that follow critical books citations, incidentally, reflect the combined total of the text plus acknowledgments, preface, and introductions that, though numbered in roman numerals, were found to have some significance.

Items unavailable for examination are indicated by an asterisk preceding the entry number. In such cases, I have noted the source of my information. As for foreign language items, I decided to include those available in French and German to give at least an impression of the international interest in Thomas.

Finally, a few words about the index are in order. It interfiles authors' names and titles. Under Thomas's name, there are important subheadings, namely his works and the primary critical aspects of the

vii

man and his art. As exhaustive as the index is, however, it can't
serve as a complete substitute for a systematic examination of the
bibliographical entries themselves. Many entries, reflecting the
nature of the subject, wind up covering a multitude of aspects.
Thus, the index attempts to refer to the most important, not all,
issues of the individual entries.

During the writing of this work, I had some help for which I am
grateful. I wish to thank the administrators and staffs of the following libraries: Appalachian State University, Clemson University,
Converse College, Davidson College, Florida State University, Furman
University, University of North Carolina at Chapel Hill, University
of North Carolina at Greensboro, University of South Carolina, University of Texas, and Wake Forest University. Most of all, I wish
to thank Professor Karen Carmean for invaluable research help and
support.

Introduction

During the last half century the reputation of Dylan Thomas has had a peculiar history. Until he died in 1953 at the age of thirty-nine, it actually rose steadily and consistently both in England and the United States. In England his reputation owed something to the fact that he was a familiar voice on the B.B.C. and that he was perceived as something of a rebel against the entrenched classical, intellectual tradition represented by T.S. Eliot and W.H. Auden. With few exceptions, he was applauded for writing a new kind of poetry, one that was particularly marked by passion, lyricism, and experimental language. There were some outspoken detractors, notably Geoffrey Grigson, David Holbrook, and the Scrutiny writers. They faulted Thomas for the apparently willful obscurity and the perceived intellectual shallowness of his poems. Many critics, however, and especially fellow-poets came to his defense. Among his more prominent English champions were Edith Sitwell, Stephen Spender, and William Empson. These three figures, incidentally, like many other of Thomas's readers, were won over after initial disapproval of his early, highly ambiguous poetry.

In the United States, Thomas's stock was rising even higher, especially once he started to give reading tours. As a result of these tours, he became something of a culture hero, certainly among young poetry lovers. To many academicians and fellow-poets, he represented the welcome voice of poetic renewal. Such figures as Conrad Aiken, Karl Shapiro, and John Malcolm Brinnin were particularly outspoken in their praise of Thomas; but it seemed that just about the whole American literary world was drawn to him and applauded his creative example. His example of personal behavior was a different matter. During these tours, Thomas behaved quite unconventionally, and stories about his drinking, womanizing, and all-round irresponsible behavior began to circulate. Gossip about his notorious acts took root, and the Thomas "legend" began to grow. Nevertheless, until the very end of his life, this personal reputation didn't seriously interfere with his poetic reputation. In the United States he was generally praised as a still developing young writer of difficult but splendid lyric poetry.

Everything changed dramatically in 1953. The Collected Poems volume came out, and it was met with nearly universal approval. Some

critics even began to consider him as possibly the major poet who
would now give a center to the contemporary poetic scene. This was
also the year when <u>Under Milk Wood</u> appeared, a play-for-voices wel-
comed as an example of unusual dramatic brilliance. Moreover, critical luminaries like Elder Olson were elevating Thomas's stature
through full-length studies of his work. Then he suddenly died.

For several years thereafter Thomas became the hot literary
topic, with the written commentary about his various aspects eventually growing to enormous proportions. As far as sheer numbers of
items are concerned, the nature of the man, or often the legend,
dominated the discussion until rather recently. It seems that Thomas
knew or met just about everyone connected to the literary world, and
these persons, being writers, all apparently felt they had a special
understanding of the man that they must share. Thus a flood of
reminiscences, tributes, and descriptive episodes followed Thomas's
death, eventually culminating in several full-length biographies and
biographical memoirs. Because the life Thomas led was, to say the
least, unusual for a poet, all the biographical material that has
sprung up around his memory has had a destructive side effect. The
story of his life, which every year became more legendary, was certainly interesting. But its sensational notoriety became so powerful
in the end that it had a distorting influence on the appreciation of
his creative achievements.

Fortunately, ever since Thomas first appeared as a published
poet, there were always those critics and commentators who thought the
work ultimately more important than the personality of the man or the
legend. Through the years, they have found in Thomas a great variety
of subjects and aspects that are fascinating and worthy of serious
discussion. Some of these are rather recent appreciations--for
example, his talents in the areas of radio, film, and children's
literature. But, all along, the main body of serious criticism
focusing on his work has grown up around four categories: Thomas's
craft, religion, Welshness, and influential reputation. Because
these categories (in addition to his life and fame) have been of
primary critical interest, they are subheaded under Thomas's name in
the index.

Looking back at the enormous bibliography that has grown up
around Thomas, one has to be impressed by the vitality of the subject. The most important question, however, has still not been
resolved, and may not be for many years to come. Most people now
agree that Thomas was an important poet who influenced his time.
But what about his future reputation? Will he eventually be judged
as a major poet of timeless value? The next wave of Thomas scholarship will perhaps answer one of the most intriguing literary ques-
tions of our age.

Writings by Dylan Thomas

18 Poems. London: Sunday Referee & Parton Bookshop, 1934
Twenty-five Poems. London: J.M. Dent, 1936
The Map of Love. London: J.M. Dent, 1939
The World I Breathe. Norfolk, Conn.: New Directions, 1939
Portrait of the Artist as a Young Dog. London: J.M. Dent; Norfolk,
  Conn.: New Directions, 1940
Deaths and Entrances. London: J.M. Dent, 1946
Selected Writings of Dylan Thomas. New York: New Directions, 1946
In Country Sleep and Other Poems. New York: New Directions, 1952
Collected Poems, 1934-1952. London: J.M. Dent, 1952; New York:
  New Directions, 1953
The Doctor and the Devils. London: J.M. Dent; New York: New
  Directions, 1953
Under Milk Wood. London: J.M. Dent; New York: New Directions, 1954
Quite Early One Morning. London: J.M. Dent; New York: New
  Directions, 1954
A Prospect of the Sea and Other Stories and Prose Writings. London:
  J.M. Dent, 1955
Adventures in the Skin Trade and Other Stories. New York: New
  Directions, 1955
Letters to Vernon Watkins. London: J.M. Dent; New York: New
  Directions, 1957
The Beach of Falesá. New York: Stein & Day, 1963; London:
  Jonathan Cape, 1964
Twenty Years A-Growing. London: J.M. Dent, 1964
Rebecca's Daughters. London: Triton; Boston: Little, Brown, 1965
Me and My Bike. New York: McGraw-Hill; London: Triton, 1965
Selected Letters of Dylan Thomas. London: J.M. Dent, 1966
The Notebooks of Dylan Thomas. New York: New Directions, 1967
Dylan Thomas: The Poems. London: J.M. Dent, 1971
Dylan Thomas: Early Prose Writings. New York: New Directions, 1971
Selected Poems of Dylan Thomas. London: J.M. Dent, 1974
The Death of the King's Canary. New York: Viking, 1976 (with John
  Davenport)
A Child's Christmas in Wales. London: J.M. Dent, 1978
Dylan Thomas: The Collected Stories. London: J.M. Dent, 1983
A Visit to Grandpa's and Other Stories. London: J.M. Dent, 1984
The Collected Letters of Dylan Thomas. London: J.M. Dent, 1985
The Outing. London: J.M. Dent, 1985

Writings about Dylan Thomas, 1934–1985

1934

1   "Our Literary 'Gangsters'; Young Poet Attacks Modern Writers."
    Sunday Referee, 30 December, p. 3.
        Quotes Thomas's views on contemporary writers. They mostly
    move around "in gangs," lacking "the strength to stand and fight
    as individuals."

2   "Poet's Corner." Sunday Referee, 25 November, p. 16.
        Covers prize-winning commentary by A.E. Trick about "Foster
    the light." Thomas is distinguished as the "best exponent" of
    those modern poets who treat words like "vials" into which mean-
    ing is poured.

3   SITWELL, EDITH. Aspects of Modern Poetry. London: Duckworth,
    pp. 149-50.
        Criticizes the style of "Our eunuch dreams." Claims that
    the "thick" and "muddy" language defeats criticism.

4   WILLIAMS, J.D. "Our Young Poets." South Wales Evening Post,
    19 November, p. 4.
        Anticipates an up-coming volume of poetry by Thomas and
    claims that he "is now definitely placed by critics among our
    'coming men.'"

1935

1   ENGLE, PAUL, and LEWIS, CECIL DAY. "Modern Poetry--English
    and American." Listener 13 (15 May):852-54.
        Discuss the situation of modern poetry, with Lewis select-
    ing "Especially when the October wind" for special consideration.

2   HAWKINS, DESMOND. Review of 18 Poems. Time and Tide 16
    (9 February):204, 206.
        Sees 18 Poems as a breakthrough volume of poetry. Credits
    Thomas with "being the first considerable poet to break through
    fashionable limitation and speak an unborrowed language" since
    the Audenesque domination.

1

3   PARSONS, I.M. "New Verse." Spectator 154 (26 April):704.
    Reviews 18 Poems, noting the impressively "complex and
    exotic vocabulary" which has the danger of sliding into
    obscurity.

4   Review of 18 Poems. European Quarterly, February, p. 274.
    Praises 18 Poems as "one of the most remarkable books of
    poetry" of recent years.

5   Review of 18 Poems. Listener 13 (27 February):381.
    Praises Thomas's "purely poetic force."

6   Review of 18 Poems. Times Literary Supplement, 14 March,
    p. 163.
    Admits that Thomas's language is "peculiar," yet applauds
    the poet's "imaginative audacities," especially when he is trans-
    forming the human condition into physiological or mechanical
    terms, or when he expresses "the correspondence between the
    forces informing the macrocosm and the microcosm."

7   ROBERTS, MICHAEL. Review of 18 Poems. Criterion 14 (April):
    496-99.
    Calls Thomas "the most striking of the new poets" appearing
    the past year. Although there is some exaggerated interest in
    the technical side of language, he must be admired for the way he
    is able to "stamp a traditional metre with an honest contemporary
    accent" and for his ability to exploit the subconscious subject
    and pattern.

8   SITWELL, EDITH, and HERRING, ROBERT. "A Correspondence on the
    Young English Poets." Life and Letters Today 13 (December):
    16-24.
    Praises Thomas as one of the young poets who "seems to me
    [to Edith Sitwell] to show most remarkable promise." "He has not
    found himself yet, for he is entangled in a perfect web of com-
    plexes, mainly about the human body."

9   TRICK, A.E. "The New Poetry." South Wales Evening Post,
    12 January, p. 4.
    Characterizes Thomas's poetry as having the quality of
    "granite--hard, shed of all romantic illusions."

10 WILLIAMS, J.D. "Gossip of the Day: Poems of Dylan Thomas."
    South Wales Evening Post, 1 January, p. 4.
    Puts Thomas "at the spear-head" of the latest movement in
    modern poetry.

                                1936

1   E., J.H. "Analysis of Poetry." Poetry Review 27 (November-
    December):486.
    Comments on Twenty-five Poems in the course of discussing
    the current state of poetry and criticism. Thomas is recognized

for having "outstanding talent" and "fine emotions," but he is
criticized for a lack of reason and intellectualism.

2   GRIGSON, GEOFFREY. "A Letter from England." Poetry
    (November):101-3.
        Comments unfavorably on Thomas's second volume of poems,
    going so far as to say that "twenty-four twenty-fifths of them
    are psychological nonsense put down with a remarkable ineptitude
    in technique."

3   Review of Twenty-five Poems. Times Literary Supplement,
    19 September, p. 750.
        Complains that Thomas's idiom can be as obscure as a
    "foreign tongue." But the impressive "originality" of his
    language can certainly be appreciated in such "simpler" poems as
    "This bread I break" or in the "magnificent" lyric "And death
    shall have no dominion."

4   ROBERTS, MICHAEL. "The Brassy Orator." London Mercury 34
    (October):555.
        Reviews Twenty-five Poems, faulting Thomas with slipping
    into "mere riot of noise" at times because he has a tendency to
    let "purely verbal associations . . . run away with him."

5   SITWELL, EDITH. "Four New Poets." London Mercury 33
    (February):386-88.
        Praises Thomas as a young poet of great promise. He is
    sometimes "a prey to his subconscious self, and consequently
    obscure; but from that subconscious self rise . . . lines which
    are transmuted by his conscious self into really great poetry,
    whose truth has been lived with the most profound intensity."

6   WILLIAMS, J.D. "The New Poems of Dylan Thomas." Herald of
    Wales, 19 September, pp. 1, 12.
        Reviews Twenty-five Poems. Admits that, being a "child of
    the Victorian Day," he is often out of his depths with Thomas's
    poetry; but he can still be "thrilled" by some of the splendid,
    eloquent imagery.

                                1937

1   ARMITAGE, GILBERT. Review of Twenty-five Poems. English
    Review 64 (February):255-56.
        Reviews Thomas's second volume of poetry, complimenting
    him on his genuine talent and vision but complaining about the
    obscure and surrealistic qualities of the verse.

2   BONNEROT, LOUIS. Review of Twenty-five Poems. Études
    anglaises 1 (January):79-80.
        Comments on the obscurity found in Thomas's second volume
    of poetry.

1938

1   MacNEICE, LOUIS. Modern Poetry: A Personal Essay. London:
     Oxford University Press, p. 160.
        Complains about Thomas's obscurity and apparent incoherence,
     but praises him for having more humanity than "the official
     surrealists."

2   SAVAGE, D.S. "London Letter." Poetry, February, pp. 277–88.
        Points to Thomas as the "outstanding" figure among the
     young poets of the time.

3   TREECE, HENRY. "Dylan Thomas and the Surrealists." Seven 3
     (Winter):27–30.
        Notes some "apparent coincidences" between Thomas and the
     surrealists.

1939

1   FITZGERALD, WILLIAM. "Make It New--Or Else!" Poetry 53
     (January):209–14.
        Reviews the 1938 edition of New Directions, praising in
     the process Thomas's story "The Orchards" as the most successful
     prose piece in the volume.

2   GRIGSON, GEOFFREY. "Poetry Politics in London: Continued."
     Poetry 54 (April):52–54.
        Reacts to D.S. Savage's claims that Thomas "forced" his way
     into the pages of New Verse and that he along with George Barker
     represented the "two most vital forces" in contemporary English
     poetry.

3   HAWKINS, DESMOND. "Recent Poetry." Spectator 163
     (25 August):300–301.
        Given The Map of Love, Thomas "is still difficult to
     assess, but the abundance of his gifts is unquestioned." His
     imagery is the "self-consistent idiom of a distinctive vision."

4   HAYS, H.R. "Surrealist Influences in Contemporary English and
     American Poetry." Poetry 56 (July):202–9.
        Places Thomas on the periphery of contemporary surrealist
     writers. The surrealist influence on him "seems to have taken a
     purely rhetorical form."

5   LEWIS, SAUNDERS. Is There An Anglo-Welsh Literature?
     Cardiff: Guild of Graduates of University of Wales, pp. 4–5.
        Submits that Thomas doesn't properly belong to the Anglo-
     Welsh tradition. He "is obviously an equipped writer, but there
     is nothing hyphenated about him." Thomas "belongs to the
     English."

6   MUIR, EDWIN. <u>The Present Age from 1914</u>. London: Cresset
    Press; New York: McBride, 1940, pp. 220-21.
        Finds that Thomas's poetry has the magic of "Celtic genius"
    filled, like George Barker's, with decadence.   While praised for
    having lines of "extraordinary beauty and imaginative force," the
    writing is finally criticized for being too obscure in meaning.

7   READ, HERBERT.   "The Map of Love." <u>Seven</u> 6 (Autumn):19-20.
        Proposes that with <u>The Map of Love</u> Thomas has proved his
    "poetic genius."   He has now matured to the point where he has
    complete mastery of his art.

8   _____.   "The Present State of Poetry: In England." <u>Kenyon</u>
    <u>Review</u> 1 (Autumn):359-69.
        Looks at the contemporary poetry scene in England and
    doesn't find too many hopeful signs for the future.   But Thomas
    is one of them, particularly since he represents a turn to an
    intense awareness of the less intellectual nature of the art.
    His writing calls for "an acute awareness of contemporary images
    and rhythms . . . which are at the same time primeval and
    elliptical."

9   Review of <u>The Map of Love</u>. <u>Listener</u> 22 (19 October):780, 782.
        Notes the uniqueness of Thomas's poetry.   Thomas is a
    "bard."   He is a nonintellectual who "expresses elemental pas-
    sions and extreme conditions of human existence . . . in an
    enlarged and primitive Welsh landscape."

10 Review of <u>The Map of Love</u>. <u>Times Literary Supplement</u>,
    26 August, p. 499.
        Begins by emphasizing Thomas's "extraordinary imaginative"
    talent but goes on to complain that his vision tends to be
    "excessively subjective."   The least successful pieces are
    "clotted with the figurative" and project "visionary chaos."

11 RICE, PHILIP BLAIR.   "Twenty-five Directions." <u>Kenyon Review</u>
    1 (Winter):109-11.
        Isolates Thomas as "the most gifted and original" poet
    represented in James Laughlin's 1938 edition of <u>New Directions</u>.
    Based, however, on the evidence of such verse as "Poem for
    Caitlin," Thomas is influenced too obviously by Hopkins and the
    earlier Auden, and his style tends to be "extremely rococo."

12 SAVAGE, D.S.   "Poetry Politics in London." <u>Poetry</u> 53
    (January):200-208.
        Distinguishes Thomas and George Barker as "probably the two
    most vital forces in English poetry today."

13 TYLER, PARKER.   "The Poetic Athlete." <u>Seven</u> 4 (Spring):20-25.
        Responds to Henry Treece's discovery of surrealistic quali-
    ties in Thomas's poetry (see Treece, 1938.3).   Thomas is a writer
    who "shares with the Surrealists their subconscious fantasy
    without dealing in any sense with their aesthetic irony, their
    disguised ethical pre-occupation."

1940

1   AIKEN, CONRAD. "A Rocking Alphabet." Poetry 56 (June):59-61.
Celebrates Thomas as a "restorer and re-creator" of language "at its most vascular and vital." Welcomes his influence after the "monkish snobbism" of Eliot and Pound. Reprinted: 1940.1; 1968.1.

2   _____. "Poetry: 1940 Model." New Republic 102 (22 April): 540-41.
Reprint of 1940.1.

3   BATES, H.E. Review of Portrait of the Artist as a Young Dog. Fortnightly 148 (July):111-12.
Dismisses Portrait of the Artist as the work of "the young puppy of contemporary poetry." Thomas "chases" his "tail" and seems "to suffer from the slightly cock-sure impression that he is doing it for the first time."

4   BERRYMAN, JOHN. "The Loud Hills of Wales." Kenyon Review 2 (Autumn):481-85.
Comments on the distinctive qualities of Thomas's poetry while reviewing The World I Breathe. The "unmistakable signature" of this poet is the "exciting," fresh use of diction. His new language can be difficult, but the charge of obscurity against him has been exaggerated.

5   DREW, ELIZABETH, and SWEENEY, JOHN L. "The Nineteen Thirties." In Directions in Modern Poetry. New York: W.W. Norton, pp. 110-12 passim.
Claims that Thomas depends "directly" on the Christian and Celtic traditions, "spinning this heritage into a vital human symbolism."

6   EDEL, LEON. "The Poet as Journalist." Poetry 58 (July):219.
Reviewing Oscar Williams's anthology New Poems: 1940, he makes a complimentary mention of Thomas's "physical verse."

7   FITTS, DUDLEY. "Poetry." Saturday Review 22 (11 May):20.
Reviews The World I Breathe, praising Thomas's virtuosity but finding him lacking in substance, and hence not a "great" poet.

8   FLEMING, EDWARD VANDERMERE. "The Old and the New." Poetry Review 31 (January-February):38-40.
Heaps contempt on the poetry in The Map of Love. Thinks it is "turgid" nonsense that "will never do." But the prose pieces, though "not pleasant reading," reveal "traces of strange, imaginative power" remindful of Poe.

9   GRIGSON, GEOFFREY. "New Poetry." Horizon 1 (January):57-59.
Reviews The Map of Love, finding some "ripe nonsense" but also some improvement in Thomas's craft.

10   HAUSER, MARIANNE. "Sketches of Youth." New York Times Book
      Review, 29 December, pp. 4, 14.
         Reviews Portrait of the Artist, calling special attention
      to the way the stories gain "clarity and form" by means of a
      successful joining of "style and mood."

11   "Literary Young Man." Times Literary Supplement, 6 April,
      p. 173.
         Reviews Portrait of the Artist, admitting that Thomas has
      a highly original and imaginative way with language but complain-
      ing that the stylistic effects don't make up for "so bodiless an
      illusion of experience." In a novel, "something steadier and
      more whole of vision is needed."

12   MAYNARD, THEODORE. "The New Artificiality." Virginia
      Quarterly Review 16 (Spring):311–14.
         Dismisses Thomas as one of the young poets (along with
      Kenneth Patchen, Muriel Rukeyser, and Revel Denney) whose reputed
      originality is "only sedulously sought novelty." In The World I
      Breathe, everything is "graceful; nothing sticks."

13   MELLERS, W.H. "The Bard and the Prep-School." Scrutiny 9
      (July):76–80.
         Reviews Portrait of the Artist, objecting to its roman-
      tically adolescent quality. The problem with Thomas "grown up"
      resides in the fact that "his interests . . . are identical with
      those of . . . the child. Because he is in fact no longer a
      child he feels that he must needs falsify these . . . desires,"
      with the result that his writing "becomes pivoted on himself, an
      orgy of self-commiseration."

14   Review of Portrait of the Artist as a Young Dog. Nation 151
      (23 November):512.
         Calls it a "rare book" about "unfolding sensibility."

15   RITCHEY, JOHN. "The World of Poetry." Christian Science
      Monitor, 23 November, p. 12.
         Recommends Portrait of the Artist as a way to discover the
      motivations that lie behind Thomas's more difficult poems.

16   ROSENFELD, PAUL. "Decadence and Dylan Thomas." Nation 150
      (23 March):399–400.
         Criticizes the writing in The World I Breathe for the
      decadent, "drunken" way in which Thomas sacrifices meaning "to
      the splendors of form, sonority, sensuous effect." Finds that
      the essentials of "emotive and intuitive meanings" hardly exist
      in the poetry.

17   SCARFE, FRANCIS. "The Poetry of Dylan Thomas." Horizon,
      November, pp. 226–39.
         Notices that Thomas's poetry, from the early years, has
      three "dominant points of contact" (Joyce, the Bible, and Freud)
      and that his habits of language and mythology can be discovered
      through these influences, so that the "key" to understanding

Thomas's world is to take into account the linguistic, mythologi-
cal, and psycho-pathological sources. Adds that his "outstanding
merit" resides in his "rich vocabulary, his sensual appreciation
of words, his intense persuasive idiom" that show him "reaching
towards all that is most living in our language." Reprinted:
1942.1; 1960.5.

18   "Story Contrasts." Times (London), 6 April, p. 11.
      Reviews Portrait of the Artist. The stories are told with
great "clarity and animation," in a style that has "the beauty
to be found in a well-designed instrument that is well cared for
and often used."

19   SYMONS, JULIAN. "Obscurity and Dylan Thomas." Kenyon Review
      2 (Winter):61–71.
      Finds Thomas's poetry too willfully obscure, the result of
the attempt to "conceal" through mannered technique the funda-
mentally "simple matter" of his poetry. His poems often are
"jokes, rhetorical intellectual fakes of the highest class."
Like Swinburne, he lacks exactness, suggesting a great deal while
actually saying little.

20   THOMPSON, DUNSTAN. "Time for Terror." New Republic 102
      (1 April):447–48.
      Finds some "false notes" in The World I Breathe, but also
praises Thomas's work for being "exceedingly rich and strange."

21   TREECE, HENRY. "An Apocalyptic Writer and the Surrealists."
      In The New Apocalypse. Edited by J.F. Hendry. London:
      Fortune Press, pp. 49–58.
      Considers Thomas in the context of the New Apocalypse
"movement" and surrealism, which he criticizes for tending to be
an exercise in Freudian psychotherapeutics.

22   TYLER, PARKER. Review of The World I Breathe. Fantasy 6,
      no. 4:71–73.
      Looking at The World I Breathe, the critic comes to the
conclusion that Thomas's "problem" is how far the sexual theme
can be "mentalized" by means of "elaborate metaphoric-analogic
reconstruction" without proving "tiresome" to both reader and
poet.

23   VERSCHOYLE, DEREK. "Mr. Dylan Thomas." Spectator 164
      (5 April):496.
      Reviews Portrait of the Artist. Although Thomas tends to
be wordy at times, he still gives us a vivid depiction of "the
adolescent life of a neurotic and tormented boy."

1941

1   BATES, H.E. The Modern Short Story: A Critical Survey. London: Thomas Nelson, p. 211.
      Notes the uniqueness of Thomas's "dream-fantasy" stories, crediting him with pointing the short story form in a new direction by way of his "lavish poetic delirium."

2   BREIT, HARVEY. "View of the World." Poetry 59 (December): 160.
      Comparing him to George Barker, he feels that Thomas "seems imprisoned in his morbidity."

3   BYRNE, BARRY. Review of Portrait of the Artist as a Young Dog. Commonweal 33 (10 January):307.
      The surrealistic quality of the writing makes it seem dated.

4   DUBOIS, ARTHUR E. Review of Portrait of the Artist as a Young Dog. Fantasy 7, no. 1:75-76.
      Praises the stories for the "real but strange characters" and "self-conscious prose." But complains that the book "adds nothing to technique or sophistication" as far as the art of autobiographical fiction is concerned.

5   FRASER, GEORGE SUTHERLAND. "Apocalypse in Poetry." In The White Horseman. Edited by J.F. Hendry and Henry Treece. London: Routledge, pp. 3-31.
      Categorizes Thomas as one of the Apocalyptic poets because he "responds to a situation" instead of "a play of ideas." He, like others of the Apocalyptic movement, is a "romantic" whose work reflects the disintegration of society.

1942

1   SCARFE, FRANCIS. "Dylan Thomas: A Pioneer." In Auden and After. London: Routledge & Sons, pp. 101-17.
      Reprint of 1940.17. Reprinted: 1960.5.

1943

1   AVISON, MARGARET. Review of New Poems. Canadian Forum 23 (September):143.
      Reviewing New Poems leads this critic to exclaim that Thomas's poetry "calls for attack." "A new expression is being forged in these pages, the din and flying sparks thicken in the air."

2   BENÉT, WILLIAM ROSE. "The Season's Poetry." <u>Saturday Review</u> 26 (16 October):23-24, 64.

Glancing at the newly published poetry, he mentions Thomas as "a young man still to watch."

3   DAICHES, DAVID. "Contemporary Poetry in Britain." <u>Poetry</u> 62 (June):150-64.

Discussed as part of the Apocalypse movement, Thomas is noted for his "great significance" in restoring passionate imagery and "intensity of utterance" to English poetry.

4   FITTS, DUDLEY. "The New Poetry." <u>Saturday Review</u> 26 (28 August):8-9.

Rates Thomas below Wallace Stevens, but finds that <u>New Poems</u> is far superior to <u>The World I Breathe</u>. Now Thomas "no longer gives the impression of addressing himself solely to the anesthetist."

5   GREGORY, HORACE. "Three Younger Poets in Review." <u>New York Times Book Review</u>, 25 July, p. 19.

Finds that in <u>New Poems</u>, Thomas sustains the "promise of his early poems" in a "brilliant" fashion. Though at times he seems to lose control of precisely what he desires to say, his readers "are rewarded by the presence of a definite personality."

6   Review of <u>These Are the Men</u>. <u>Documentary News Letter</u> 4 (February):174-75.

Praises Thomas's contribution (as the author of the commentary and verse) to the documentary film. His language "cuts like a knife into the pompously bestial affectations" of the Nazis depicted.

7   RODITI, EDOUARD. "The Unspoken Word." <u>Poetry</u> 63 (October): 48-50.

Complains about Thomas's obscurity, which brings on the feeling that "the poet is often confusing or misleading himself almost as much as the reader."

<u>1944</u>

1   AIKEN, CONRAD. "The New Euphuism." <u>New Republic</u> 110 (3 January):26-27.

Declares that Thomas, with his violent love of language, led the reaction against the "dehydrated" fashion represented by Eliot and Auden.

2   GHISELIN, BREWSTER. "Use of a Mango." <u>Rocky Mountain Review</u> 8 (Spring):111-12.

Reviews <u>New Poems</u>, emphasizing Thomas's tendency to "squeeze" his lines with "meaning and often with unusual matter." Compares the demands his poetry places on the imagination to those brought on by Wallace Stevens's work.

3   STEARNS, MARSHALL W. "Unsex the Skeleton: Notes on the
Poetry of Dylan Thomas." Sewanee Review 52 (July-September):
424-40.
   Makes an early case for the importance of Thomas as an
influential, original poet. Provides a systematic discussion of
his major themes (man, sex, and religion) and predominant technique (dialectical imagery). Reprinted: 1945.5; 1960.33.

4   UNTERMEYER, LOUIS. "Eight Poets." Yale Review 33 (Winter):
348-51.
   Compares Thomas with Kenneth Patchen for the originality
and excitement to be discovered in New Poems. While Patchen
achieves excitement "by sheer force," Thomas achieves it "by
leaping images and wild associations."

5   WANNING, ANDREWS. "Poetry in Wartime." Partisan Review 11
(Spring):212-13.
   Reviews New Poems, expressing some disappointment with the
conscious "progress toward logical lucidity." Compared to
earlier poems, the new ones appear more "contrived and rhetorical" and have a less "explosive" nature.

1945

1   HOFFMAN, FREDERICK J. Freudianism and the Literary Mind.
Baton Rouge: Louisiana State University Press, pp. 295-99.
   Discovers the influence of Freud in the young writer.
Thomas's "insight into the unconscious self is linked with a
maturing sensitivity to the mystery and charm of sex" and to "a
certain paralyzing hesitation to realize it fully." Reprinted:
1959.10.

2   HORAN, ROBERT. "In Defense of Dylan Thomas." Kenyon Review
7 (Spring):304-10.
   Defends Thomas in letter form against the charge of being
a baroque verbalizer more interested in intricate style than
theme and meaning. He has instead a remarkable imagination that
"transforms, actively, rather than describes, passively, the
objects of his attention." "It is in an effort to bring the
diverse and almost uncontrollable poles of his observations and
sympathy into the same poem . . . that he strikes the fundamental
problem of composition and experience." Reprinted: 1960.33.

3   "Officer and Sten Gun." Welsh Gazette, 12 April, p. 6.
   Reports on a shooting spree by an Army captain inadver-
tently involving Thomas.

4   STEARNS, MARSHALL W. "Dylan Thomas's 'After the funeral.'"
Explicator 3 (May): item 52.
   Explicates "After the funeral," noting that the poem falls
into two sections: the depiction of the burial and praise of the
beloved dead.

5   ____. "Unsex the Skeleton: Notes on the Poetry of Dylan
     Thomas." In Transformation Three. Edited by Stefan Shimanski
     and Henry Treece. London: Lindsay Drummond, pp. 145-58.
     Reprint of 1944.3. Reprinted: 1960.33.

                              1946

1   BRINNIN, JOHN MALCOLM. "Dylan Thomas' Poems." New York Times
     Book Review, 8 December, p. 24.
          Declares that, with the publication of The Selected
     Writings of Dylan Thomas, it was evident that Thomas had extended
     England's great poetic tradition through his "revolutionary uses
     of poetic craft and sensibility." His essential method is that
     of "metaphorical logic--successive 'explosions of meaning,'
     rather than a point-by-point distribution of thematic elements."

2   COBLENTZ, STANTON A. "What Are They--Poems or Puzzles?" New
     York Times Magazine, 13 October, pp. 24, 50-51, 53.
          Depicts Thomas as one of the writers behind the unfortunate
     tendencies of modern poetry to gravitate toward obscurity, freak-
     ishness, ugliness, exhibitionism, and chaos. Instead of follow-
     ing the honored tradition of conveying "high thoughts and pro-
     found feelings," modern poetry has chosen instead to "shock and
     startle."

3   "Passionate Pilgrim." Time 48 (2 December):112.
          Reviews New Direction's publication of The Selected
     Writings. The selections illustrate that Thomas is the "most
     spectacular and distinguished younger poet" in Britain. His
     writing is full of "word magic and feverish, often fervent pas-
     sions," all finally dedicated to celebrate sensual man and joyful
     existence. The introduction by John L. Sweeney is a very helpful
     summary of the poet's beliefs and background (see Sweeney,
     1946.12).

4   Review of Deaths and Entrances. Wind and the Rain 3 (Autumn):
     159-62.
          Compares Thomas's poetry in Deaths and Entrances with
     Robert Graves's in Poems, 1938-1945. "To leave the rapt
     ecstasies of Dylan Thomas's personal vision for the more ob-
     jective world delineated by Robert Graves is to find ourselves
     at once in a more temperate zone; and some natures will feel this
     a considerable advantage."

5   Review of The Selected Writings. New York Herald Tribune Book
     Review 23 (15 December):20.
          Notes that John L. Sweeney (see Sweeney, 1946.12) finds
     Thomas to be a poet who tries "fearlessly" to discover and ex-
     press his selfhood.

6   Review of The Selected Writings. New Yorker 22 (21 December): 99.
    Notes that Thomas's surrealistic tendencies are less obvious than they were previously.

7   RHYS, KEIDRYCH. "Contemporary Welsh Literature." British Annual of Literature 3:17–22.
    Links Thomas with a renaissance of contemporary Welsh literature. Sees Thomas as basically an urban writer.

8   SAVAGE, D.S. "The Poetry of Dylan Thomas." New Republic 114 (29 April):618–22.
    Greets the publication of Deaths and Entrances as further evidence of Thomas's being a major poet whose work "provides a touchstone for current poetic practice and appreciation." A brief survey of his development begins by stressing the fact that he is "first of all a maker" of "verbal structures." Reprinted: 1960.33.

9   SEYMORE, WILLIAM KEAN. "Poets and Pretenders." Poetry Review 37 (April-May):126–29.
    Complains about the prevalence of pretentious, self-consciously clever writing masquerading as poetry. Points to Thomas's Deaths and Entrances as exemplifying "lucubrations without light."

10 SPENDER, STEPHEN. "Dylan Thomas, George Barker, David Gascoyne." In Poetry Since 1939. London: Longmans, Green, pp. 44–50.
    Declares that Thomas is something of a genius and that he is one of the poets of the younger generation reacting against "a conscious and intellectual" way of writing and choosing instead "the involuntary, the mysterious, the word-intoxicated, the romantic and the Celtic."

11 _____. "Poetry For Poetry's Sake and Poetry Beyond Poetry." Horizon 13 (April):233–34.
    Sees Thomas as an "opaque" poet who mainly "writes poetry for poetry's sake." To him "every vivid impression for which he can find a suitable image is poetry." His "virtues" are "words, rhetoric, violent imagery."

12 SWEENEY, JOHN L. Introduction to Selected Writings of Dylan Thomas. New York: New Directions, pp. vii-xxiii.
    Notes the paradox of Thomas's religion. He had a "devout" nature but he was anything but conventional in his religion.

13 "Symbolism of To-Day." Times Literary Supplement, 9 March, p. 116.
    Reviews Deaths and Entrances. Compared with his earlier poetry, Thomas now writes with greater "clarity and fervid observation." The poet's love of language is pronounced, as is his "inherent religious respect." More deeply than before, he is

13

"the Celt seriously inquiring with a sensual rationalism into man's existence in the scheme of things."

14 TREECE, HENRY. "Gerard Manley Hopkins and Dylan Thomas." In How I See Apocalypse. London: Lindsay Drummond, pp. 129-39.
Claims that Thomas is the only poet worth mentioning who was influenced both in style and subject matter by Hopkins. Draws his conclusion in large part by placing selected passages and works from the two poets against each other. Reprinted: 1960.5.

15 TURNER, W.J. "A Major Poet." Spectator 176 (8 February):148, 150.
Reviews Deaths and Entrances, concluding that this is the work of a "major" poet. Thomas is praised for being original yet traditional, imperfect yet exceptional, "with the unmistakable fire and power of genius."

16 WILLIAMS, OSCAR, ed. A Little Treasury of Modern Poetry. New York: Charles Scribner's Sons, pp. 25 passim.
Defends Thomas against the charge of writing poems of obscure nonsense. Praises him for bringing back poetry marked by the release of immediate emotions and anthologizes ten selections to illustrate the importance of this new writer.

17 WRIGHT, DAVID. Review of Deaths and Entrances. World Review, June, p. 69.
Praises Thomas's new volume of poetry for containing some of the best poems of the decade. Special praise is given to Thomas's "profound apocalyptic imagery."

1947

1 ARMSTRONG, MARTIN. "The Spoken Word." Listener 38 (16 October):695.
Comments on Thomas's reading ability. "At his best" he is a "fine performer," but he sometimes has a "lack of control."

2 BERRYMAN, JOHN. "Lowell, Thomas, etc." Partisan Review 14 (January-February):81-82.
Reviews The Selected Writings and declares that here is "one of the three best poets writing in England." Thomas follows the unwritten law that fine poets "do not develop." His poems as a whole are "about breaking loose," and it's a "delight" to see how he expresses this theme with continuing "intensity and freshness."

3 BUNKER, ROBERT. Review of Selected Writings. New Mexico Quarterly Review 17 (Summer):385-86.
Applauds New Directions for opening their new series of "selected writings" with the Thomas volume.

4 "Eleventh Letter." <u>Poetry</u> (London) 11 (September-October): 5-8.
    Responds to an attack on Thomas by Geoffrey Grigson.

5 EMPSON, WILLIAM. "Death and Transfiguration." <u>Nation</u> 164 (22 February):214-16.
    Prefers Thomas's early poems because they have the concentration of "exploding bombs," but, looking at the <u>Selected Writings</u> volume, also sees some evidence that the poet's work indicates further development in the future.

6 FIEDLER, LESLIE. "The Latest Dylan Thomas." <u>Western Review</u> 11 (Winter):103-6.
    Considers Thomas's revolutionary influence on "taste and sensibility." His writing offered the alternatives of "the self rather than the state, the myth rather than history, romantic love rather than comradeship, the apocalyptic awareness of death rather than the millenial hope of salvation."

7 GREGORY, HORACE. "Romantic Heritage in the Writings of Dylan Thomas." <u>Poetry</u> (March):326-36.
    Points out Thomas's neoromantic and regional influences, the links between his prose and poetry, and the "charm" of his unusual imagination. Thomas's remarkable sense of "immediacy" and unity is also emphasized. Reprinted: 1954.18; 1960.5.

8 HAYWARD, JOHN. <u>English Poetry</u>. Cambridge: Cambridge University Press, p. 132.
    Shows the first edition copy of <u>18 Poems</u> in this catalog of primary editions of the works of English poets.

9 LEWIS, C. DAY. <u>The Poetic Image</u>. London: Jonathan Cape; New York: Oxford University Press, pp. 122-28.
    Discusses Thomas's revolutionary technique by placing a poem of his against one by Hopkins. Suggests that Thomas's technique works best when the experience he is depicting is most "purely inward."

10 LLOYD, L.C. "On the Air." <u>Spectator</u> 178 (20 June):717.
    Praises Thomas's radio broadcast <u>Return Journey</u>, an autobiographical description of bomb-shattered Swansea.

11 LOWELL, ROBERT. "Thomas, Bishop, and Williams." <u>Sewanee Review</u> 55 (Summer):493-503.
    Compares Thomas to such poets as Pound, Hart Crane, Wallace Stevens, and Hopkins, declaring him to be a "dazzling obscure writer who can be enjoyed without understanding." "As a formal metrician, Wallace Stevens is the only living poet who can hold a candle to him." His poetry is "about light--the ecstasy of experiencing it, the agony of its deprivation, and the agony of its attainment." His main flaws are repetition, redundancy, and overloading.

15

12   MOSS, HOWARD. "Ten Poets." <u>Kenyon Review</u> 9 (Spring):290-98.
      Considers the publication of <u>Selected Writings</u> an important
event because it offers proof that here is a major poet whose
work has permanent value. Like such other "genuine creators" as
Robert Lowell and William Carlos Williams, he doesn't merely
interpret reality but constructs it. The "most original" English
poet since Hopkins, he uses a remarkable language to concentrate
primarily on the "duality of birth and death."

13   ROSS, ALAN. "Poetry: The Contemporary Landscape." <u>World
Review</u>, April, pp. 55-59.
      Includes Thomas in the discussion of the most important
current poetic figures and movements. Thomas's "timelessness,
his concern with the fundamental themes of human existence . . .
are stamped with the power of his rich personality."

14   TINDALL, WILLIAM YORK. <u>Forces in Modern British Literature</u>.
New York: Knopf, pp. 351-55 passim.
      Comments on Thomas's debts to Hegel, Empson, and, particu-
larly, Freud. Notes that his poetry falls into three recog-
nizable periods--the early Freudian poems of "womb and tomb";
the war-years poems of "ritualistic celebration of renewal"; and,
following his "reluctant acceptance" of growing domestic respon-
sibilities, the poems belonging to the so-called "period of
humanity." Reprinted: 1956.45.

1948

1   ABBOTT, CHARLES, ed. <u>Poets at Work: Essays Based on the
Modern Poetry Collection at the Lockwood Memorial Library,
University of Buffalo</u>. New York: Harcourt, Brace, pp. 164
passim.
      Contains a facsimile of a worksheet of "Ballad of the
Long-legged Bait" and occasional observations by other writers.

2   ASTRE, GEORGES-ALBERT. "Un jeune et grand poète anglais."
<u>Critique</u> 4 (January):21-29.
      Reviews <u>Deaths and Entrances</u>, <u>Selected Writings</u>, and
<u>Portrait of the Artist</u> and decides that this is the work of the
"most astonishing" English poet of the day. His images are found
to be brilliant.

3   GLOVER, C. GORDON. "Poet in a Pub." <u>Band Wagon</u>, October,
pp. 37-39.
      Interviews Thomas, who was then living close to Oxford.

4   GRIGSON, GEOFFREY. "How Much Me Now Your Acrobatics Amaze."
In <u>The Harp of Aeolus and Other Essays</u>. London: George
Routledge & Sons, pp. 151-60.
      Discusses Thomas in the context of what is referred to as
the new romanticism "without reason." Seen as a "psychological
curiosity," Thomas is taken to task for writing muddled poetry
that is essentially "inhuman and glandular." Reprinted: 1960.5,
33.

5   HUDDLESTONE, LINDEN. "An Approach to Dylan Thomas." Penguin
    New Writing 35:123-60.
        Surveys Thomas's development and accomplishments. He
    "writes against what he fears," and he "writes of what he felt
    and reasoned of elemental truth."

6   KORG, JACOB. "The Short Stories of Dylan Thomas."
    Perspective 1 (Spring):184-91.
        Looks at the eleven stories contained in The World I
    Breathe. These stories, like Thomas's poems, are seen as "the
    difficult and obscure expressions of spiritual conflict." The
    main source for the obscurity in these prose pieces is the "fact
    that imagined things are expressed in the language of factual
    statement instead of the language of metaphor."

7   LEWIS, E. GLYN. "Dylan Thomas." Welsh Review 7 (Winter):
    270-81.
        Examines the religious aspect. Concludes that he is cer-
    tainly a religious poet, but not in any conventional sense. His
    religion celebrates a "profane existence; it is imbued with an
    intense . . . feeling of unity of all forms of existence." He
    reveals a "thirst to return to primitive . . . cosmic life."
    Reprinted: 1960.33.

8   RHYS, ANEURIN. "Dylan Thomas: A Further Estimate." Poetry
    Review 39 (April-May):214-16.
        Complains that years of reading Thomas's poetry have still
    not answered the question of whether he is "a buffoon with a
    flair for poetry or a poet with a taste for buffoonery." The
    problem with his "cataclysmic vocabulary" is that it may be
    "verbally exciting" but it usually remains obscure.

9   TINDALL, WILLIAM YORK. "The Poetry of Dylan Thomas."
    American Scholar 17 (Autumn):431-39.
        Declares that Thomas is the "best and most magical" English
    poet since Yeats started to write. Compared to Yeats's "gran-
    deur," T.S. Eliot's "austerity," and W.H. Auden's "chumminess,"
    he writes with "more than Elizabethan abundance." His primary
    themes are "the nature of myth, the fall and regeneration of
    man, and the writing of a poem." Reprinted: 1964.53.

                              1949

1   BULLOUGH, GEOFFREY. "Surrealism, the New Apocalypse, Etc."
    In The Trend of Modern Poetry. Edinburgh: Oliver & Boyd,
    pp. 213-21.
        Places Thomas in the surrealistic tradition. Points out
    that the movement of his poetry is "centrifugal," with words
    breeding words, brought on by a fertility of imagination that is
    "sometimes fine" but sometimes "burns too furiously."

17

2   COMFORT, ALEX. "An Exposition of Irresponsibility." In A
     New Romantic Anthology. Edited by Stefan Schimanski and
     Henry Treece. London: Grey Walls Press, p. 33.
        Refers to Thomas in the context of a discussion about
     poetic responsibility.

3   COX, R.G. "The Cult of Dylan Thomas." Scrutiny 16
     (September):247-50.
        Reviews Henry Treece's Dylan Thomas, finding it another
     example of the poet's admirers's failure to explain their en-
     thusiasm in a convincing way. Although Thomas "shows undoubted
     poetic gift," his work completely lacks "organization and disci-
     pline." "The much-vaunted romantic subjectivism looks for the
     most part like an excuse to avoid the trouble of precise
     communication."

4   EVERY, GEORGE. "The Impact of Joyce." In Poetry and Personal
     Responsibility. Viewpoints, 14. London: SCM Press,
     pp. 32-40.
        Comments on Joyce's influence on Thomas. He "owes much" to
     the novelist's way of expressing a "dream world" based on sub-
     conscious exploration. His poetry, like Finnegans Wake, contains
     the "impulse to combine contradictory images in order to express
     a felt contradiction." Like Joyce, he tries to "immerse" his
     personal identity in the existence prior to birth.

5   FRANKENBERG, LLOYD. "Dylan Thomas." In Pleasure Dome: On
     Reading Modern Poetry. Boston: Houghton Mifflin, pp. 316-23.
        Stresses the influence of Blake and Joyce on Thomas's
     poetry and prose. The "vehement," exalted element of fantasy of
     his writing can be seen to follow three stages: in the first he
     writes about fantasy; in the next he alternates fantasy and
     reality; finally he composes "more purely in or from" fantasy.
     Reprinted: 1968.6.

6   JONES, NOEL A. "Dylan Thomas as a Pattern." British Annual
     of Literature 6:12-16.
        Warns that Thomas is a dangerous influence. His example
     could corrupt younger writers.

7   "The Making of a Poet." Times Literary Supplement, 22 July,
     p. 476.
        Complains that Henry Treece's Dylan Thomas is a weak work
     when it comes to dealing with the poet's influences, his prose
     writings, and his more recent poems. But is impressed by the
     account of the atmosphere that existed when Thomas published his
     first volume of poems.

8   Review of Dylan Thomas. Listener 41 (19 May):861.
        Compliments Henry Treece's study of Thomas for its "honest
     and detailed appraisal," which presumably will go far to help
     establish this poet as the "most original and naturally gifted"
     of his period.

9   REXROTH, KENNETH, ed. Introduction to The New British Poets.
     Norfolk, Conn.: New Directions, pp. xvii-xx.
          Recalls the "tolerant but embarrassed" critical "racket"
     that originally met Thomas's poetry. Also lists the main ele-
     ments that influenced his unique idiom: Hopkins, Hart Crane,
     Rimbaud, Welsh poetry, the Old Testament, omnivorous "boyish"
     reading, and (especially in his later poems) Vaughan and Herbert.
     Reprinted: 1960.5.

10   SPENDER, STEPHEN. "Dylan Thomas." New Statesman 37
     (18 June):650-52.
          Reviews Henry Treece's Dylan Thomas, criticizing it as the
     work of a violently "partisan" writer who fails to provide any
     new understanding of the special kind of poetry written by
     Thomas. What is needed is an analysis, for example, of Thomas's
     extreme opaqueness.

11   TREECE, HENRY. Dylan Thomas: "Dog among the Fairies."
     London: Lindsay Drummond, 158 pp.
          Finds that there is a significant, unconscious imbalance
     between Thomas's emotional and intellectual experience and his
     technique. This lack is the most prominent of Thomas's various
     flaws, but it's also the source of the powerful charm that has
     made him a "cataclysmic force among those poets deadened by
     traditionalism, or made ineffectual by hypersensitivity."
     Reprinted in part: 1960.5; revised reprint: 1956.46.

                                1950

1   AIVAZ, DAVID. "The Poetry of Dylan Thomas." Hudson Review 3
     (Autumn):382-404.
          Attempts to explain the artistic logic behind Thomas's
     difficult style and to reveal his basic vision. Concludes that,
     contrary to some of his detractors, Thomas is actually a "poet
     who thinks; he deserves to be read as much for his sense as for
     his sound and fury." Reprinted: 1960.33.

2   ALLOTT, KENNETH, ed. Introduction to The Penguin Book of
     Contemporary Verse. Harmondsworth: Penguin Books, pp. 11-27,
     224-26.
          Contains some critical commentary on Thomas in the context
     of looking at the contemporary poetry scene.

3   BAUM, BERNARD. "Dylan Thomas: An Unpurged Image." Poetry 75
     (March):357-60.
          Calls Henry Treece's Dylan Thomas "unfortunate" because,
     written in a fragmentary and poorly balanced way, it leaves the
     reader wondering whether this poet was essentially one of
     "inspired genius" or "profound cerebration."

4   BERGONZI, BERNARD. "Stopping the Rot--IV." <u>Nine</u> 2 (Summer): 201-2.
Comments on Thomas's obsessive use of Freudian ideas and images, particularly in his early poems.

5   BREIT, HARVEY. "Talk with Dylan Thomas." <u>New York Times Book Review</u>, 14 May, p. 19.
Gives the interviewer the impression that Thomas is "one of the passing breed of spiritual anarchists." Reprinted: 1956.7; 1960.5.

6   DAICHE, DAVID, and CHARVAT, WILLIAM, eds. <u>Poems in English, 1530-1940</u>. New York: Ronald Press, pp. 744-45.
Contains explicatory notes on selected anthologized poems by Thomas. "There is a fierceness about Thomas's use of natural imagery that is like nothing else in English poetry."

7   GIOVANNINI, G. "Thomas' 'The force that through the green fuse.'" <u>Explicator</u> 8 (June): item 59.
Explicates the poem and declares that it expresses a variation on the theme of "life (and love) cankered by death."

8   HYNES, SAM. "Thomas' 'From love's first fever to her plague.'" <u>Explicator</u> 9 (December): item 18.
Explicates the poem, stressing the Freudian imagery used to express the theme of human development.

9   JOHNSON, S.F. "Thomas' 'The force that through the green fuse.'" <u>Explicator</u> 8 (June): item 60.
Explicates the poem, calling it a creation that amounts to a "generalized élan vital."

10   McLAREN, FLORIS. "Dylan Thomas in Vancouver." <u>Contemporary Verse</u>, Spring, pp. 26-27.
Describes Thomas's visit to Vancouver.

11   WERRY, RICHARD. "The Poetry of Dylan Thomas." <u>College English</u> 11 (February):250-56.
Surveys Thomas's poetic art and attempts to evaluate his significance in literary history. Stresses the fact that Thomas's poetry is personal and that its "fountainhead" is the subject of death.

<u>1951</u>

1   DEUTSCH, BABETTE. "The Orient Wheat." <u>Virginia Quarterly Review</u> 27 (Spring):221-36.
Notes Thomas's connection with the Apocalypse movement, the influence of his Welsh background, and various similarities with other poets, particularly Hart Crane and Hopkins. Focuses on key lines taken from <u>Selected Writings</u> to illustrate the exceptional quality of his poetry.

2   MILES, JOSEPHINE. The Primary Language of Poetry in the
    1940s. Berkeley: University of California Press, pp. 390,
    447–48.
        Offers a word-count analysis of Thomas's poetry.

3   PINTO, VIVIAN De SOLA. Crisis in English Poetry: 1880–1940.
    London: Hutchinson's Universal Library, pp. 202–4.
        Places Thomas in the "New Romanticism" movement appearing
    between the two world wars, finding him to be the most bril-
    liantly lyrical young poet of the nineteen-thirties.

4   PRYS-JONES, A.G. "Anglo-Welsh Poetry." Dock Leaves 2
    (January):5–9.
        Surveys the Anglo-Welsh poetry scene. Thomas "has cer-
    tainly brought new vitality into the English tradition, and has
    exercised a marked influence over a number of his younger
    contemporaries."

5   RANSOM, JOHN CROWE. "The Poetry of 1900–1950." Kenyon Review
    13 (Summer):445–54.
        Surveys the poetry scene of the first half of the twentieth
    century, finally attempting to categorize the era's poets as
    major or minor figures. Thomas causes an "embarrassing predica-
    ment" because (like Housman, Auden, and Wallace Stevens) he
    doesn't seem to quite fit the definition of a major poet, that
    is, a writer whose "deliverances" are obviously of "vital human
    importance" and are "freshly produced" in impressive numbers.

6   TREECE, HENRY. "Apocalypse Revisited." World Review, July,
    pp. 22–28.
        Looks at the beginning of the so-called Apocalyptic move-
    ment and traces its development and eventual demise. Comments
    on Thomas's relation to it.

                                    1952

1   BOGAN, LOUISE. "Verse." New Yorker 28 (2 August):65–66.
        Reviews In Country Sleep, proclaiming that in these new
    poems Thomas's "bardic side" is in strong evidence. Notes that
    he has broken free of some earlier technical problems, so that
    now he is especially successful in expressing the sexual and
    joyous mysteries of life.

2   BREIT, HARVEY. "Talk with Dylan Thomas." New York Times
    Book Review, 17 February, p. 18.
        Tells the interviewer that poetry consists of "statements
    made on the way to the grave." Thomas also indicates that his
    favorite poet of the century is Thomas Hardy. Reprinted:
    1956.7; 1960.5.

3   CARTER, THOMAS H. Review of In Country Sleep. Shenandoah 3
     (Spring):24-26.
          Finds that the lyric poet shows a "new depth in compassion"
     in his most recent poems. He also exhibits certain qualities one
     had come to expect of his work: "the packed line, the incredible
     energy behind the poetry, and . . . the rich imagery" that is
     "perhaps a little more truthful than reality."

4   DEUTSCH, BABETTE. "A Poet Singing On His Way." New York
     Herald Tribune Book Review 28 (23 March):4.
          Reviews In Country Sleep, hailing these poems for their
     celebration of the "riches of the sensual world" and their
     "declaration of joy in the teeth of the dark."

5   _____. Poetry in Our Time. New York: Henry Holt & Co.,
     pp. 330-44 passim.
          Considers Thomas as a religious poet. Like Hart Crane, he
     was "possessed" by a "revivalist's" fervor. The "difficulty" of
     Thomas's poetry is the result of his combining private references
     with Christian tradition, Welsh mythology, and Freudian psychol-
     ogy. Moreover, he was "more alive to the music of his meaning
     than to the meaning of his music." Though some of his work is
     flawed by "indecipherable" ambiguity, his best poetry gives us
     "the most direct kind of apprehension with an immediacy and
     intimacy foreign to the adult mind." Reprinted: 1963.6.

6   DURRELL, LAWRENCE. "Poetry in the Thirties." In Key to
     Modern British Poetry. London: Peter Neville, pp. 196-208.
          Contrasts Thomas and William Empson, showing how their
     approaches differ radically and how this discovery in turn yields
     insight into the work of both. Thomas, less interested than
     Empson in expressing intellectual content, tends to compress his
     lines until they are like "ideograms for thought or emotion."
     His poetry is also especially marked by sensuality, incantation,
     symbolic ambiguity, and prophetic tendency.

7   EDMAN, IRWIN. "The Spoken Word." Saturday Review 35
     (29 November):68-69.
          Feels that Thomas's melodious, ardent readings recorded on
     the Caedmon label make the poetry printed on a page "dull in
     comparison."

8   FRANKENBERG, LLOYD. "Controlled Abandon." New York Times
     Book Review, 6 April, p. 4.
          Reviews In Country Sleep, calling the author "one of the
     most dramatic of lyric poets." Thomas "leashes, lashes and
     releases his emotions in a whirl of crescendos."

9   FRASER, GEORGE SUTHERLAND. "Craft and Sullen Art." New
     Statesman 44 (29 November):640, 642.
          Reviews Collected Poems, concluding that this collection
     should "consolidate and raise" Thomas's reputation. The evidence
     is that he is the "most masterly verse craftsman of his genera-
     tion" and that he is both a "narrow" and "deep" poet guided by
     important themes.

10   GILLETT, ERIC. "A Christmas Box." <u>National and English</u>
     <u>Review</u> 139 (December):369.
        Reviews <u>Collected Poems</u>, recommending the work for the
     "clear-cut and striking" inspiration. "Unlike some of his con-
     temporaries he is not afraid of beauty."

11   GREENHUT, MORRIS. "Opinion." <u>Beloit Poetry Journal</u> 2
     (Summer):28–29.
        Reviews <u>In Country Sleep</u> and thinks that the poet's "usual
     affirmations" are no longer as convincing as they were in his
     earlier poetry. The critic detects a mounting desperation as
     Thomas realizes the loss of vitality. His "belief" now "depends
     on reiterated and increasingly exaggerated affirmation."

12   GREGORY, HORACE. "The 'Romantic' Heritage in the Writings of
     Dylan Thomas." <u>Poetry and Poverty</u> 1:22–30.
        Discovers Thomas's regional influence, unusual imagination,
     and his "affinity to a larger, unevenly gifted body of 'neo-
     romantic' literature" by looking at several samples of his work.
     He has a great gift for "immediacy" that is somewhat flawed by
     its exhaustive intensity.

13   HUMPHRIES, ROLFE. "Verse Chronicle." <u>Nation</u> 174 (19 April):
     389–90.
        Reviews <u>In Country Sleep</u>, finding it somewhat "contrived"
     at times, but also rich in "energy" and imagination. In compar-
     ing Wallace Stevens's poetry to Thomas's, the critic finds that
     the exuberance of the American has "less sense of moisture."

14   "Interview with Dylan Thomas." <u>Occident</u>, Spring, pp. 5–6.
        Student-sponsored and directed interview.

15   JOHNSON, S.F. "Thomas' 'The force that through the green
     fuse.'" <u>Explicator</u> 10 (February): item 26.
        Explicates the poem, emphasizing the biblical echoes.

16   _____. "Thomas' 'The Hunchback in the Park' and 'On the
     Marriage of a Virgin.'" <u>Explicator</u> 10 (February): item 27.
        Explicates the poems, pointing out how both "present
     dramatically an intense glorification of the natural and the
     physical" by means of the "consciousness of a particularized
     character."

17   McDONALD, GERALD D. Review of <u>In Country Sleep</u>. <u>Library</u>
     <u>Journal</u> 77 (15 March):533.
        Praises the volume for its "customary resonance, vitality,
     and exaltation."

18   MACKWORTH, CECILY. "Dylan Thomas et la double vision."
     <u>Critique</u> 19 (June):500–516.
        Reviews <u>Collected Poems</u>, <u>A Prospect of the Sea</u>, <u>Portrait of</u>
     <u>the Artist</u>, and H. Bokanowski and M. Alyn's <u>Dylan Thomas</u>. The
     divided, paradoxical poet is praised for the tumultuous beauty of
     the language and the fundamental mystery characteristic of his
     work.

19   MAYHEAD, ROBIN. "Dylan Thomas." Scrutiny 19 (Winter):142-47.
     Finds much to criticize in reviewing Collected Poems. At
best, Thomas's employment of language indicates "an agreeable
minor talent." At worst, he has a mannered habit of "clutching
at the apparently striking image" that occurs "without working
out . . . its implications or a proper consideration of its
appropriateness." Violence takes the place of precise imagination.

20   MEYER, GERARD PREVIN. "Lissom Celtic Tropes." Saturday
     Review 35 (21 June):17-18.
     Praises the poems in In Country Sleep particularly for
their "aural art." Their music plays upon the inner ear like
"splendid pyrotechnics." A biographical overview is attached to
the review essay.

21   POPKIN, HENRY. "Poets as Performers: The Revival of Poetry-
     Reading." Theatre Arts 36 (February):27, 74.
     Notes that Thomas, despite his "difficult" poetry, brings
in the largest crowds of all the poets then taking part in a
resurgence of public readings.

22   ROETHKE, THEODORE [Winterset Rothberg]. "One Ring-Tailed
     Roarer to Another." Poetry, December, pp. 184-86.
     Reviews In Country Sleep, calling the writer a "rare
heedless fornicator of language" who expresses himself with "the
voice of angels and ravens." Reprinted: 1960.33.

23   "Salute to a Poet." Times Literary Supplement, 28 November,
     p. 776.
     Applauds the appearance of Collected Poems as an important
"event" in the midst of a disappointing British poetry scene.
Drawing on selected lines from some of Thomas's best poems
(especially "Fern Hill" and "Poem in October"), concludes that
here was "essentially a religious poet" who actually "celebrates
whatever God has made." Also comments on such important issues
as Thomas's autobiographical, romantic, and Welsh aspects and
the problems of his obscurity.

24   SPENDER, STEPHEN. "A Romantic in Revolt." Spectator 189
     (5 December):780-81.
     Reviews Collected Poems, declaring that Thomas "represents
a romantic revolt against this classical tendency" that has
formed around the "theological views" of Auden and Eliot.

25   SWEENEY, JOHN L. "Intimations of Mortality." New Republic
     126 (17 March):18, 22-23.
     Reviews In Country Sleep, noting that the "technique and
method" of the new poems are "confirmatory rather than explora-
tory." Still thinks of Thomas as the exceptional poet who
writes for both the eye and the ear.

26 WILDER, AMOS NIVEN. "Man and Nature in Dylan Thomas." In
    Modern Poetry and the Christian Tradition. New York: Charles
    Scribner's Sons, pp. 100-102.
        Points out Thomas's surrealistic "treatment" of nature and
    compares his method to that of Norman Nicholson.

                                1953

1   ADAMS, PHOEBE. "Symbols and Metaphors." Atlantic Monthly 191
    (May):79-80.
        Reviews Collected Poems, praising Thomas as the foremost
    lyricist among contemporary poets. He is a "warlock" who can
    take an old theme and turn it "magically new."

2   AGREE, JAMES. "A Dylan Thomas Screen Play." New York Times
    Book Review, 6 December, p. 38.
        Reviews The Doctor and the Devils, complimenting the script
    for its functional storytelling, its "highly playable" dialogue,
    and its imagined form. Above all, the story is told with sincere
    humanity and thus shows that Thomas "could not work for money
    without also working with love."

3   ARLOTT, JOHN. "Dylan Thomas." Spectator 191 (13 November):
    534.
        Gives Thomas's obituary. This poet "lived to live and to
    write; there his integrity was absolute."

4   BARTLETT, PHYLLIS. "Thomas' 'Among Those Killed in the Dawn
    Raid was a Man Aged a Hundred.'" Explicator 12 (December):
    item 21.
        Explicates the poem as a celebration in which the two
    primary symbols are the sun (standing for life) and the cage
    (standing for the body).

5   BREIT, HARVEY. "Farewell and Hail." New York Times Book
    Review, 22 November, p. 8.
        Pays tribute to Thomas's memory. His "violence" was
    "always morally motivated." His poetry was something mysterious
    and familiar, like a whole, dense, dark, alien mapped world."

6   CARRUTH, HAYDEN. "Poetry Chronicle: Parnassus Stormed."
    Partisan Review 20 (September-October):576-77.
        Reviews Collected Poems, finding the work to be impressive
    as a whole, but irksome on occasion. The poems's "freshness and
    originality" can become an "anomaly" that can lead one to believe
    that behind Thomas's "childlike attitudes" exists a "fractious-
    ness and malevolence that is destructive beyond any recognizable
    motivation." Despite his genius, his language is too often more
    "disconcerting than compelling."

7   CLANCY, JOSEPH P. "Dylan Thomas: Promise Clipped." <u>America</u>
    90 (12 December):295-96.
        Looks at the achievement of Thomas. The main concern of
    his poetry was an "awareness of a dynamic universe, where the
    essential drives of nature . . . are simultaneously destructive
    and constructive." The main limitation of his writing is a
    tendency toward the "too great intensifying of each part of the
    poem."

8   COFFMAN, STANLEY K. Review of <u>Collected Poems</u>. <u>Books Abroad</u>
    27 (Autumn):436.
        Comments on the poetry's development toward a "more easily
    apprehended logical structure." The poems are still difficult,
    yet they have the lyrical, poetic quality lacking in so much
    other "difficult" poetry.

9   CORMAN, CID. "Dylan Thomas: Rhetorician in Mid-Career."
    <u>Accent</u> 13 (Winter):56-59.
        Indicates that Thomas's poetic development is limited by an
    increasingly desperate dependency on rhetoric. Uses "Over Sir
    John's hill" as one of the crucial poems revealing the essential
    facts that Thomas employs "distinctly elemental language" to
    eulogize the "hot-and-cold inevitable ends." Reprinted: 1960.33.

10 DAICHES, DAVID. Review of <u>Collected Poems</u>. <u>Yale Review</u> 42
    (Summer):625-27.
        Remarks that, unlike T.S. Eliot, Thomas "accepts man as he
    is." At his most characteristic, he writes poetry that is like a
    "grand hailing of experience." The feeling sometimes arises that
    his creations depend on hit-or-miss chance; but when he "regis-
    ters a hit, the sheer poetic power generated is enormous."

11 DAVENPORT, JOHN. "Dylan Thomas." <u>Twentieth Century</u> 153
    (February):142-46.
        Declares that Thomas's poetry deserves to be judged "on the
    highest level." Agrees with Stephen Spender that Thomas "repre-
    sents a romantic revolt against the classicist tendency" and
    speculates that his "rhetorical urge" can be traced to his Welsh
    background. His primary themes are the "eternal ones" of life
    and death.

12 _____. "Dylan Thomas." <u>Twentieth Century</u> 154 (December):
    475-77.
        Speculates that Thomas's position will ultimately be "un-
    assailable" because of the influence he had on fellow poets.

13 DOBRÉE, BONAMY. "Two Experiments." <u>Spectator</u> 190 (12 June):
    764.
        Praises <u>The Doctor and the Devils</u> for its visual sense and
    its "hard-hitting, vivid prose."

14   "Dylan Thomas, 39, Welsh Poet, Dies." New York Times,
      10 November, p. 31.
          Reports Thomas's death of "cerebral ailment," followed by
      a summary of his life and career.

15   "Film-Script." Times Literary Supplement, 29 May, p. 351.
          Reviews The Doctor and the Devils, finding it to be an
      example of "applied" writing that will be interesting primarily
      to film students. Speculates that the expressionistic presenta-
      tion of dialogue may work well on the screen.

16   FRASER, GEORGE SUTHERLAND. The Modern Writer and His World.
      London: Derek Verschoyle, pp. 41 passim.
          Places Thomas in Rimbaud's tradition of poets whose "mad-
      ness" represents a trust in the emotional, subjective approach as
      the way to apprehend truth and reality. Reprinted: 1965.18.

17   FREMANTLE, ANNE. "Death of a Poet." Commonweal 59
      (18 December):285–86.
          Takes an over-view of the poet's career and life, and finds
      that the "typical" Thomas was a combination of the "slightly
      truculent, partly pagan, yet wholly reverential."

18   GRADDON, JOHN. "The Interior Life." Poetry Review 44 (April-
      June):338–40.
          Compares the "grudging and partial recognition" of Thomas
      by critics with the kind of reception that met Ezra Pound.
      Thomas is a "Celt, with a song." His writing is essentially the
      "projection of a personality in process of finding universality,
      not only in many people but in . . . the poet himself."

19   GRINDEA, MIRON, ed. "Our Dylan Thomas: Memorial Number."
      Adam International Review 238:80 pp.
          Contains items about the man and his work. The contribu-
      tors commemorating the poet include such luminaries as Igor
      Stravinsky, George Barker, and Augustus John. The bulk of the
      numbers consists of offerings that are personal reminiscences
      and tributes. Selected items reprinted: 1960.5, 33; 1963.8.

20   HAYES, RICHARD. "Poets in the Theater." Commonweal 58
      (26 June):297–98.
          Reviews the performance of Under Milk Wood at the Poetry
      Center. Proclaims it as a "triumph" of poetic verse.

21   HEWES, HENRY. "The Backward Town of Llareggub." Saturday
      Review 36 (6 June):24-25.
          Praises Under Milk Wood as the "richest" and "earthiest"
      performance of the theater season. Describes the effectiveness
      of Thomas's role, and provides a brief history of the growth of
      the play for voices. Quotes Thomas as saying that he regarded
      the version as still incomplete and that he already had a dif-
      ferent ending in mind, where he follows "lots of characters into
      the night until the last lover has left the wood."

22   HIGHET, GILBERT. "Two Poets." Harper's Magazine 206 (May):
      96.
         Uses a poem to comment on Thomas's Collected Poems, ending
      with the words "prickly promise."

23   JANES, ALFRED. "World's End." Gower 6:6.
         Provides a brief memorial of the poet.

24   JOHNSON, GEOFFREY. "The Acid Test." Poetry Review 44 (April-
      June):340-43.
         Reacts to the praise that many critics heaped on Collected
      Poems. Believes that "this over-praise bordering on idolatry"
      does the poet a "vicious disservice" because he is generally be-
      ing flattered for the wrong reasons, especially for his idiosyn-
      cratic style. In addition to its "bombastic" style, Thomas's
      poetry is criticized for "monotonously egocentric" and intel-
      lectually shallow content. Reprinted: 1960.33.

25   JOHNSON, PAMELA HANSFORD. "Seventeen Further Memoirs." Adam
      International Review 238:24-25.
         Remembers the courtship days when Thomas looked to her
      "like a brilliant, audacious child." Reprinted: 1960.5, 33.

26   JONES, GLYN. "Three Anglo-Welsh Prose Writers." Rann 19
      (April):1-5.
         Considers Thomas along with two other Anglo-Welsh writers--
      Gwyn Thomas and Caradoc Evans.

27   KORG, JACOB. "Thriller into Art." Nation 177 (14 November):
      413.
         Praises The Doctor and the Devils for the way Thomas turns
      a lurid thriller into a "dignified" creation. A significant
      moral issue takes shape without sacrificing the basic excitement
      of the story.

28   L., B. Review of Collected Poems. English 9 (Spring):149-50.
         Praises the volume as one that must place Thomas "at the
      forefront" of the poets of his generation. This is a poet who
      "makes his readers work," but hardly ever in vain.

29   "A Lesson in Anatomy." Time 62 (5 October):110.
         Praises The Doctor and the Devils as a script that contains
      the best qualities of fiction and drama. Moreover, Thomas man-
      ages to speak out for the "dignity of human life" without forcing
      the characters to make "tiresome speeches about it."

30   McDONALD, GERALD D. Review of Collected Poems. Library
      Journal 78 (15 August):1334.
         Calls Thomas a great poet with a voice that is the "most
      enlivening" heard in contemporary poetry.

31   ____. Review of The Doctor and the Devils. Library Journal
        78 (15 December):2214.
        Finds Thomas's adaptation to be "vividly presented" and a
        work with "real literary distinction."

32   MacNEICE, LOUIS. "The Strange, Mighty Impact of Dylan
        Thomas' Poetry." New York Times Book Review, 5 April,
        pp. 1, 17.
        Calls Thomas "perhaps the most startling phenomenon" in an
        age of "startling poetic experiment." He is "sheer downright
        Bard." The meaning of the various selections in Collected Poems,
        the volume under review, emerges "not so much . . . in the
        rational sense as myth." Like Blake, Thomas bases his "prophetic
        revelations" on "songs of innocence."

33   MERWIN, W.S. "The Religious Poet." Adam International Review
        238:73-78.
        Depicts Thomas as a "great religious" poet whose work con-
        sistently shows him attempting "at times desperately, to find
        and come to grips with his subject, finding it, and making it
        into a poetry of celebration." As the poetry becomes increas-
        ingly dramatic, so does the complexity and power of Thomas's
        vision. Reprinted: 1960.5, 33.

34   MEYER, FRANK. Review of Collected Poems. American Mercury,
        July, p. 143.
        Pans Thomas's collection because he finds that the poet's
        "virtuosity" has resulted only in "variations more complex on
        the single theme of himself."

35   NEMEROV, HOWARD. "The Generation of Violence." Kenyon Review
        15 (Summer):477-83.
        Looking at Collected Poems, one can discover a number of
        poems that are failures, but a few are truly "beautiful." In
        most of the selections, whether successful or not, Thomas has
        tried "to make the order of association do the work of and in
        part replace the order of narrative."

36   "Poetry and Protest." Poetry and Poverty 4:39-40.
        Reviews Collected Poems, discovering that a look at
        Thomas's development reveals how much he was influenced by the
        romantic climate of the forties.

37   "Poets Attend Rites for Dylan Thomas." New York Times,
        14 November, p. 17.
        Reports that nearly 400 people attended a funeral service
        held for Thomas in Greenwich Village, including such literary
        luminaries as Tennessee Williams, Muriel Rukeyser, John Berryman,
        and Babette Deutsch.

38 RAINER, DACHINE. Review of Collected Poems. Commonweal 58
    (15 May):159-61.
    Praises Thomas for his remarkable language but also for his
celebration of man's "dignity" and his "reverence for the
Absolute." States that Thomas is "second only to Yeats and Blake
as a radical romantic."

39 Review of Collected Poems. New Yorker 29 (10 October):160.
    Remarks on Thomas's progress from his early phase as a
"roaring boy" to his current status as a "master of effects."

40 Review of The Doctor and the Devils. New Statesman 45
    (27 June):786.
    Believes that Thomas's film script is a clear improvement
on the original, James Bridie's The Anatomist. Vivid and elo-
quent, the script should succeed on the screen if a good director
with a taste for horror were found.

41 RIGGS, THOMAS. "Recent Poetry--a Miscellany." Nation 176
    (2 May):376-77.
    Praises the "superb, strange lyrics" gathered in Collected
Poems. Thomas is described as having a "bardic consciousness,"
and his best poems are seen as "inward hymns to an indwelling
vitality."

42 ROLO, CHARLES J. "Ends and Means." Atlantic Monthly 192
    (November):110-11.
    Finds The Doctor and the Devils to be a "gripping,
imaginatively written drama" that should transfer well to the
screen.

43 SAMPSON, PAUL. "Macabre Tale." Washington Post, 20 December,
    p. 6B.
    Reviews The Doctor and the Devils, calling it a "strange
mixture of fresh, poetic descriptive writings and stale movie
cliches."

44 SCOTT, WINFIELD TOWNLEY. "The Script of a Screenplay." New
    York Herald Tribune Book Review 30 (29 November):16.
    Calls the publication of The Doctor and the Devils un-
necessary except as a curiosity piece, noting that Thomas formed
a mixture of two previous versions of the story--Robert Louis
Stevenson's atmospheric short story "The Body Snatchers" and
James Bridie's psychological play The Anatomist.

45 _____. "A Wild Man Bound." Saturday Review 36 (11 April):
    29-30.
    Reviews Collected Poems, finding the content of the poems
"pretty simple and unvaried." His writing is the result of a
"few vividly felt intimations of mortality--time and change,
death existing in the seed, death itself." Thomas does show
signs, though, of wishing to control his "fine frenzy" with
"responsibility."

46   SCRIVEN, R.C.   Review of The Doctor and the Devils.   Punch,
      17 June, p. 725.
            Praises Thomas's version of the Burke and Hare murders for
      its combination of "brilliant description and sparse, first-rate
      dialogue."

47   SHUTTLEWORTH, MARTIN.   "Without Apologies."   New Statesman 45
      (7 February):144-45.
            Describes a literary luncheon given in honor of Thomas, who
      is celebrated as a "truly intuitive" poet by A.L. Rowse.   Re-
      printed: 1960.5.

48   SITWELL, EDITH.   "The Love of Man, the Praise of God."   New
      York Herald Tribune Book Review 29 (10 May):1, 14.
            Reviews Collected Poems, praising Thomas especially for his
      lyrical ability to condense essence.   This poet's voice is unique
      in the way it contains the spirit of the origin of created
      "things."

49   SWEENEY, JOHN L.   "The Round Sunday Sounds."   New Republic 128
      (6 April):24-25.
            Finds that there is "something prayerful and distinctly
      non-conformist" about almost all of the selections in Collected
      Poems.   Suggests that to get a full picture of Thomas, one must
      take his prose into account, too, because it shows his creative
      vision in a "different angle of reflection."

50   TINDALL, WILLIAM YORK.   "Burning and Crested Song."   American
      Scholar 22 (Autumn):486, 488, 490.
            Reviews Collected Poems, concluding that the volume pro-
      vides sufficient evidence that Thomas, with the possible excep-
      tions of Eliot and Stevens, is the finest living poet.   Notes
      that the poetry falls into three recognizable periods.

51   "Trial and Error."   Times (London), 16 May, p. 5.
            Reviews The Doctor and the Devils, praising the script for
      the "vigorous" dialogue and the "lively" shooting directions.
      The treatment tends, however, to dwell on the gruesome, and it
      is sometimes repetitive.

52   WATKINS, VERNON.   "Mr. Dylan Thomas: Innovation and Tradi-
      tion."   Times (London), 10 November, p. 11.
            Delivers an obituary survey of Thomas's life and career.
      "None has ever worn more brilliantly the mask of anarchy to con-
      ceal the true face of tradition."   He was a person and poet
      "narrow and severe with himself and wide and forgiving in his
      affections."

53   "Welsh Rare One."   Time 61 (6 April):112.
            Gives the popular perception of "untidy" poet, then follows
      with a review of Collected Poems.   Thomas, like Hamlet, "thinks
      in soliloquy" and "wrestles with the dilemma of self-
      consciousness."   At his worst, he "can and does riffle his

images and similes like a cardsharp." At his best, he "makes
his poetry toe the line of his creed: 'Man be my metaphor.'"

54   WILLIAMS, A.R. "Dictionary for Dylan Thomas." Dock Leaves 3
     (Winter):30-36.
     Using his own lengthy experience of reading Thomas's
poetry, suggests that if one works hard and has a good dictionary
he will find that the "apparent nonsense" of the writing is "only
superficial." Concludes, however, by doubting that the kind of
labor Thomas's poetry demands is justifiable in a modern poet.

                               1954

1   ALLEN, WALTER. "Words in Spate." New Statesman 48
     (6 November):586.
     Praises Quite Early One Morning as an "enchanting collec-
tion" showing how potent Thomas's language was in areas other
than poetry. The most valuable pieces are his reminiscences of
childhood and some items of impressionistic reporting. He "kept
undimmed the innocent eye of childhood."

2   ARLOTT, JOHN. "Writing for Radio." Spectator 192 (9 April):
     441-42.
     Celebrates the "glorious quality of fun" found in Under
Milk Wood. "Even at its richest, no single word is extravagant."

3   ARROWSMITH, WILLIAM. "Meander and Milk Wood." Hudson Review
     7 (Summer):291-96.
     Compares Under Milk Wood with T.S. Eliot's The Confidential
Clerk. Thomas's work is a great success and Eliot's is a failure
because Thomas "has taken the full risk of everything he had--his
convictions, his skills and his faith--and put them passionately
to work" while Eliot has taken only the risks of "time and judg-
ment." "Where Eliot is ascetic, Thomas is eleusinian."

4   _____. "The Spoken Word." Listener 51 (4 February):236.
     Admits to being "spellbound from start to finish" when
first hearing the radio broadcast of Under Milk Wood. Thomas's
complex poetic language has finally "become available to the
public imagination" without giving up anything at all of its
"new-minted brilliance."

5   _____. "The Wisdom of Poetry." Hudson Review 6 (Winter):
     597-600.
     Using the publication of Collected Poems as an opportunity
for reassessment, concludes that Thomas's main subject is the
"praise of Process" and that he is "our most consistently and
extravagantly primitive poet" whose work ultimately suffers from
a lack of "civilized virtues." Reprinted: 1960.5.

                                32

6   ASSELINEAU, ROGER. "Dylan Thomas." Études anglaises 7
(January):89-100.
      Believes that with the appearance of Collected Poems it was
now possible to think of Thomas as one of the major poets of the
age.

7   ATKINSON, BROOKS. "Platform Drama." New York Times, 16 May,
sec. 2, p. 1.
      Finds Under Milk Wood to be a "notable" work for three
reasons: its original form, its vigorous writing and characterization, and its apparent similarity with Our Town. Whereas Our
Town has a theme, Under Milk Wood lacks one, although it is a
"trenchant portrait" of Thomas's mind.

8   AURY, DOMINIQUE. "Dylan Thomas." La nouvelle revue française
3 (1 February):306-7.
      Gives an obituary notice. Thomas lived, as it were, for
death.

9   BANYARD, GRACE. "The Voice on the Air." Fortnightly 176
(December):431.
      Reading Quite Early One Morning makes the critic recall the
hypnotic effect of Thomas's voice coming over the radio.

10   BARO, GENE. "Magic in His Prose, Too." New York Herald
Tribune Book Review 31 (19 December):3.
      Reviews Quite Early One Morning, praising the collection as
a "delightful and moving book." Composed in a prose that is a
"magical instrument," the collection is dominated by two distinct
moods: the "sheer bubbling sense of fun" and the "sense of
nostalgia for the transitoriness and frailty of life."

11   BARRETT, MARY ELLIS. "A Luncheon with Dylan Thomas."
Reporter 10 (27 April):45-48.
      Recalls an earlier interview with the "dumpy figure" who
at least "looked and sounded" like a real lyric poet.

12   BOLLIER, E.P. "Love, Death and the Poet--Dylan Thomas."
Colorado Quarterly 2 (Spring):386-407.
      Sets out to describe the "essential" Thomas. He was a
"reshaper of language, an explorer of man's dark beginnings" who
attempted to "know himself and make peace with his past before
judging the world." He moved from being an objective examiner
of man's fate to someone able to "look beyond the country of his
skull" into the reality of others.

13   BOOTHROYD, J.B. "No Telly-Belly for Larry Gib." Punch 226
(3 March):282-83.
      Gives a "dual" (dialogue) "commemoration" of Under Milk
Wood and the Ideal Home Exhibition.

14   BREIT, HARVEY. "Dylan Report." New York Times Book Review,
     18 April, p. 8.
         Reports on the growing Dylan Thomas Fund and notes that
     13,500 copies of Under Milk Wood were sold by Dent in England
     within three weeks of publication.

15   BRINNIN, JOHN MALCOLM. "The Talent of Genius." New Republic
     130 (25 January):19.
         Praises The Doctor and the Devils for its effective way of
     suggesting real emotion and for its "superb visual sense."

16   BROOKS, ELMER L. "Thomas' 'Among Those Killed in the Dawn
     Raid was a Man Aged a Hundred.'" Explicator 12 (June):
     item 49.
         Explicates the poem in primarily realistic terms.

17   BROWN, ALAN. Review of The Poetry of Dylan Thomas. Canadian
     Forum 34 (September):140.
         Reviews Elder Olson's study of Thomas's poetry. Suggests
     that Olson has applied too much ingenuity in analyzing the
     poetry (particularly the sonnet sequence), in the process making
     the "firepower" of the poems quite "harmless."

18   BYLER, W.S., ed. Yale Literary Magazine, November, pp. 2-34.
         Included in the special issue on Thomas are articles that
     focus on personal reminiscences, his poetic art, his dramatic
     art, his romantic heritage, and several poems and testaments
     celebrating his memory and achievement. Selected items re-
     printed: 1960.5, 33; 1963.8. Reprint of 1947.7.

19   CAMPBELL, ROY. "Dylan Thomas--The War Years." Shenandoah 5
     (Spring):26-27.
         Remembers Thomas with great affection. He was "the finest
     comrade and companion . . . and a real man, in spite of being a
     poet."

20   CANE, MELVILLE. "Are Poets Returning to Lyricism?" Saturday
     Review 37 (16 January):8-10, 40-41.
         Argues that the poetic tide is turning from essentially
     intellectual to lyrical poetry, with Thomas being one of the
     prime examples of this trend.

21   CHRISTOPHER, Sister MARY. Review of The Poetry of Dylan
     Thomas. Catholic World 180 (November):159-60.
         Compliments Elder Olson's study for elucidating the poet's
     art while accepting the unavoidable characteristic obscurity of
     the work.

22   CORBETT, HUGH. Review of The Doctor and the Devils. Books
     Abroad 28 (Autumn):438.
         Finds the script to have special interest in the way it
     depicts a brilliant, ruthless scientist. It has "tragedy in-
     cisively portrayed" through the "rich, true-toned word magic" of
     an outstanding poet.

23 CORMAN, CID. "A Note on Dylan Thomas." Origin 12 (Spring): 256–58.
Defends Thomas against such "blackwashing" attackers as Kenneth Rexroth. Thomas may have "often said more than he meant, but he always meant to be candid."

24 CRUTTWELL, PATRICK. "Letter from England." Hudson Review 7 (Summer):272–75.
Dismisses Thomas's work as "meaningless mannerisms" and claims to see the beginning of a reaction against his kind of writing.

25 DAICHES, DAVID. "The Poetry of Dylan Thomas." College English 16 (October):1–8.
Gives a general assessment of Thomas's poetry. Counters the belief on the part of some critics that he was a "whirling romantic" or a "metaphysical imagist" by offering evidence that he was instead a poet using a complex craft to "create a ritual of celebration." Reprinted: 1956.12; 1958.9; 1960.10; 1966.8.

26 DAVIES, PENNAR. "Sober Reflections on Dylan Thomas." Dock Leaves 5 (Winter):13–17.
Declares that Thomas should ultimately be seen as a "gifted entertainer, a phenomenon" in the history of this century's "publicity" and, finally, as "an interesting minor poet."

27 DAVIES, ROBERTSON. "Not for Mrs. Jones the Gas." Saturday Night 69 (26 June):24–25.
Makes the case that, in The Doctor and the Devils and Under Milk Wood, Thomas revealed the "authentic voice of a dramatic poet of high quality . . . who has not yet reached his fullest development."

28 DAWEDEIT, GLENDY. "Poet and Novelist Try Change of Pace." Washington Post, 12 December, p. 6B.
Finds that Thomas's contradictory personality shows itself plainly in Quite Early One Morning and that the "plum-pudding richness" of his imagery doesn't always enhance his prose pieces.

29 "Dylan Thomas and the Spoken Word." Times Literary Supplement, 19 November, p. 731.
Praises Quite Early One Morning for its great variety and depth. Thomas's contribution to broadcasting is compared to Chaplin's to silent film. He was especially adept at evoking the excitement of childhood by means of narrative and an "exact and intuitive" use of language. In his broadcasts "all the echoes and vitality of his extremely sociable life" can be discovered, anticipating Under Milk Wood, his final "masterpiece."

30   "Dylan Thomas (1914-1953)." <u>Poetry</u> 83 (January):244-45.
Expresses sense of loss at the sudden death of Thomas, a
poet of "such peculiar genius" that his poems usually "had a
sharp effect" even before being understood.

31   "Dylan Thomas's Last Work." <u>Times Literary Supplement</u>,
5 March, p. 148.
Gives <u>Under Milk Wood</u> a positive review, even if its expressed vision of life does seem adolescent. "Nowhere is
Thomas's delight in performing conjuring tricks with words more
evident," and his use of techniques particularly appropriate for
radio is masterly throughout the piece.

32   "Dylan Thomas's Last Work." <u>Times</u> (London), 6 March, p. 8.
Reviews <u>Under Milk Wood</u>, calling it probably the most
imaginative and skillfully designed piece for radio yet. Instead
of being a poet with "a message," Thomas was a "peculiarly sensitive register of feeling." He was primarily an artist of
evocation.

33   "Dylan Thomas's Play." <u>Times</u> (London), 26 January, p. 6.
Reviews the B.B.C. presentation of <u>Under Milk Wood</u>.
Although "not in the least theatrical," it is an impressive
"evocative" creation of "gossiping characterization."

34   EBERHART, RICHARD. "Saucy Love of Life." <u>New York Times Book
Review</u>, 9 May, p. 5.
Finds the distinguishing quality of <u>Under Milk Wood</u> to be
the "immediate intelligibility" of the writing. "It is a garish
show and panorama of a day," containing a "joyful, positive love
of life" that Rabelais would have certainly loved.

35   _____. "Time and Dylan Thomas." <u>Virginia Quarterly Review</u> 30
(Summer):475-78.
Reviews Elder Olson's <u>The Poetry of Dylan Thomas</u>. Praises
it as an intelligent book, but disagrees with Olson's position
that Thomas's most difficult, "prolix" poems happen to be his
best.

36   EMPSON, WILLIAM. "<u>Collected Poems</u> and <u>Under Milk Wood</u>." <u>New
Statesman</u> 47 (15 May):635-36.
Believes that, when he died, Thomas was preparing to become
a dramatist and that the early poems represent the "permanent
challenge" and the "decisive part" of his writing as a whole.
Reprinted: 1960.5; 1966.8.

37   FITTS, DUDLEY. "The Bard of Wales." <u>Saturday Review</u> 37
(1 May):30.
Reviews Elder Olson's <u>The Poetry of Dylan Thomas</u>, praising
it for its success in separating the meaning of the poems from
the distorting legend of the poet. In searching for meaning,
the critic uses paraphrase, but he uses this approach with the
knowledge that poems "simply are" and that a paraphrase should
act "not as a crutch, but a shove."

38   FRASER, GEORGE SUTHERLAND. "Grasping a Whole." New Statesman
      48 (18 September):330.
          Reviews Elder Olson's The Poetry of Dylan Thomas. Finds
      Olson's neo-Aristotelian approach faulty at those times when the
      desire for "tidy" interpretation leads to oversimplification; but
      is impressed by Olson's "non-verbal" means of analyzing the
      structural and symbolic elements of Thomas's sonnet sequence.

39   GARLICK, RAYMOND, ed. "A Dylan Thomas Number." Dock Leaves 5
      (Spring):51 pp.
          Editorializes that the "true face of tradition" in Thomas's
      poetry "may well prove to be that family face which is becoming
      more familiar . . . as the legitimate descent of Anglo-Welsh
      poetry." The journal's special number contains items dealing
      with Thomas's broadcast work, his Welsh background, his peculiar
      genius, and the distinction of Under Milk Wood. Some tributes
      and poems are also contained. Selected poem reprinted: 1963.8.

40   GHISELIN, BREWSTER. "The Extravagant Energy of Genius."
      Western Review 18 (Spring):245-49.
          Offers the view that Thomas's obscurity is not due to a
      lack of intelligent meaning. To deal with the problem of clari-
      fying his most difficult poems, the critic suggests as the best
      approach a "rationale of approach" instead of explications of
      individual poems.

41   GILLETT, ERIC. "A Wonder of Words." National and English
      Review 142 (April):235-36.
          Praises Under Milk Wood as "one of the most important"
      additions to our literature made by radio. Notes some of the
      influences that helped make the radio play and recalls with
      pleasure the first "superb" radio broadcast produced by Douglas
      Cleverdon.

42   GRAVES, ALLEN WALLACE. "Difficult Contemporary Short Stories:
      William Faulkner, Katherine Anne Porter, Dylan Thomas, Eudora
      Welty and Virginia Woolf." Ph.D. dissertation, University of
      Washington, 187 pp.
          Analyzes selected contemporary short stories by methodi-
      cally assessing their central obscurities and then discussing
      whether or not these obscurities are artistically justified. The
      stories by Thomas investigated are "The Burning Baby," "The
      Orchards," and "Patricia, Edith and Arnold." Essays focusing on
      each of the selected authors discuss in detail their strategic
      use of obscurity. See Dissertation Abstracts International 14
      (1954):2067.

43   GREGORY, HORACE. "The Romantic Heritage of Dylan Thomas."
      Yale Literary Review, November, pp. 30-34.
          Reprint of 1947.7.

44   HABART, MICHEL. Review of Collected Poems. Critique 10
      (January):85–87.
         Reviews the volume with the praise that this is the work of
      a splendid poet who will be missed. The collection reveals a
      "remarkable continuity" of poetic art and inspiration.

45   HALSBAND, ROBERT. "Cinema by Dylan Thomas." Saturday Review
      37 (6 March):38.
         Reviews The Doctor and the Devils. Praises the "vivid
      visual effect" of the scenario.

46   "Harvard Library Gets Poet's MSS." New York Times,
      26 December, p. 60.
         Reports on Oscar William's presentation to Harvard of a
      collection of Thomas's original correspondence and manuscripts,
      including the worksheets and final copy of "Prologue."

47   HOLROYD, STUART. "The Celtic Genius in Modern Poetry."
      Poetry Review 45 (January–March):21–26.
         Declares that the Celtic poet is currently more important
      in English literature than ever before. Surveys the creative
      activity of the Celtic countries, ending with a celebration of
      Thomas. His poetry "possesses that soaring quality which is
      almost mystical in that it cannot be apprehended intellectually."

48   _____. "A Great Humanist." Poetry Review 45 (July–
      September):165–67.
         Praises Under Milk Wood for the "generosity" with which it
      represents the divine nobility of man. It's "one of the sanest"
      works of literature of our time because it is based on a "whole
      philosophy of values."

49   HOWARD, D.R. "Thomas' 'In my Craft or Sullen Art.'"
      Explicator 12 (February): item 22.
         Explicates the poem, indicating the central importance of
      the word "sullen." The word is used by Thomas to stress the fact
      that his art results from an exceedingly careful process of
      painstaking construction.

50   HUMBOLDT, CHARLES. "The Tragedy of Dylan Thomas." Masses
      and Mainstream, September, pp. 53–56.
         Reviews Elder Olson's The Poetry of Dylan Thomas.

51   HYNES, SAM. "Dylan Thomas: Everybody's Adonais." Commonweal
      59 (26 March):628–29.
         Speculates on the reasons behind the great public mourning
      following Thomas's death. The main reason may have been that he
      represented the popular "notion" of what a poet is supposed to be
      like. When the "wailing" will finally fade, the "miraculous,
      wonderful words" of the poet will remain.

52   JONES, DANIEL. Preface to "Under Milk Wood": A Play for
      Voices. New York: New Directions, pp. vii–xi.
         Gives a brief history of the antecedents and development of
      the radio play.

53   JONES, DANIEL; ROETHKE, THEODORE; MacNEICE, LOUIS; ADIX,
      MARJORIE; and BARKER, GEORGE. "Dylan Thomas: Memories and
      Appreciations." Encounter, January, pp. 9-17.
         Recollections and tributes by people who met and knew
      Thomas personally, including essays by Daniel Jones describing
      their creative friendship and by Louis MacNeice praising his
      "great bardic virtues of faith, joy, and craftsmanship." Re-
      printed in part: 1960.5, 33.

54   JOOST, NICHOLAS. "And He Sang in His Chains Like the Sea."
      Commonweal 60 (14 May):151.
         Praises Elder Olson's The Poetry of Dylan Thomas for its
      intelligent, painstaking criticism. In Olson's hands "Aristote-
      lian esthetic is a useful and adaptable critical instrument."

55   KNAUBER, CHARLES F. "Imagery of Light in Dylan Thomas."
      Renascence 6 (Spring):95-96, 116.
         Argues that Thomas's use of light is essentially religious
      in nature. The "evolutionary manifestation of God" is defined by
      Thomas as "man's growth in Him."

56   KORG, JACOB. "A Changed Dylan Thomas." Nation 178
      (24 April):360-61.
         Looks at Under Milk Wood and Elder Olson's The Poetry of
      Dylan Thomas, drawing the conclusions that, starting as a mystic,
      Thomas was becoming more and more dramatic and ethical in his
      later works. Praises Olson's exegesis on Thomas's religious
      sonnets in particular.

57   _____. "Sounds of Laughter." Nation 179 (25 December):
      552-53.
         Praises Quite Early One Morning for its dominant mood of
      "wicked fun." Selected for special praise are Thomas's pieces on
      childhood and on the business of poetry.

58   LEBERT, GORDON. Review of The Poetry of Dylan Thomas.
      Quarterly Journal of Speech 40 (October):349.
         Recommends Elder Olson's book as the "best study yet" of
      Thomas's poetry. It's a "readable, close examination" of a
      difficult poet.

59   McDONALD, GERALD D. Review of Under Milk Wood. Library
      Journal 79 (15 June):1232.
         Praises the radio play as an "enkindling work" that is
      "full of great promise" for the stage.

60   McDONNELL, THOMAS P. "The Emergence of Dylan Thomas."
      America 91 (21 August):500-502.
         Considers the development and impact of Thomas's poetry.
      His main influence was to restore a "human and emotional" charac-
      ter to poetry. In general, Thomas "emerged from the early morass
      of semi-automatism" to a more approachable and public "communi-
      cative art."

61   MACLURE, MILLAR. Review of Under Milk Wood. Canadian Forum
     34 (November):191.
        Calls Under Milk Wood a "painting for the ear." The char-
     acters "are the way being alive" must have appeared to Thomas.

62   MacNEICE, LOUIS. "Sometimes the Poet Spoke in Prose." New
     York Times Book Review, 19 December, p. 1.
        Finds the selections in Quite Early One Morning to be
     valuable mainly for revealing Thomas's "catholic tastes, his
     innocence and his integrity." Refers to Hugh Griffith's com-
     parison of Thomas to a Shakespearean Fool.

63   MAUD, RALPH N. "Dylan Thomas's Poetry." Essays in Criticism
     4 (October):411-20.
        Recognizes that a true appreciation of Thomas's poetry can
     only follow an understanding of the poet's distinct craft. Thus
     an attempt is made to explain the method and imagery that lead
     to meaning. It's important to understand at the start that the
     basic unit of Thomas's poetry is invariably the "short rhetori-
     cally coherent phrase."

64   ____. Review of The Poetry of Dylan Thomas. Western
     Humanities Review 8 (Spring):165-66.
        Criticizes Elder Olson's study for its "forced ingenuity"
     which fails to convince.

65   "Memories & Martyrs." Time 64 (27 December):68-69.
        Reviews Quite Early One Morning. This "fragmentary prose
     footnote" by the brilliant poet won't have much influence on his
     reputation.

66   MONTAGUE, JOHN. "A First Response." Shenandoah 5 (Spring):
     28-31.
        Believes that Thomas was "almost alone" in "making real
     poetry" out of his struggle to find his way through darkness
     "towards some measure of light." The "narrowness of scope"
     amounted to his "preservation."

67   NICHOLSON, NORMAN. "The Inward Eye." Fortnightly 176 (July):
     48-49.
        Discusses the practice of radio listening, pointing to
     Under Milk Wood as a work that "exploited to the full" the visual
     force of the radio. Doubts, however, that this radio play proves
     that Thomas was potentially a great dramatist.

68   OCHSHORN, MYRON. "The Love Song of Dylan Thomas." New Mexico
     Quarterly Review 24 (Spring):46-65.
        Argues that the "dialectical tilt" between birth and death
     informs all of Thomas's poetry. Looks at some of the other
     characteristic qualities of his verse as well.

69   OLSON, ELDER. The Poetry of Dylan Thomas. Chicago:
      University of Chicago Press, 166 pp.
         Focuses intensely on Thomas's original use of language,
      thus revealing that (at least until the later poems) this was
      essentially a symbolist writer who was concerned with a "night-
      mare universe" that he experienced subjectively. A bibliography
      by William H. Huff is included. Reprinted in part: 1960.5;
      1966.8.

70   _____. "The Poetry of Dylan Thomas." Poetry 83 (January):
      213-20.
         Reviews Collected Poems, finding some problems in the
      poetry but ultimately praising the writer for the "genius already
      manifest." Confronts the major issue of Thomas's "difficulty."
      It's due to Thomas's "unusually powerful and original concep-
      tions" which are "formulated in symbols difficult in themselves
      and complex in their interrelations"; dramatic points-of-view
      presented with "deliberate" or even "studied" ambiguity; con-
      scious exploitation of "formal enigma"; and his working in a
      strange creative tradition. Reprinted: 1960.33.

71   OLSON, ELDER; DENNY, REVEL N.; and SIMPSON, ALAN. "The
      Poetry of Dylan Thomas." University of Chicago Round Table
      849 (18 July):1-12.
         Discusses the distinct achievements of Thomas, focusing on
      Olson's study.

72   "On Under Milk Wood." Daily Telegraph, 8 September, p. 1.
         Reports on the B.B.C.'s production of the play-for-voices.

73   PANTER-DOWNES, MOLLIE. "Letter from London." New Yorker 29
      (6 February):67-68.
         Reports on the "Homage to Dylan Thomas" program organized
      to honor the dead poet. Much of the literary and artistic London
      crowd turned up at the Globe, and the program included such par-
      ticipants as Edith Evans, Richard Burton, and Louis MacNeice.

74   PESCHMANN, HERMANN. "Dylan Thomas, 1912-1953: A Critical
      Appreciation." English 10 (Autumn):84-87.
         Surveys Thomas's career and attempts a final evaluation.
      Although Thomas is a difficult poet, he should be remembered for
      deeply affecting readers' hearts and minds by means of the "most
      dynamic and exultant" verse of our age.

75   PIKE, STEPHEN. "Not Good Enough." Poetry Review 45 (July-
      September):164-65.
         Dismisses Under Milk Wood as simply a "well-turned
      trifle." Too much of the writing "degenerates" into sentimental
      prose-poetry and the content consists of mere variations of a
      worn-out theme.

76   PRESCOTT, ORVILLE. "Books of the Times." New York Times, 15 December, p. 29.
Praises some of the selections in Quite Early One Morning, especially for their zest and eloquence, but finds others "verbose and tiresome" or just plain trivial. The best items are the reminiscences of Thomas's childhood.

77   _____. Review of Under Milk Wood. New York Times, 28 April, p. 29.
Discovers a "Joycean eloquence" in the radio play, but ultimately finds it to be a work overly pretentious and too "confused" to be a total success.

78   REID, ALASTAIR. "A First Word." Yale Literary Magazine, November, p. 20.
Recalls being struck by Thomas's intense obsession with words. Reprinted: 1960.5, 33.

79   "Report and Summary." College English 15 (April):421.
Summarizes the gist of two recent publications on Thomas—Elder Olson's The Poetry of Dylan Thomas and a "rhapsodic" piece by Edith Sitwell (see 1954.88).

80   Review of The Doctor and the Devils. New Yorker 30 (6 March): 120.
Praises Thomas's script for avoiding verbal or visual cliches.

81   ROLO, CHARLES J. "Reader's Choice." Atlantic Monthly 194 (July):82-83.
Calls Under Milk Wood a "small masterpiece" that celebrates life in a "rollicking, fantastical" manner. The "verbal pyrotechnics" imply a "deity disporting . . . with the elements he rules."

82   ROWLANDS, SHEILA. "The Literary Topography of Laugharne." Dock Leaves 5 (Winter):38-40.
Suggests that the surroundings and the topography of Laugharne have a magical quality and that the place comes out repeatedly in Thomas's poetry.

83   RUSSELL, FRANCIS. "Twisting Counterpoint of Thought." Christian Science Monitor, 6 May, p. 11.
Complains that Thomas's poetry "lacked coherency." His poetic world is a "private one of private symbols." Finds that in Under Milk Wood he finally succeeded in becoming more objective, but that it nevertheless remains a work that "apprehends rather than comprehends."

84   SALTER, WILLIAM. "Look and Listen." New Statesman 47 (6 February):159-60.
Applauds the B.B.C. presentation of Under Milk Wood. All along Thomas was attempting to express the "daedal dance" of

existence, and in his play-for-voices he succeeded in doing so
"on a larger scale than anywhere else." Parallels between
Thomas and Robert Burns are also emphasized.

85   SCOTT, WINFIELD TOWNLEY. "The Death, and Some Dominions of
     It." Yale Literary Magazine, November, pp. 13-14.
        States that Thomas had two powerful nostalgias: "back to
     childhood and forward to oblivion." Reprinted: 1960.5.

86   _____. "Poet of a Lost Eden Recaptured in Wales." New York
     Herald Tribune Book Review 30 (23 May):4.
        Reviews Under Milk Wood and Elder Olson's The Poetry of
     Dylan Thomas. Finds Thomas's prose play to be a minor work com-
     parable to Whittier's "Snow Bound," though he praises its vital
     delight in language. Olson's book is marked especially for its
     work on Thomas's religious sonnets sequence.

87   SEYMORE-SMITH, MARTIN. Review of Collected Poems. Black
     Mountain Review 1 (Spring):57-58.
        Criticizes Thomas for essentially having little to say.
     Almost all of his poems consist of "series of generalizations."

88   SITWELL, EDITH. "Dylan Thomas." Atlantic Monthly 193
     (February):42-45.
        Appraises Thomas's best poetry in the course of this
     affectionate obituary.

89   SMITH, HARRISON. "Whose Is the Guilt?" Saturday Review 37
     (13 March):24.
        Speculates that our society was the ultimate cause of
     Thomas's premature death.

90   SOLOMON, I.L. "Welsh Winesburg." Saturday Review 37
     (3 July):18.
        Praises the "mischievous, bawdy, delightful" quality of
     Under Milk Wood, noting at the same time that the writing re-
     flects the "devilish" influence of adolescence that plagued
     Thomas throughout his life.

91   SPENDER, STEPHEN. "Dylan Thomas." Britain Today, January,
     pp. 15-18.
        Looks at Thomas's poetry in light of his death.

92   _____. "Greatness of Aim." Times Literary Supplement,
     6 August, p. vi.
        Compares Thomas and W.H. Auden. Both attempted to inject a
     vision of life derived from "whole experience" into poems made
     and formed with that aim. Thomas can be seen as the "outstanding
     contemporary Romantic example" while also being a Christian;
     Auden can be seen as "anti-Romantic," yet he is less classical
     than "dogmatic." Thomas is "opaque" and Auden "transparent."
     Reprinted: 1955.79.

93   _____. "A Literary Letter from London." New York Times Book Review, 10 January, p. 14.
     Explains the reputation of Thomas as the last of the "new writers" as the result of his being a combination of an "individualist, innovator, and traditionalist" all at once.

94   STANFORD, DEREK. Dylan Thomas: A Literary Study. London: Neville Spearman; New York: Citadel Press, 194 pp.
     Discusses Thomas's reception among his contemporary critics. Analyzes the "autotelic" style used to create poems always concerned with memory and sensation. Speculates in a postscript about Thomas's ultimate place in English poetry. Reprinted in part: 1960.5.

95   "Sudden Magic." Newsweek 44 (20 December):86.
     Discovers in Quite Early One Morning a "rich sampling" of Thomas's characteristic "sensuousness" leading into mysticism and comedy. The pieces invoking childhood are especially magical.

96   SWEENEY, JOHN L. "The Gardener and the Prince." Shenandoah 5 (Spring):20-23.
     Points out that man was the "master metaphor" in Thomas's work and that he "acknowledged the fatherhood of Adam" with unusual compassion.

97   THWAITE, ANTHONY. "Fragments of a Legend." Spectator 193 (12 November):586.
     Reviews Quite Early One Morning. Thinks that the apparent haphazard way in which this book was put together is an injustice to Thomas.

98   TOMLINSON, CHARLES. "Scholarship and Dylan Thomas." Spectator 193 (20 August):235-36.
     Reviews Elder Olson's The Poetry of Dylan Thomas. Criticizes Olson's "academic fashion" of reading the poetry. "The text, when reached, is smothered under a load of terms."

99   TYNAN, KENNETH. "Prose and the Playwright." Atlantic Monthly 194 (December):72, 74, 76.
     Considers the state of modern poetic drama and sees Under Milk Wood as an unusually successful work because Thomas avoided the "fatal urge" of aspiring toward self-conscious verse.

100   WALTERS, RAYMOND, Jr. "Trade Winds." Saturday Review 37 (20 February):8, 10.
     Describes the efforts going on to settle which version of Under Milk Wood should be marked as the authorized one and reports on the progress of the Dylan Thomas Fund.

101   WELLS, HENRY W. "Voice and Verse in Dylan Thomas' Play." College English 15 (May):438-44.
     Submits that Under Milk Wood introduces both a new kind of drama and poetry. The drama is new in being for voices, the poetry in employing an innovative order of versification.

102   WILLIAMS, FORREST. "Detour to Laugharne." Colorado Quarterly
      3 (Summer):94–95.
         Discovers that Thomas could write with "completely genuine
      naturalism" by comparing the actual Laugharne with the observa-
      tions of some of the poems Thomas wrote there.

103   WOODCOCK, GEORGE. "Dylan Thomas and the Welsh Environment."
      Arizona Quarterly 10 (Winter):293–305.
         Argues that the kind of poetry Thomas wrote could only have
      come from a Welsh environment. "In its language and imagery, its
      mythology and its strange combination of mysticism and carnality"
      Thomas's poetry represented "the expression of an ancient tradi-
      tion emerging volcanically" into the middle of the English cul-
      ture that had attempted to bury it.

104   _____. "Notes on the Poetry, No. 2 (Dylan Thomas and the
      Welsh Scene)." Poetry and Poverty 7:20–25.
         Believes that Thomas, while "almost a total individualist,"
      was not as self-obsessed as is commonly believed. The "compas-
      sion that emerges from so many poems of his middle period about
      the victims of war and the martyrs of solitude and oddity" repre-
      sents "a kind of dialectical swing away from his silence about
      the tragedies of the Depression years."

105   ZINNES, HARRIET. Review of The Poetry of Dylan Thomas. Books
      Abroad 28 (Autumn):481.
         Objects to Elder Olson's argument that Thomas's sonnets are
      necessarily unified, but still applauds the "sensitivity and
      erudition" the critic brings to his readings of Thomas's diffi-
      cult poetry.

                                  1955

1   ADAMS, ROBERT MARTIN. "Taste and Bad Taste in Metaphysical
     Poetry: Richard Crashaw and Dylan Thomas." Hudson Review 8
     (Spring):61–77.
        Comparing him to Richard Crashaw, the author notes that
     Thomas's religious sonnets follow metaphysical impulses and
     methods revealing a powerful tendency toward the baroque and
     grotesque. Reprinted and adapted: 1966.8; 1971.1.

2   AMIS, KINGLSEY. "Thomas the Rhymer." Spectator 195
     (12 August):227–28.
        Takes a critical look at A Prospect of the Sea.

3   BANYARD, GRACE. "Deaths and Entrances." Contemporary Review
     188 (September):214–15.
        Notes that Thomas's reputation is undergoing a change, with
     new emphasis being placed on his prose. Welcomes the publication
     of A Prospect of the Sea as a representative selection, particu-
     larly reflective of Thomas's concerns with death and madness.

4   BARO, GENE. "The Orator of Llareggub." Poetry 87 (November):
     119-22.
         Finds that although Under Milk Wood is deficient as
     theater, it has the enduring strengths of Thomas's vibrant lan-
     guage and charm. What finally distinguishes it is Thomas's
     "great humane compassion."

5   _____. "The Poignant World of Dylan Thomas." New York Herald
     Tribune Book Review 31 (12 June):4.
         Finds that Adventures in the Skin Trade and some other
     stories included in this volume form a "vein of pure gold" in the
     tradition of Dickens. As a whole, however, Thomas's writing is
     often marked by "troublesome imprecision" even though he shows
     some characteristic brilliance in dealing with the "eternal"
     themes of life, love, and death.

6   BARRETT, MARVIN. Review of Adventures in the Skin Trade.
     Harper's Magazine 211 (July):89.
         Finds that, although Thomas tended to overwrite in prose,
     he does offer extended samples of masterly descriptive writing.

7   BOYD, BEVERLY. Review of Quite Early One Morning. Catholic
     World 180 (February):396-97.
         Notes that the prose in the volume tends to be, like
     Thomas's poetry, obscure but also "deep, and very beautiful."

8   BOYLE, KAY. "A Declaration for 1955." Nation 180
     (29 January):102-4.
         Recalls a meeting with a young Thomas, and still retains
     the feeling of "the quality of tenderness . . . behind the savage
     impact of his gaze."

9   BREIT, HARVEY. "In and Out of Books." New York Times Book
     Review, 18 December, p. 8.
         Believes New Direction's publication of A Child's Christmas
     in Wales by itself to be especially fortunate because "by its
     simple power of poetic radiance" the story clears the poet of
     many ugly and painful details that too often cling to him.

10   BRINNIN, JOHN MALCOLM. "Cockles, Brambles, and Fern Hill."
     Atlantic Monthly 196 (November):50-55.
         Follows a preview published in the October issue (see
     Brinnin, 1955.12) with another selected part of Brinnin's forth-
     coming Dylan Thomas in America (see Brinnin, 1955.11). The
     selection focuses on a 1953 visit to Thomas's home in Wales.

11   _____. Dylan Thomas in America: An Intimate Journal.
     Boston: Little, Brown & Co., 305 pp.
         Written by the man who acted as sponsor, agent, and all-
     around guide during Thomas's reading tours of the United States,
     the book describes both the extraordinary readings and personal
     behavior of the poet. Essentially, Brinnin tries to account for
     what he perceived to be Thomas's generosity of mind and soul
     mixed with an extreme sense of loneliness and a tendency toward

self-degradation, concluding that the "briefest review" of the
man's emotional existence would imply that "no man was ever more
adept in killing what he loved, or suffered more in the conse-
quence." Reprinted in part: 1960.5.

12   _____. "Dylan Thomas in Wales." Atlantic Monthly 196
        (October):37–44.
        Previews part of Brinnin's forthcoming Dylan Thomas in
America (see Brinnin, 1955.11). The selection focuses on a
1951 visit to Thomas's home in Wales. A dissenting note by
Caitlin Thomas is appended.

13   BROSSARD, CHANDLER. "The Magic of Dylan Thomas." Commonweal
        62 (10 June):262–63.
        Reviews Adventures in the Skin Trade, finding many things
to praise in the collection because it's marked throughout by
Thomas's "devout" imagination.

14   CAMPBELL, ROY. "Memories of Dylan Thomas at the B.B.C."
        Poetry 87 (November):111–14.
        Reminisces about his experiences with Thomas both as friend
and poetry program reader. Although Thomas had trouble reading
"correct" poets like Dryden and Pope, he was the "best all round
reader of verse that I ever produced."

15   COLLIER, KAY. Review of Adventures in the Skin Trade. Truth,
        16 September, p. 1162.
        Offers a critical response to the publication of the frag-
ment of the novel.

16   CRAMPTON, MICHAEL. "New Novels." New Statesman 50
        (10 September):305–6.
        Reviews Adventures in the Skin Trade. Although the frag-
ment is "uneven" stylistically, it is also "pure joy, a Thurber
fantasy of domestic life."

17   DAVIE, DONALD. Articulate Energy: An Inquiry into the Syntax
        of English Poetry. London: Routledge & Kegan Paul,
        pp. 126–28 passim.
        Suggests that Thomas "exploits a pseudo-syntax" because,
though formally precise, his poetry "offers" but fails to "mime"
the mind's process.

18   DAVIES, ROBERTSON. "Portrait of the Artist at Extreme
        Length." Saturday Night 70 (5 February):12–13.
        Praises Portrait of the Artist and Quite Early One Morning
as "two golden little books" that give us the "distilled essence
of a poet's life."

19   DAWEDEIT, GLENDY. "Poet Gave the Legend an Assist."
      Washington Post, 7 August, p. E6.
         Speculates that at least part of Thomas's popularity was
      due to a "modern nostalgia for a poet in the grand tradition of
      eccentricity." Finds that Derek Stanford's Dylan Thomas helps
      one understand the poet, but that this critical work pales next
      to the "candor" of Adventures in the Skin Trade.

20   ____. "A 'Tell-All' Memoir by a Friend." Washington Post,
      20 November, p. E6.
         Reviews John Malcolm Brinnin's Dylan Thomas in America,
      finding it to be the kind of account sure to "swell the legend."
      The best parts are those that reveal the "tormenting mental
      process" preceding Thomas's "suicidal round."

21   DAWSON, S.W. "Mr. Maud on Dylan Thomas." Essays in Criticism
      5 (April):187–89.
         Believes that Ralph Maud makes a critical mistake in his
      writing on Thomas when he accepts the poet's "divorce" of lan-
      guage "from its roots in experience" as a sign of poetic origi-
      nality.

22   "Design for Living." Times (London), 15 September, p. 13.
         Gives a brief review of Adventures in the Skin Trade. It's
      a "slight" work that will "titillate rather than satisfy" the
      poet's admirers.

23   "Dylan Thomas: An Application for Reinterment." Times
      (London), 21 October, p. 5.
         Reports on the application for the reinterment of Thomas's
      body in the grounds of the Boat House in order to better accom-
      modate the "pilgrims."

24   FRASER, GEORGE SUTHERLAND. "Artist as a Young Dog." New
      Statesman 49 (11 June):812.
         Praises Emlyn Williams's stage portrayal of Thomas. The
      actor shows how worthy of perpetuation the Thomas legend is.
      An important part of the "truth" about Thomas is the legendary
      "card, the young dog, the wide boy from Swansea with a bottle on
      his finger, the brilliant minor writer of excellent comic tales."
      Reprinted: 1960.33.

25   GARDINER, HAROLD C. "Welsh Chanter's Spell." America 92
      (1 January):363.
         Reviews Quite Early One Morning, praising the "tone and
      flavor" of the "remarkable thought and language."

26   GHISELIN, BREWSTER. "Some Help for the Readers of Dylan
      Thomas." Western Review 19 (Winter):145–47.
         Reviews Elder Olson's The Poetry of Dylan Thomas, finding
      it largely unsatisfactory because of the critic's frequent fail-
      ure to support some key contentions about the poet. The most
      impressive thing about the study is the believable emergence of

Thomas as a lyrical poet of "limited" and "uneven" production and range but of great "tragic" force.

27 GILLETT, ERIC. "The World Within the Skull." National and English Review 144 (January):45-46.
     Reminisces about working experiences with Thomas after looking at Quite Early One Morning. There was no "more vital and sincere" speaker than Thomas in the B.B.C. studio.

28 GOODFELLOW, DOROTHY W. "Dylan Thomas, 'The Boy of Summer.'" In Lectures on Some Modern Poets. Carnegie Series in English, 2. Pittsburgh: Carnegie Institute of Technology, pp. 77-90.
     Stresses the "nightmarish" nature of Thomas's work, an aspect that points to existentialism.

29 GRADDON, JOHN. "The Book of the Year: An Editorial Symposium." Poetry Review 46 (January-March):39.
     Chooses Under Milk Wood as the year's most important book because "it acted as a catalyst" in resolving and reevaluating critical attitudes fluctuating since the 1920s.

30 GRAVES, ROBERT. "These Be Your Gods." In The Crowning Privilege. London: Cassell & Co., pp. 119-22, 138-42.
     Objects to the practice of making idols of living poets and argues that Thomas (who was generally considered to be one of the idols along with Yeats, Pound, Eliot, and Auden) was "drunk on melody, and what the words were he cared not." Reprint of 1955.31. Reprinted in part: 1956.18-19; 1960.5.

31 _____. "These Be Your Gods, O Israel." Essays in Criticism 5 (April):129-50.
     Attacks Thomas as the last in a list of modern idols (see Graves, 1955.30). Reprinted: 1955.30. Reprinted in part: 1956.18-19; 1960.5.

32 HAMILTON, EDITH. "Words, Words, Words." Saturday Review 38 (19 November):15-16, 52-53.
     Using Jean Ingelow as a comparative starting point, depicts Thomas as in the forefront of modern poetry's trend away from clarity and reason and toward the point where "we can give up trying to fit meanings to words."

33 HEATH-STUBBS, JOHN, and WRIGHT, DAVID, eds. Introduction to The Faber Book of Twentieth Century Verse. London: Faber & Faber, pp. 24-25, 28.
     Notes Thomas's role in bringing back "innocence" and "elaborate, formal and rhetorical" technique to English poetry.

34 HEWES, HENRY. "The Author." Saturday Review 38 (19 November):17.
     Gives a biographical sketch of John Malcolm Brinnin, author of Dylan Thomas in America.

35   HICKS, GRANVILLE. "Dylan Thomas and George Orwell--So
      Different, Yet in One Way So Alike." New Leader 38
      (26 December):16-17.
         Reviews John Malcolm Brinnin's Dylan Thomas in America,
      giving the work credit for providing some of the information
      necessary to understand Thomas's "decline" in his later years.
      Like George Orwell, Thomas was a "born" dissenter, and this
      quality "proved fatal."

36   "Interpretations of Dylan Thomas." Times Literary Supplement,
      7 January, p. 10.
         Compares the strengths and weaknesses of Elder Olson's The
      Poetry of Dylan Thomas and Derek Stanford's Dylan Thomas.
      Olson's work is a "triumph of structure analysis," employing the
      original method of approaching the poems by way of "dramatic
      plotting" instead of verbal texture. This method's main problem
      is that "it makes Thomas often look tidier than he is." Stan-
      ford's work is useful mainly as a companion reader. He approaches
      the poems by means of their texture and "atmosphere" instead of
      structure. His readings are "particularly intelligent about the
      religious element" in the poems, but he ultimately fails to
      address the ambiguous quality of that faith.

37   JARRELL, RANDALL. "The Year in Poetry." Harper's Magazine
      211 (October):96.
         Finds that Under Milk Wood is exceedingly successful in
      expressing "directly and funnily and lovingly" the joy of
      living.

38   JENNINGS, ELIZABETH. "Thomas the Novelist." Spectator 195
      (7 October):462-63.
         Reviews Adventures in the Skin Trade. Praises the fragment
      both for its "extraordinary eloquence" and its creation of an
      "extremely interesting" autobiographical protagonist.

39   JOOST, NICHOLAS. "The Wit, Flamboyance and Faith of Dylan
      Thomas." Commonweal 61 (7 January):387.
         Reviews Quite Early One Morning, finding the collection to
      be especially useful in helping to illuminate "some of the most
      remarkable poetic work" of the last fifty years.

40   KNAUBER, CHARLES F. "Wales and the Sea." Renascence 8
      (Autumn):52-54.
         Reviews Under Milk Wood. Says that the triumph of the
      radio play is the "recognition of the insatiability and degen-
      eration" of the passions that preoccupy the characters.

41   KORG, JACOB. Review of Adventures in the Skin Trade. Nation
      181 (30 July):102.
         Praises the "energetic" quality of this uncompleted novel.

42 KUNITZ, STANLEY, and COLBY, VINETA, eds. Twentieth Century
   Authors: First Supplement. New York: H.W. Wilson,
   pp. 990-91.
   Links Thomas's "impassioned" writing with his personality.

43 LASK, THOMAS. "Welsh Poet's Play on Disks." New York Times,
   23 October, sec. 2, p. 16.
   Recommends the Westminster recording of Under Milk Wood for
   its excellent representation of the text and the planned effect.
   The recorded play is "as simple and moving as a folk dance."

44 LAURENTIA, Sister M. "Thomas' 'Fern Hill.'" Explicator 14
   (October): item 1.
   Explicates the poem as one whose strength depends on a
   symmetrical union of the symbol of the farm and the theme of
   time.

45 LERNER, L.D. "The Life and Death of Scrutiny." London
   Magazine 2 (January):76.
   Comments on Scrutiny's "disgraceful" dismissal of Thomas as
   a "very minor poet."

46 "Looking for Trouble." Times Literary Supplement,
   30 September, p. 569.
   Reviews Adventures in the Skin Trade, concluding that the
   fragment of the projected novel proves that Thomas had a genius
   for comedy. There is doubt that, had he lived, Thomas could have
   ever controlled his "natural comic sense" to bring about the
   "ordered construction of a considerable work"; nevertheless, the
   comedy is "superior" even to that found in Under Milk Wood.

47 LOUGÉE, DAVID. "The Worlds of Dylan Thomas." Poetry 87
   (November):114-15.
   Claims that Thomas was both a great poet and prose writer.
   Emphasizes that a distinguishing feature of the prose is "what
   can only be called a deep sense of fun."

48 McDONALD, GERALD D. Review of Dylan Thomas: A Literary
   Study. Library Journal 80 (15 February):458-59.
   Recommends Derek Stanford's study as a "useful" aid for
   anyone reading Thomas's "difficult" poetry.

49 _____. Review of Dylan Thomas in America. Library Journal 80
   (15 October):2232.
   Praises John Malcolm Brinnin's account for its forthright-
   ness in dealing with some of the unattractive aspects of the
   poet.

50 MacLAREN-ROSS, J. "New Novels." Listener 54 (25 August):307.
   Reviews A Prospect of the Sea. Recommends the book for its
   many items of "absorbing interest," especially the satirical
   essay "How to Be a Poet."

51   MacLURE, MILLAR. Review of A Prospect of the Sea. Canadian
      Forum 35 (November):188.
         Recommends the volume as an antidote to the explosion of
      writing about Thomas after his death. Here is a chance to be
      "caught" again by his "suffering, cocky imagination." Both the
      subconscious and the "pastoral" pieces are essential to an
      understanding of the poems.

52   MacNEICE, LOUIS. "Book Reviews." London Magazine 2 (May):
      106-9.
         Reviews recent books about and by Thomas. Believes that
      Elder Olson's The Poetry of Dylan Thomas is essentially flawed by
      forced ingenuity. Derek Stanford's Dylan Thomas comes in for
      some praise for its "honest" and discriminating work on the dif-
      ficult poems. Quite Early One Morning has "limitations" that
      "proved assets" in Thomas's poetry.

53   MARTZ, LOUIS L. "New Poetry: In the Pastoral Mode." Yale
      Review 44 (Winter):301-9.
         Discusses the pastoral quality of Under Milk Wood. Finds
      that in theme and method Thomas fulfilled the "marvellous prom-
      ise" of a dreamed Eden.

54   MAUD, RALPH N. "Dylan Thomas Astro-Navigated." Essays in
      Criticism 5 (April):164-68.
         Reviews Elder Olson's The Poetry of Dylan Thomas, finding
      it to be unpersuasive because the critic fails to "match the
      poet in accuracy" and thus surpasses him in "ingenuity." The
      astronomical interpretations in particular seem strained and
      ultimately invalid.

55   _____. "Dylan Thomas' Manuscripts in the Houghton Library."
      Audience, 4 February, pp. 4-6.
         Describes the manuscripts of Thomas's poems found in the
      Houghton Library.

56   _____. "A Note of Dylan Thomas's Serious Puns." Audience,
      15 April, pp. 5-7.
         Comments on Thomas's tendency to use puns for significant
      purposes.

57   _____. "Thomas' 'Sonnet I.'" Explicator 14 (December):
      item 16.
         Explicates the first sonnet of the "Altarwise by owl-light"
      sequence as a religious sonnet depicting the newly crucified
      Christ and the impending Resurrection.

58   MEYERHOFF, HANS. "The Violence of Dylan Thomas." New
      Republic 133 (11 July):17-19.
         Remembers seeing Thomas give one of his public readings.
      It started with terrible awkwardness, but once Thomas began
      reading the poems, he was a "being transformed." "He read as if
      it were an act of worship." Adventures in the Skin Trade, the

book under review, shows the "pagan," the "deeply poetic," and
the sad sides of Thomas.

59 MOODY, J.N. Review of Adventures in the Skin Trade.
    Commonweal 63 (2 December):242.
        Recommends the book for its "dazzling" and exuberant"
    writing.

60 MOORE, GEOFFREY. "Dylan Thomas." Kenyon Review 17 (Spring):
    258-77.
        Attempts to clarify the achievement of Thomas by placing
    him in the context of his "physical and spiritual environment"
    and against the developing tradition of modern poetry. The
    ultimate conclusion is that he wrote the most memorable cele-
    bratory, affirmative poetry since Hopkins. Reprinted: 1960.33.

61 "Mr. Emlyn Williams as Dylan Thomas." Times (London), 19 May,
    p. 3.
        Reviews Emlyn Williams's presentation of "Dylan Thomas
    Growing Up." The one-man interpretation of readings of the
    poet's work was an "immense success" because, by means of a very
    "artful naivety," Williams created a "human figure of the
    enigmatic poet."

62 OBOLER, ELI M. Review of Adventures in the Skin Trade.
    Library Journal 80 (July):1594.
        Recommends the book, particularly "The True Story" con-
    tained in the volume. The latter is seen as a classic of short
    fiction.

63 PORTER, KATHERINE ANNE. "His Poetry Makes the Difference."
    New York Times Book Review, 20 November, p. 5.
        Finds John Malcolm Brinnin's Dylan Thomas in America a
    "very honorable attempt" to tell his side of the story straight,
    a story "of disgrace and disaster and death" that followed high
    hopes of success.

64 PRESCOTT, ORVILLE. "Books of the Times." New York Times,
    15 November, p. 31.
        Calls John Malcolm Brinnin's Dylan Thomas in America "one
    of the saddest books of recent years." The account makes one
    feel "astounded that such a human wreck" as Thomas could have
    composed poems "at all."

65 "Prose Writings by Dylan Thomas." Times Literary Supplement,
    5 August, p. 446.
        Reviews A Prospect of the Sea. Edited by Daniel Jones,
    this volume of stories and essays is primarily valuable for
    revealing the writer at work during a transitional, exploratory
    period when he was discovering, using, and controlling his
    "volcanic" imagination while his life was moving from adolescence
    toward manhood and maturity.

66   READ, HERBERT. "The Drift of Modern Poetry." Encounter 4
      (January):3-10.
         Considers the general course of modern poetry, eventually
      focusing on Thomas as an example of "new Romanticism." His
      "images were threaded to . . . human, universal themes, to which
      he gave a fresh, contemporary expression." But, like many of his
      fellow poets of the time, he presented thoughts that were "static
      convictions rather than the products of a philosophical activity."

67   Review of Adventures in the Skin Trade. Virginia Quarterly
      Review 31 (Autumn):ci.
         Praises the collection for its lyrical language and
      "authentic fancy."

68   Review of Dylan Thomas. New Statesman 49 (15 January):82.
         Recommends Derek Stanford's study as a "serious work of
      criticism" whose main value lies in the "honest attempt" to
      elucidate the poetry, particularly its lyrical nature.

69   Review of A Prospect of the Sea. New Statesman 50
      (20 August):223-24.
         Notes that the collection falls into "unequal halves." The
      first part, written between 1934 and 1938, represents Thomas as
      surrealist; the second, written between 1947 and 1953, reveals
      him as a humorist. "The comic Thomas survives much better than
      the surrealist."

70   Review of Under Milk Wood. Virginia Quarterly Review 31
      (Winter):xvi.
         Compares the play for voices to an example of expressionist
      drama.

71   ROLO, CHARLES J. "Reader's Choice." Atlantic Monthly 196
      (July):81.
         Reviews Adventures in the Skin Trade, finding many of the
      selections slight yet always marked by Thomas's genius with
      language.

72   ROSENTHAL, M.L. "The Friend of the Poet." Nation 181
      (17 December):539-40.
         Calls John Malcolm Brinnin's Dylan Thomas in America an
      "invaluable" account, particularly for the insights it gives of
      what results when a "natural" like Thomas is placed in the "world
      of genteel literary professionalism."

73   "The Saddest Book." Newsweek 46 (28 November):118, 120-21.
         Reviews John Malcolm Brinnin's Dylan Thomas in America.
      Describes it as the "saddest" book published during the year, one
      that doesn't have the "style" that might have transformed the
      "sordidness" of the poet's final days into tragedy.

74   SCHWARTZ, DELMORE. "With a Deep-Set Romantic Attitude." <u>New York Times Book Review</u>, 22 May, pp. 4, 20.
    Points out that <u>Adventures in the Skin Trade</u> reveals Thomas's extreme romanticism to have been an attitude applied "toward all experience and not merely a mood congenial to the writing of poetry." This work of fiction offers a "meaningfulness comparable to . . . Keats' letters and Yeats' memoirs."

75   SCOTT, WINFIELD TOWNLEY. "Candid Memoir of Dylan Thomas on His Way to Self-Destruction." <u>New York Herald Tribune Book Review</u> 32 (20 November):1, 15.
    Reviews John Malcolm Brinnin's <u>Dylan Thomas in America</u>, noting the extraordinary frankness that is not marked in any sense by the "scandalous or malicious." Finds the account to be the "most harrowing revelation of self-destruction" since that of Hart Crane.

76   _____. "The Lyric Marvel." <u>Saturday Review</u> 38 (8 January): 17-18.
    Reviews <u>Quite Early One Morning</u>, noting that when Thomas turned from poetry to prose, he "rarely turned very far," the remarkable exuberance for language existing in both kinds of writing. The "autobiographical dithyrambs" of the volume's first part are the most significant and compelling; the less personal pieces of the second part are often slight, being important mainly for showing Thomas at work as a professional.

77   SHAPIRO, KARL. "Dylan Thomas." <u>Poetry</u> 87 (November):100-110.
    Recalls the outpouring of anguish that followed the death of Thomas and attempts in light of that passionate response to estimate the achievement of his fellow poet. He disagrees with those who linked Thomas with the traditions of Bohemia or the high symbolists. Seeing him instead as a "lone wolf" who actually represented a turning away from all the poetic schools, Shapiro agrees with the common view that Thomas was the "best lyric poet of our time." While noting that Thomas's technique is derivative, he points out that, "through the force of emotion," the "iron of English" is bent into an impressive personal idiom. After listing those poems he believes will have a permanent life, he notes that Thomas's few happy poems are among the best and almost always the simplest while the despairing ones are "among the most rewarding, the richest in feeling, and the most difficult to hold." Reprinted: 1960.5, 31, 33; 1966.8.

78   _____. "The Truth Outside the Rules." <u>Encounter</u> 4 (May): 87-88.
    Declares that Thomas belongs to a group of poets who have broken away from "immobile myth-makers" and are writing vital poetry "intimate" with the age. These poets (including Spender, MacNeice, and Day Lewis along with Thomas) are writing the best "human" poetry of the time.

79 SPENDER, STEPHEN. The Making of a Poem. London: Hamish
    Hamilton, pp. 35–44.
    Reprint of 1954.92.

80 "The Spoken Word." Time 65 (2 May):104.
    Surveys the current popularity of voice recordings, start-
    ing with the Caedmon release of Thomas reading "grandly," filling
    the air "with a sweet Welsh tumult."

81 "Time's Books: The Legend of Dylan Thomas." Time 65
    (30 May):90, 92, 95.
    Speculates that Thomas's popularity can be explained by the
    fact that he gave people what they expected from poetry ("joy")
    and a poet (a legendary "romantic"). A survey of his reputation
    and life leads to the conclusion that while he had a wild and
    ribald side, he was also the "lonely misanthrope who saw the
    world and himself with intolerable clarity." Believes that the
    recently published Adventures in the Skin Trade enhances his
    "legend."

82 TREWIN, J.C. "Greek and Welsh." Illustrated London News,
    19 March, p. 520.
    Praises the Vanbrugh Theatre presentation of Under Milk
    Wood for showing how visuals can be used successfully to augment
    the power of the language in Thomas's play-for-voices.

83 "The Two Literatures of Wales." Times Literary Supplement,
    5 August, p. xii.
    Distinguishes between Anglo-Welsh and Welsh literature.
    Describing Thomas as a Welsh writer is the result of being
    ignorant of the "great corpus" of living literature written in
    Welsh. Thomas's considerable influence was in Anglo-Welsh writ-
    ing, the other important literary tradition alive in Wales. Goes
    on to describe various distinctive qualities of true Welsh lit-
    erature and mentions a number of its practitioners.

84 TYLER, PARKER. "Then Was my Neophyte a Scriptist." Poetry
    87 (November):116–18.
    Reviews The Doctor and the Devils. Although it's clear
    that Thomas is here mainly "working for a living," the script is
    nevertheless impressive, particularly in its "remarkably sentient
    graph of lens-likely images."

85 UNTERMEYER, LOUIS. "Dylan Thomas." In Masters of the Modern
    World. New York: Simon & Schuster, pp. 753–57.
    Provides a biographical essay that emphasizes Thomas's
    impassioned life and work. His poetry "has the virtue of over-
    abundance."

86 _____. "Poet's Portrait as a Doomed Man." Saturday Review 38
    (19 November):16–17.
    Reviews John Malcolm Brinnin's Dylan Thomas in America,
    calling it an extraordinary book that, though limited to Thomas's

last and worst years, provides a "sharp, candid" portrait of a
"tragically troubled and self-doomed" man.

87   WATKINS, VERNON. "A Poem by Dylan Thomas." Times (London),
     2 August, p. 9.
        Corrects the general impression that Thomas wrote "Do not
     go gentle into that good night" in memory of his father. The
     poem was addressed to his father.

88   WEEKS, EDWARD. "The Morning of the Poet." Atlantic Monthly
     195 (January):78.
        Reviews Quite Early One Morning, suggesting that this
     "scintillating" volume by "one of the finest lyric poets" of this
     age is particularly valuable because it's the next best thing to
     an autobiography.

89   WEST, ANTHONY. "A Singer and a Spectre." New Yorker 30
     (22 January):106-8.
        Reviews Quite Early One Morning, finding the best pieces
     providing a "tremendous lark" while being at the same time
     "fundamentally extremely serious." Thomas "knew his art and
     craft" better than most of his fellow-poets, and he "used it
     more naturally."

90   WHITE, WILLIAM. "A Book Review." Papers of the Bibliograph-
     ical Society of America 49:90-93.
        Reviews Elder Olson's The Poetry of Dylan Thomas, focusing
     on the usefulness of William H. Huff's bibliographical section.

91   WOODCOCK, GEORGE. Review of Quite Early One Morning. Arizona
     Quarterly 11 (Spring):79-81.
        Notes some unevenness of quality in the volume, but con-
     cludes by praising Thomas's prose for its "vigor and directness."

92   ZINNES, HARRIET. Review of Quite Early One Morning. Books
     Abroad 29 (Summer):309.
        Finds some of the material to be merely frivolous, but
     recommends the collection nevertheless because it does contain
     certain "delightful" pieces that illustrate Thomas's humor, per-
     sonal warmth, and stylistic "bombast."

93   _____. Review of Under Milk Wood. Books Abroad 29 (Spring):
     176.
        Praises Thomas's play-for-voices as the "culmination" of
     the writer's genius for sensuous language, humor, and honest
     depiction of "genuine" life.

1956

*1 ALGREN, NELSON. "An Intimate Look at Dylan Thomas." Chicago
    Sun-Times, 1 January.
        Recollects a meeting with Thomas and comments on John
    Malcolm Brinnin's Dylan Thomas in America, a book that "needed
    doing." The one disappointment about Brinnin's book was that it
    "offered no insight into what was driving" him. See Maud,
    1970.14, p. 194.

2   "Anglo-Welsh Attitudes." Times Literary Supplement, 1 June,
    p. 328.
        Surveys the flowering of Anglo-Welsh literature that took
    place during the second quarter of this century against a back-
    drop of social upheaval. Compares Thomas's short stories with
    those of Gwyn Thomas and Glyn Jones, but emphasizes that "while
    he shared their exuberance and perceptiveness," he was different
    in the way he "transmuted experience so that it became vivid,
    odd, intensely real."

3   ASSELINEAU, ROGER. "Comptes rendus." Études anglaises 9
    (July–September):272–74.
        Reviews Quite Early One Morning, Adventures in the Skin
    Trade, and A Prospect of the Sea. Suggests that these posthu-
    mously published works will reinforce Thomas's reputation.

4   BANYARD, GRACE. "The Gates of Hell." Contemporary Review
    189 (June):380.
        Praises John Malcolm Brinnin's Dylan Thomas in America as
    an account full of "terrible" wisdom and truth about the poet's
    nature and genius.

5   BERGH, TONY VAN DEN. "Signifying Nothing." Poetry Review 47
    (July–September):165–66.
        Pans John Malcolm Brinnin's Dylan Thomas in America, an
    account that tells us nothing beside the known fact that the poet
    was a drunkard.

6   BLISSETT, WILLIAM. "Dylan Thomas: A Reader in Search of a
    Poet." Queen's Quarterly 63 (Spring):45–48.
        Gives a personal account of the progress from being intro-
    duced to Thomas's poetry, through various phases of "reading and
    misreading," to the present response to his work.

7   BREIT, HARVEY. The Writer Observed. Cleveland: World,
    pp. 123–25, 231–33.
        Reprint of 1950.5.

8   CASILL, R.V. "The Trial of Two Poets." Western Review 20
    (Summer):241–45.
        Reviews John Malcom Brinnin's Dylan Thomas in America. The
    author fails to "justify" the poet's anguish with authentic com-
    passion. Using a "curiously Prufrockian tone," Brinnin is seen

"swinging between civilized extremes of repulsion at Thomas's crude gregariousness and attraction to his impenetrable lone-liness."

9   CONNOLLY, THOMAS E. "Thomas' 'And death shall have no dominion'" Explicator 14 (February): item 33.
     Explicates the poem as one that "emphatically" denies spiritual or physical death as the end of existence.

10   CORKE, HILLARY. Review of Dylan Thomas in America. Encounter 6 (May):89-90.
     Recommends the last fifty terrifying pages of John Malcolm Brinnin's account as a warning against the poet's excesses.

11   "Drink and the Devil." Times Literary Supplement, 11 May, p. 284.
     Reviews John Malcolm Brinnin's Dylan Thomas in America. Although written with evident and even painful sincerity, the account doesn't serve the subject well. The worst fault of the writer is a naïveté "at times bordering upon the fatuous," which led him to conclude that the poet was a "sort of Jekyll and Hyde," "ill-behaved but endearing drunk." Brinnin was also wrong to believe that Thomas's financial worries weren't really responsible for his unhappiness and that when he died the poet's creative gifts were failing.

12   DAICHES, DAVID. "The Poetry of Dylan Thomas." In Literary Essays. London: Oliver & Boyd, pp. 50-61.
     Reprint of 1954.25. Reprinted: 1958.9; 1966.8.

13   DARLINGTON, W.A. "Dylan Thomas' Under Milk Wood Staged." New York Times, 22 August, p. 25.
     Reports on the performance of Under Milk Wood at the Edinburgh Festival. Compares the play unfavorably with Our Town and speculates that a "visual interpretation" gets in the way of its brilliant words.

14   DAVENPORT, JOHN. Review of Dylan Thomas in America. Twentieth Century 159 (July):608-10.
     Criticizes John Malcolm Brinnin's book not for playing with facts but for giving an account lacking in humor. Brinnin is "shocked that a genius could be a clown, a conscious" one at that. Concludes that the "repulsive middle-class society, with its lack of patronage, killed Dylan Thomas as much as himself did."

15   "Experiment in Verse." Times Literary Supplement, 17 August, p. iii.
     Surveys the conservative, "safe" quality of the time's poetry, indicative of a strong reaction against the kind Thomas and other members of the modern movement wrote. Compares selected passages by Thomas and Donald Davie to show that the "safe" way may not be the best way, that by taking greater risks Thomas reached a "greater prize" than his counterpart.

16   G., J. "Dylan Thomas: Selections from the Verse of Dylan
     Thomas." High Fidelity 6 (July):58.
     Finds the display of Thomas's self-destructive tendencies
     presented in the first part of Caedmon's recording of his verse
     offensive, but concludes that the selected reading of his major
     poetry is "perhaps sufficient compensation."

17   ____. "Dylan Thomas: Under Milk Wood." High Fidelity 6
     (June):71-72.
     Reviewing Caedmon's release of Under Milk Wood, states a
     preference for the Westminster Argo recording of this unconven-
     tional play that is "full of the excitement of the theatre."

18   GRAVES, ROBERT. "These Be Thy Gods, O Israel--I." New
     Republic 134 (27 February):16-18.
     Reprinted from 1955.31. Reprinted: 1960.5.

19   ____. "These Be Thy Gods, O Israel--II." New Republic 134
     (5 March):17-18.
     Reprinted from 1955.31. Reprinted: 1960.5.

20   GREGORY, HORACE. "A Legacy in Lyrics." New York Times Book
     Review (16 December):4-5, 22.
     Welcomes Henry Treece's enlarged and revised edition of
     Dylan Thomas: "Dog among the Fairies." Believes it deserves
     special praise for the author's "lack of pretentions, for his
     candor, for his knowing limitations of critical speculation."
     While his case is sometimes flawed, especially by a certain lack
     of imaginative logic, this critic is nevertheless on the mark in
     emphasizing the essential lyric quality of Thomas's poetry.

21   GILLETT, ERIC. "A Protest and Some Pleasures." National and
     English Review 146 (May):281-82.
     Reviews John Malcolm Brinnin's Dylan Thomas in America.
     Objects to its "untimely" publication even if it is an honest and
     "brilliant" book.

22   HARDWICK, ELIZABETH. "America and Dylan Thomas." Partisan
     Review, Spring, pp. 258-64.
     Speculates on how much harm was done to Thomas by the
     adoration that met him in America, dwelling especially on the
     record provided by John Malcolm Brinnin's "obsessive" book,
     Dylan Thomas in America. Reprinted: 1960.5.

23   HASSAN, IHAB B. "Thomas' 'The tombstone told when she died.'"
     Explicator 15 (November): item 11.
     Explicates the poem as an elegy that reconciles the "ob-
     jective fact of mortality" with the writer's "passionate appre-
     hension of the fact of existence."

24   HEWES, HENRY. "Edinburgh 1956." Saturday Review 39
     (6 October):39.
     Describes a staged performance of Under Milk Wood, sug-
     gesting that the play-for-voices might be even more successful

if it were turned into a documentary film that would free the piece to be both a "visual as well as an auditory poem."

25   HOWARD, D.R. "Then I Slept." Renascence 9 (Winter):91-96.
     Reviews John Malcolm Brinnin's Dylan Thomas in America and A Child's Christmas in Wales. Complains that Brinnin's account "dwells too much on unimportant things." Warns of the "pernicious" mistake of "lumping together the mind and the persona" of Thomas. The tale by Thomas is "witty, fast-paced, droll."

26   HUNT, K.W. Review of Dylan Thomas in America. English Journal 45 (April):232.
     Struck by the freshness of much of the recalled details, but complains that John Malcolm Brinnin's account does at times become repetitious and "inconsequential."

27   JENKINS, DAVID CLAY. "Writing in Twentieth Century Wales: A Defense of the Anglo-Welsh." Ph.D. dissertation, State University of Iowa, 351 pp.
     Examines the roots and primary qualities of Anglo-Welsh writing and discusses the most prominent Welsh writers against this background. Thomas's "Welshness" is revealed and analyzed in light of selected poems and prose. A listing of Thomas's contributions to Wales supplements the study. See Dissertation Abstracts International 16 (1956):1906.

28   KEOWN, ERIC. "At the Play." Punch 231 (29 August):257-58.
     Praises the R.A.D.A. production of Under Milk Wood at the Edinburgh Festival for capturing the "darting sweep" of the radio play on stage.

29   KNIEGER, BERNARD. "Thomas' 'Sonnet I.'" Explicator 15 (December): item 18.
     Explicates the first sonnet of the "Altarwise by owl-light" sequence line by line, indicating the complex possibilities of interpretation.

30   MacLURE, MILLAR. Review of Dylan Thomas. Canadian Forum 36 (October):165.
     Pans Henry Treece's revised edition of his study. It is a "mean, thin, circuitous" piece of writing that shows that the author is no critic.

31   MacNEICE, LOUIS. "What Vomit Had John Keats." New Statesman 51 (21 April):423-24.
     Reviews John Malcolm Brinnin's Dylan Thomas in America. Grants the account some virtues but ultimately believes it's a harmful book that is bound to "prejudice potential readers" against a poet whose best work "was anything but Bohemian or irresponsible." The account seems to be the product of an egotism of love that causes a blindness to other people's feelings and the complex nature of the "beloved subject."

32   MELCHIORI, GIORGIO. "Dylan Thomas: The Poetry of Vision."
      In The Tightrope Walkers: Studies of Mannerism in Modern
      English Literature. London: Routledge & Kegan Paul,
      pp. 213-42.
          Analyzes the consciously organic quality of Thomas's poetry
      and its obsessive reliance on the sheer power of words. Consid-
      ers the various influences on his writing, coming to the conclu-
      sion that Thomas was not an isolated phenomenon. Although
      certainly an original writer, he was a part of the tradition of
      visionary poetry. He served as a "link in the chain of stylistic
      evolution from Funambulism . . . to a style akin to Baroque."

33   MICHIE, JAMES. "Book Reviews." London Magazine 2 (January):
      81-83.
          Reviews Adventures in the Skin Trade and A Prospect of the
      Sea. The unfinished novel is often very funny and is "full of
      language that wriggles with life." The prose pieces are a mixed
      bag but are full of "sharp impressionistic strokes."

34   MORGAN, W. JOHN. "Evans, Thomas and Lewis." Twentieth
      Century 160 (October):322-29.
          Believes that it's a mistake to try to make too much of the
      presence or absence of Welshness in Under Milk Wood. Thomas was
      more concerned with his characters' "humours" than their authen-
      tic Welshness. Discusses Thomas in context of the unusual situa-
      tion of Anglo-Welsh writers.

35   POWELL, ANTHONY. "Booking Office." Punch 230 (2 May):532-33.
          Reviews John Malcolm Brinnin's Dylan Thomas in America,
      praising it for its "realism."

36   RAYMOND, JOHN. "Thomas the Word-Spinner." New Statesman 52
      (29 September):372.
          Praises the New Theatre production of Under Milk Wood. The
      "boldness" of orchestration brings out the "nuance and beauty of
      the text." The play goes "piling up conceits, metaphors, bubbl-
      ing extravagances, bucket after bucket of words scooped from the
      foaming Dewi."

37   RICHARDSON, KATHLEEN VALMAI. "No Tepid Don." Poetry Review
      47 (October-December):240-41.
          Reviews J. Alexander Rolph's Dylan Thomas: A Bibliography
      and Henry Treece's second edition of Dylan Thomas. Both books
      are recommended, Treece's for the "excellent analysis" of the
      poetry and Rolph's for depicting the "mechanics" of the poet's
      "survival."

38   ROLO, CHARLES J. "Reader's Choice." Atlantic Monthly 197
      (January):84.
          Reviews John Malcolm Brinnin's Dylan Thomas in America,
      anticipating that the book will stir a lot of serious controversy
      even though it's written "out of the deepest regard" for the
      poet.

39   ROLPH, J. ALEXANDER. Dylan Thomas: A Bibliography. London:
     J.M. Dent, 115 pp.
        Lists the published writings, ending with a section on the
     gramophone recordings made by Thomas himself and of his works.
     Attaches historical notes to some of the items, particularly
     Thomas's early books, and contains notations detailing the
     textual changes that occurred between the first and latest print-
     ings of his publications. In a foreword Edith Sitwell emphasizes
     Thomas's attractive qualities.

40   SALTER, WILLIAM. "Murrow, Thomas, Sartre." New Statesman 52
     (1 September):241–42.
        Found the televised offering of the Edinburgh Festival
     stage production of Under Milk Wood disastrous. The "minor
     masterpiece" was harmed by unimaginative tinkering with the
     original.

41   SCHLAUCH, MARGARET. Modern English and American Poetry:
     Techniques and Ideologies. London: Watts, pp. 33, 35, 43
     passim.
        Refers to various lines from Thomas to illustrate a variety
     of poetic techniques—such as the use of sense transfer, activ-
     ity transfer, and miniature conceits.

42   SKELTON, ROBIN. The Poetic Pattern. London: Routledge;
     Berkeley: University of California Press, pp. 24 passim.
        Declares that there is a "supra-logical process of
     pattern-making" at work in Thomas's poetry.

43   STEIN, ARNOLD. Review of The Poetry of Dylan Thomas. Modern
     Language Notes 71 (June):455–57.
        Declares that Elder Olson's study fails to exhibit Thomas
     completely enough. As a "practicing athlete in critical logic"
     Olson comes off rather pedantic, and he limits the discussion of
     Thomas's imagination by his critical choice of symbol over
     metaphor. The poet comes out "domesticated" to the professor's
     critical attitudes.

44   "Times Book Review: The Writings of Dylan Thomas." Times
     Literary Supplement, 27 July, p. 451.
        Recommends J. Alexander Rolph's Dylan Thomas: A Bibliog-
     raphy for its careful scholarship and inclusiveness. Some minor
     errors in the text are pointed out, but as a whole it's a "fine"
     work without anything that is not valuable or is misleading.
     Highlighted is the fact that the bibliography traces all of
     Thomas's poems, from the first one printed in his grammar school
     magazine when he was eleven to the elegy he was working on before
     he died.

45   TINDALL, WILLIAM YORK. Forces in Modern British Literature.
     New York: Vintage Books, pp. 238–43 passim.
        Reprint of 1947.14.

46 TREECE, HENRY. Dylan Thomas: "Dog among the Fairies." New
    York: de Graff; London: Ernest Benn, 158 pp.
    Revised reprint of 1949.11.

47 "Under Milk Wood at Edinburgh." Times (London), 22 August,
    p. 4.
        Reviews the performance of the radio play given at Edin-
    burgh's Lyceum Theatre. Finds the adaptation of the work to the
    stage less than totally successful, since it was obviously meant
    as a work not to be read or seen but to be heard. "The view of
    life it expresses may be adolescent, but it has all the freshness
    of adolescence."

48 WATKINS, VERNON. "Dylan Thomas in America." Encounter 6
    (June):77-79.
        Reacts in letter form to John Malcolm Brinnin's Dylan
    Thomas in America and the "banal" and self-righteous reviews the
    book tended to inspire. States that Thomas's work "will remain
    his best interpreter."

49 WOODCOCK, GEORGE. Review of Dylan Thomas in America. Arizona
    Quarterly 12 (Spring):87-88.
        Faults John Malcolm Brinnin's account of Thomas in America
    for a lack of humor and a "morbid taste for scandal."

50 ZINNES, HARRIET. Review of Adventures in the Skin Trade.
    Books Abroad 30 (Spring):178.
        Discovers that Thomas's use of symbolism in the title work
    is more controlled than ever before. His prose no longer effu-
    sively fantastic, now contains the "peculiar stark and morbid
    spirit of disengagement" characteristic of modern existence.

                                1957

1   AMIS, KINGSLEY. "An Evening with Dylan Thomas." Spectator
    199 (29 November):737.
        Remembers a nearly disastrous visit made by Thomas to
    Swansea's University College. Was struck by man's shyness.
    Reprinted: 1970.1.

2   ATKINSON, BROOKS. "Theatre: Worlds of Dylan Thomas." New
    York Times, 8 October, p. 41.
        Praises Emlyn Williams's "genius" for taking the audience
    inside the character of Thomas in his performance of "A Boy
    Growing Up."

3   BAKER, A.T. "The Roistering Legend of Dylan Thomas."
    Esquire (December):201-9.
        Comments of the "public outcry" that followed Thomas's
    sudden death.

4   BARO, GENE. "Leftover Life to Kill." New York Herald Tribune
    Book Review 34 (13 October):4.
        Calls Caitlin Thomas's Leftover Life to Kill a "harrowing"
    book of "agonized and exuberant confession." As described by
    her, the marriage with the poet of a "hundred guises" was so
    violently intense and turbulent as to appear like a "permanent
    challenge."

5   BAYLEY, JOHN. "Dylan Thomas." In The Romantic Survival: A
    Study in Poetic Evolution. London: Constable & Co.,
    pp. 186-227.
        Points out the technical problems found especially in
    Thomas's early poetry, but also takes the stand that his eventual
    reputation will probably rest on the "peculiar" attempts to make
    his language mean and sound physical, to strike a balance between
    the surrealistic and positivistic approaches, and to compress and
    apprehend time in a special way. Discusses the most prominent
    and distinct stylistic habits: the tendency toward incantation,
    the focus on single words, an interest in metaphysical technique,
    the use of warring imagery, and a subjective and emotional striv-
    ing for the union of mind and matter. He possessed "the absorp-
    tion and the single-mindedness of the great Romantics. He shows
    the same steady inward gaze as Wordsworth, the same inspired
    egotism, but whereas Wordsworth attempts to trace the growth and
    movements of his mind in . . . plain lucid diction . . . Thomas
    tries to get at the mystery of his own growth and being by means
    of his own highly personal idioms and image clusters."
    Reprinted: 1966.8.

6   BEUM, ROBERT. "Syllabic Verse in English." Prairie Schooner
    31 (Fall):259-75.
        Uses selections from Thomas in the discussion of syllabic
    verse. Thomas's poems, like those of several other poets under
    discussion, incorporate "most of the devices" that characterize
    syllabic poetry.

7   BITTNER, WILLIAM. "A Little Bit of Dylan Thomas." Saturday
    Review 40 (12 October):22-23.
        Reviews Caitlin Thomas's Leftover Life to Kill. It's a
    "breathlessly emotional book" that is honest about the important
    things.

8   BOGAN, LOUISE. "Fairy Tale Reversed." New Yorker 33
    (17 October):193-94, 197.
        Reviews Leftover Life to Kill, finding Thomas's widow, in
    her attempt to confront life without her husband, to have a
    "basic good sense and the ability to discriminate," even if
    "often almost savagely repressed." The account does provide an
    almost complete picture of the complex sides of Thomas.

9   BREIT, HARVEY. "The Haunting Drama of Dylan Thomas." New
York Times Magazine, 6 October, pp. 22, 24, 26.
Reports on the growth of Thomas's posthumous fame, including the imminent Broadway productions of Under Milk Wood and
Emlyn Williams's "A Boy Growing Up." In this impressionistic
summary of Thomas's life and character, the conclusion is reached
that in him the "Pure Genius Type" had found an "ideal contemporary lodging."

10 CLANCY, JOSEPH P. "Exposed Wounds." America 98 (2 November):
139–40.
Reviews Caitlin Thomas's Leftover Life to Kill. Marked by
the "perverse drive toward self-exhibition and self-destruction"
that took hold of her husband, this is a book that "should not
have been written."

11 CLURMAN, HAROLD. "Theatre." Nation 185 (2 November):309–10.
Reviews a dramatic performance of Under Milk Wood.
Although its characters are rather shallow, it has the great
attraction of rich language and "delicious gab."

12 CULLIGAN, GLENDY. "Shrill Memoir Simply Dull." Washington
Post, 13 October, p. E7.
Dismisses Caitlin Thomas's Leftover Life to Kill as an
exceedingly emotional outpouring failing in its intention to
rebut John Malcolm Brinnin's "malicious" account of the poet.

13 DAVENPORT, JOHN. "Who Fished the Murex Up?" Spectator 199
(15 November):651.
Reviews Letters to Vernon Watkins. Some of the material
contained represents a "complete refutation of those who think
Thomas did not know what he was saying or how best to say it."

14 De BEDTS, RUTH. "Dylan Thomas and the Eve of St. Agnes."
Florida Review, Fall, pp. 50–55.
Sees a link between Thomas and Keats.

15 DURRELL, LAWRENCE. "The Shades of Dylan Thomas." Encounter
9 (December):56–59.
Recalls his acquaintance with the young Thomas. His ultimate impression was that here was both a "splendid clown and a
splendid poet" and that beneath the public personality "there was
a somebody quieter, somebody very much harassed by a gift." Reprinted: 1960.33.

16 FOELL, EARL W. Review of Leftover Life to Kill. Christian
Science Monitor, 10 October, p. 14.
Finds Caitlin Thomas's book a "morbid, secret-baring
testament" whose "vivid glimpses" of her husband are too
infrequent.

17 FRASER, GEORGE SUTHERLAND. Dylan Thomas. Bibliographical
Series, edited by Bonamy Dobrée. London: Longmans, Green &
Co., 36 pp.

Argues that Thomas's poetry has more variety in tone, style, and subject matter than is usually realized and that he is a "much less narrowly consistent poet" whose poetic method and attitude to life continued to develop up to his death. Reprinted: 1960.5, 13; 1965.17; 1977.16.

18   FULLER, JOHN G. "Trade Winds." Saturday Review 40 (16 November):8, 10, 12.
      Describes the White Horse Tavern, Thomas's favorite bar in New York, where he is recalled fondly and his ghost seems still to be "watching and listening."

19   GIBBS, WOLCOTT. "Llareggub, Serutan, Gumshoe." New Yorker 33 (26 October):95-96.
      Reviews a performance of Under Milk Wood at the Henry Miller Theatre. Finds that the attempt to "give concrete visual form" to a work the writer meant to "entrust to the imagination" was a fundamental mistake.

20   GLICK, BURTON S. "A Brief Analysis of a Short Story by Dylan Thomas." American Imago 14 (Summer):149-54.
      Gives "The Followers" a psychoanalytical reading. The impact of the story depends on the reader's response to a combination of present factors: "identification through the universality of the scopophilic component-instinct, the fear of the supernatural, the sudden feelings of guilt and confusion, and the dread of dire punishment at the hands of the dead."

21   GRAVES, ROBERT. "And the Children's Teeth are Set on Edge." New Republic 137 (28 October):15-18.
      Reviews Caitlin Thomas's Leftover Life to Kill. Concludes that Caitlin "revelled" in the "cat-and-dog life" she led with the poet whose writing resembled the "inspired hit-or-miss rhetoric of the Welsh revivalist."

22   "Grief Writ Large." Economist 183 (8 June):880.
      Reviews Caitlin Thomas's Leftover Life to Kill, calling it a "squalid" story exhibiting a great deal about the disturbed character of the woman but hardly anything about her husband.

23   GRIGSON, GEOFFREY. "Recollections of Dylan Thomas." London Magazine, September, pp. 39-45.
      Gives his version of what Thomas was like when he first appeared on the London scene. Notes Francis Thompson's influence on Thomas's poetry, which is seen as an example of "decayed romanticism." Reprinted: 1960.5.

24   HARDING, JOAN. "Dylan Thomas and Edward Thomas." Contemporary Review 192 (September):150-54.
      Using their widows's published accounts as a springboard, compares Dylan and Edward Thomas. Edward Thomas wrote with an "equilibrium on the human plane"; Dylan, at the end, was moving from the physical to the spiritual plane, and from an essentially lyrical to a dramatic way of writing.

25   HAYES, RICHARD. "In the Kingdom of Our Language." Commonweal
     67 (8 November):151.
           Believes that a staged performance of Under Milk Wood is a
     serious mistake because it tends to put literal emphasis on a
     work that should be appreciated for its "evocative power."

26   HEWES, HENRY. ". . . And death shall have no dominion."
     Saturday Review 40 (19 October):53.
           Reviews "A Boy Growing Up," a "memory jaunt" performed and
     adapted by Emlyn Williams. The climax of the performance
     stresses the "glowing radiation" of Thomas's "ephemeral exist-
     ence."

27   HOLROYD, STUART. "Dylan Thomas and the Religion of the
     Instinctive Life." In Emergence from Chaos. London:
     Gollanz; Boston: Houghton Mifflin, pp. 77–94.
           Considers Thomas as a kind of pantheist, a "psychological
     type whose religion is that of the instinctive life." Notes that
     sex, death, and prenatal life are recurring themes and that
     Thomas's "lack of interest in metaphysical issues was responsi-
     ble" both for his weaknesses and his greatness. Reprinted:
     1960.5.

28   HYAMS, C. BARRY, and REICHERT, KARL H. "A Test Lesson on
     Dylan Thomas's Poem 'The hand that signed the paper.'" Die
     Neueren Sprachen 6, no. 4:173–77.
           Offers a plan for teaching and interpreting the poem. The
     essay includes a list of questions and answers dealing with the
     important points of the poem.

*29 JONES, DANIEL. Songs from "Under Milk Wood." London: Keith
     Prowse Music Publishing Co.
           Contains Jones's settings for the play-for-voices. See
     Maud, 1970.14, p. 29.

*30 JONES, GWYN. The First Forty Years: Some Notes on Anglo-
     Welsh Literature. Cardiff: University of Wales Press.
           Underlines the irony that, despite his ambivalent Welsh-
     ness, Thomas is generally perceived to be the foremost example of
     the Anglo-Welsh tradition. See Kershner, 1976.19, p. 188.

31   JULIAN, Sister MARY. "Edith Sitwell and Dylan Thomas: Neo-
     Romantics." Renascence 9 (Spring):120–26, 131.
           Links Thomas with Edith Sitwell, particularly in having a
     "bardic sense of the function of poetry."

32   KAZIN, ALFRED. "The Posthumous Life of Dylan Thomas."
     Atlantic Monthly 200 (October):164–68.
           Dwells on the phenomenon of the Thomas "legend." Finds
     that the ultimate vision of the poetry attains the "quality of a
     worshiped and awesome natural force." Adds the "fact" that
     Thomas was a "peculiarly lovable as well as magnetically gifted
     person" who had the capacity to inspire people with the "sense of
     an unusual radiance in their lives." Reprinted: 1962.13.

33   KNIEGER, BERNARD. "Thomas' 'Light breaks where no sun
      shines.'" Explicator 15 (February): item 32.
          Explicates the poem as one being primarily about acquiring
      knowledge and its consequences.

34   KORG, JACOB. "Imagery and Universe in Dylan Thomas's
      18 Poems." Accent 17 (Winter):3-15.
          Analyzes the predominant imagery found in 18 Poems. Finds
      that Thomas's use of images is "peculiarly fitted to express the
      realities of his dialectic universe" since they function to
      "embrace antithetical meanings." A mystic like Blake, Thomas
      writes poetry that derives much of its obscurity from his sub-
      jective, cosmic vision.

35   LANDER, CLARA. "The Macabre in Dylan Thomas." Canadian Forum
      36 (March):274-75, 278.
          Compiles a considerable amount of evidence showing that
      Thomas "grew up among reminders of death" and went on to write
      as if he were watching death "from the inside looking out."

36   _____. "Of Poets and Poetry." Queen's Quarterly 64 (Summer):
      290-91.
          Dismisses Henry Treece's Dylan Thomas as a rather "super-
      ficial" book.

37   MacNEICE, LOUIS. "Fragments I Have Shored." New Statesman 53
      (8 June):741.
          Reviews Caitlin Thomas's Leftover Life to Kill. A "highly
      personal and deeply moving document," it is especially important
      for revealing that the Thomases "formed a little island of myth
      in which . . . outbreaks of violence were necessary and a tug-of-
      war was a bond."

38   MANNES, MARYA. "A Question of Timing." Reporter 17
      (14 November):39.
          Reviews a performance of Under Milk Wood and concludes that
      the substance of the play is "diluted" by complex staging and
      busy production efforts.

39   McDONALD, GERALD D. Review of Dylan Thomas: A Bibliography.
      Papers of the Bibliographical Society of America 51:98-100.
          Reviews J. Alexander Rolph's descriptive bibliography.
      Commends the "careful" work.

40   MILLER, JAMES E., Jr. "Four Cosmic Poets." University of
      Kansas City Review 23 (Summer):312-20.
          Argues that Thomas (along with Whitman, Hart Crane, and
      D.H. Lawrence) belongs to a tradition of "forceful singers" who
      are guided by a mythic vision of life's "mystic evolution."

41   "New Stage Work." Time 70 (28 October):93.
      Criticizes Douglas Cleverdon's stage version of Under Milk
Wood. Atmosphere should be the prominent feature, but it now
"plays second fiddle to antics," and the play has been turned
into a "variety show."

42   NYREN, DOROTHY. Review of Leftover Life to Kill. Library
Journal 82 (1 October):2450.
      Recommends Caitlin Thomas's book for the "intimate memo-
ries" it provides of "the century's prominent poet."

43   O'CONNOR, PHILLIP. Review of Leftover Life to Kill.
Encounter 9 (August):87.
      Comes away from Caitlin Thomas's book with the strong
impression that the Thomases were "naive persons of a kind, for
whom social identity is an adventure into unreality; profitable
but also frequently disgusting."

44   "Out of Tragedy a Legend--And Words with Wings." Newsweek 50
      (28 October):96.
      Based on the fact that Under Milk Wood and "A Boy Growing
Up" were simultaneous Broadway hits, one is tempted to speculate
that, had he lived, Thomas would have become a writer for the
theater. His characteristic "excesses" are "theatrical."

45   PANTER-DOWNES, MOLLIE. "Letter from London." New Yorker 33
      (13 July):56.
      Reports on the reception of Caitlin Thomas's Leftover Life
to Kill. People found the book to be "either deeply moving or
deeply shocking," though the basic truth to come out of the
account seems to be that Thomas and his wife "made good or bad
weather for each other."

46   PEEL, J.H.B. "The Echoes in the Booming Voice." New York
Times Book Review, 20 October, pp. 40–41.
      Evaluates Thomas's position in literature by systematically
comparing him to Hopkins, concluding that the final difference
between them is that one is a "major" and the other (Thomas) a
"minor" poet.

47   "Poet in the Making." Times Literary Supplement, 15 November,
      p. 691.
      Reviews Letters to Vernon Watkins. The volume is recom-
mended to anyone wishing to know about the effects Thomas aimed
for in his poetry. The letters "destroy the myth" of Thomas
being some kind of unconscious genius "staggering between bar and
bed." But they do confirm the view that this poet had a
"narrow" and "egotistical" artistic view and foundation. Speculates that his greatest talent might have been for transforming
everything into "fantastic comedy."

48 "Poet of Cwmdonkin Drive." <u>Times</u> (London), 12 December,
  p. 13.
   Reviews <u>Letters to Vernon Watkins</u>, recommending the volume
both for what it reveals about the poet's artistic seriousness
and his character. Thomas "knew the extent of his talent better
than many of his critics, and, when he cared to, he threw into
his life a gift for living as uncommon as his gift for verse and
prose."

49 POORE, CHARLES. "Books of the Times." <u>New York Times</u>,
  10 October, p. 31.
   Calls Caitlin Thomas's <u>Leftover Life to Kill</u> the best book
written about the poet because he is approached "obliquely" and
thus appears in a "harmony of revelation." Thomas is shown in
his "most quarrelsome and most exalted moods."

50 PORTER, KATHERINE ANNE. "In the Depths of Grief, a Towering
  Rage." <u>New York Times Book Review</u>, 13 October, pp. 3, 32.
   Reviews Caitlin Thomas's <u>Leftover Life to Kill</u>, finding it
to be a feverish, self-centered account that does nothing to
contradict the many wild legends surrounding her husband.

51 QUIGLY, ISABEL. "Child in the Dark." <u>Spectator</u> 198 (7 June):
  754.
   Reviews Caitlin Thomas's <u>Leftover Life to Kill</u>. Thinks
this book is, by comparison, a "tender and even dignified" anti-
dote to John Malcolm Brinnin's <u>Dylan Thomas in America</u>.

52 READ, BILL. "A Visit to Laugharne." Transcript of Radio
  Broadcast, Boston University's WBUR (October).
   Describing a visit to Thomas's home, the guest is struck by
the great contrast between the "boisterous public behavior" of
his friend in America and the much quieter domestic life in
Wales. Includes an example of how extensive Thomas's revisions
tended to be and notes that this poet dreaded talking about
poetry and criticism. Revised and reprinted: 1960.5.

53 "Recitation in Manhattan." <u>Time</u> 70 (21 October):56.
   Praises Emlyn Williams's "A Boy Growing Up," an impersonat-
ing recitation in which the actor and storyteller "triumphantly
become one." The "best turn" is the rendering of the first section of <u>Adventures in the Skin Trade</u>.

54 Review of "A Boy Growing Up." <u>Theatre Arts</u> 41 (December):27,
  82.
   Praises Emlyn Williams's story-telling performance based
on Thomas's prose writings.

55 RICHART, BETTE. "A Fierce Confession." <u>Commonweal</u> 67
  (25 October):94-95.
   Reviews Caitlin Thomas's <u>Leftover Life to Kill</u>. Expresses
disappointment in the book's failure to reveal very much about
her "epic" husband. Thomas "emerges from all the obscuring mists
as a folk hero still."

56 RICKEY, MARY ELLEN. "Thomas' 'The Conversation of Prayer.'"
Explicator 16 (December): item 15.
Explicates the poem as one about both man and boy approach-
ing "death and grief."

57 ROSENTHAL, M.L. "Caitlin Thomas in Capri." Nation 185
(2 November):308–9.
Dismisses Caitlin Thomas's Leftover Life to Kill as a
"pastiche of fragmentary stereotypes" that has little to do with
the question of what her husband was really like. Instead, it's
a record of a "partially realized fantasy-life" of a deeply
troubled woman.

58 RUDIKOFF, SONYA. "Elegy for a Dead Self." New Leader 40
(2 December):25.
Reviews Caitlin Thomas's Leftover Life to Kill, an unusual
elegy that is more about the "dead wife" than the dead poet.

59 THESPIS. "Theatre Notes." English 11 (Spring):146–47.
Expresses surprised pleasure at the opportunity to see how
well the "tumbling images" can come to visual life in a stage
version of Under Milk Wood produced for the Edinburgh Festival.

60 THOMAS, CAITLIN. Leftover Life to Kill. London: Putnam;
Boston: Atlantic, Little, Brown, 262 pp.
Describes the difficulties of being Thomas's wife. Highlights Thomas's puritanical streak, his superstitions about
intellectualism, his weakness when confronted by flattery, and
his domestic versus his public behavior and character. Reprinted
in part: 1960.5.

61 _____. "This Was Dylan." Atlantic Monthly 199 (June):33–38.
Previews part of Caitlin Thomas's forthcoming Leftover Life
to Kill (see Thomas, 1957.60). "If I waited a million years, I
could not forget Dylan," she wrote.

62 THWAITE, ANTHONY. "Dylan Thomas and George Barker." In
Essays on Contemporary English Poetry. Tokyo: Kenkyusha,
pp. 98–110.
Takes a chronological look at Thomas's published poems and
comes to the conclusion that "as his rage increased, his technique deteriorated." But he was a "major" poet even though his
writing contained some "carelessness, bombast and even faking."
Revised and reprinted: 1961.35.

63 "Times Book Review: The Kick of Grief." Times Literary
Supplement, 31 May, p. 336.
Reviews Caitlin Thomas's Leftover Life to Kill. Written by
an extremely temperamental person, this account is mainly sub-
jective, although an extended depiction of the married life of
the Thomases is "fascinating."

64   TODD, WILLIAM B. "Note 81. The Bibliography of Dylan
      Thomas." Book Collector 6 (Spring):71-73.
         Offers supplementary information to J. Alexander Rolph's
      bibliography. James Campbell adds a further note (note 82,
      pp. 73-74) on issues of Thomas's The Map of Love.

65   "Two of a Kind." Time 70 (14 October):122, 125.
         Reviews Caitlin Thomas's Leftover Life to Kill. It's a
      "searingly candid chronicle" that reveals the self-destructive
      romantic temperament possessed by both husband and wife.

66   WAIN, JOHN. "Dylan Thomas: A Review of His Collected Poems."
      In Preliminary Essays. London: Macmillan & Co.; New York:
      St. Martin's Press, pp. 180-85.
         Having read Collected Poems, Wain concludes that while this
      was the work of a "fine, bold, original, and strong poet,"
      Thomas had two problems that kept him from being truly great:
      a limited subject matter and a technique that at times seems
      "quasi-automatic." Reprinted: 1960.5; 1966.8.

67   _____. "English Poetry: The Immediate Situation." Sewanee
      Review 65 (Summer):353-74.
         Taking stock of the state of contemporary English poetry,
      declares that after Auden left for America, a new generation of
      writers turned to Thomas for leadership. The Thomas "myth became
      as important as the Auden myth."

68   WATKINS, VERNON. Introduction to Letters to Vernon Watkins.
      New York: New Directions, pp. 11-21.
         Gives a background of the letter-writing friendship with
      Thomas.

69   WEBSTER, MARGARET. "A Look at the London Season." Theatre
      Arts 41 (May):32, 92-93.
         Points to Under Milk Wood as one of the highlights of the
      season, although the West End production is "cluttered" with too
      much scenery and character acting. The credits for the New
      Theatre production are given.

70   WHITTEMORE, REED. "The 'Modern Idiom' of Poetry, and All
      That." Yale Review 46 (Spring):357-71.
         Expresses a dissatisfaction with the tendency of modern
      poetry to drift toward self-conscious complexity at the expense
      of clarity. Thomas is one of the poets whose poetry appears to
      be "stitched and unstitched with the curious aim of forcing the
      reader to note that the 'modern idiom' of poetry is unmistakably
      the idiom of poets."

71   WILLIAMS, EMLYN. "Studying Dylan Thomas." New York Times,
      6 October, sec. 2, p. 3.
         Describes the preparation behind Emlyn Williams's "A Boy
      Growing Up" performance, and its principal ambition--to re-
      create the "warm and simple and richly comic side" of Thomas.

72   WILLIAMS, WILLIAM CARLOS. Selected Letters. New York:
       McDowell, Obolensky, pp. 278, 287–88.
         Muses over the different kind of poetry Thomas writes
compared to the characteristic American verse.

<h2 style="text-align:center">1958</h2>

1   BROOKE-ROSE, CHRISTINE. "Book Reviews." Twentieth Century
      163 (March):280–81.
        Reviews Letters to Vernon Watkins and George Sutherland
Fraser's Dylan Thomas. The Letters volume is especially valuable
in showing how much pain Thomas took with his writing. Fraser is
commended for evaluating Thomas's achievement with "great acumen
and fairness."

2   _____. A Grammar of Metaphor. London: Secker & Warburg,
      pp. 320–23 passim.
        Analyzes Thomas's unusual use of syntax in the context of
discussing fifteen important poets.

3   CAHOON, HERBERT. Review of Letters to Vernon Watkins.
      Library Journal 83 (15 February):601.
        Recommends the volume because it provides insights not only
into Thomas's poetry but also his "remarkable" personality.

4   CECIL, DAVID, and TATE, ALLEN, eds. Modern Verse in English:
      1900–1950. New York: Macmillan, pp. 34, 36, 40, 641.
        Surveys the contemporary English poetry scene and mentions
Thomas as an example of a romantic reaction against cerebral
modes.

5   CIARDI, JOHN. "Dylan Thomas." Saturday Review 41
      (15 November):50.
        Comments on the Caedmon record set of Thomas reading his
poetry. The recordings provide evidence that Thomas "possessed
one of the most extraordinary rhythmic and verbal gifts of the
century." He was "our most overwhelming combination of poet,
actor, and ham."

6   _____. "The Real Thomas." Saturday Review 41 (1 March):18,
      31.
        Considers the Letters to Vernon Watkins volume to be espe-
cially valuable for their allowing to emerge the "real" Thomas:
"the poet and friend at home in himself" who, above everything
else, enforced the "discipline" of his art "upon himself."

7   CLAIR, JOHN A. "Thomas' 'A Refusal to Mourn the Death, by Fire,
      of a Child in London.'" Explicator 17 (December): item 25.
        Explicates the poem, stressing Thomas's integration of
structure with symbolism and imagery.

8   CONDON, RICHARD A. "Thomas' 'Ballad of the Long-legged
     Bait.'" Explicator 16 (March): item 37.
     Explicates the poem as one that is mainly a meditation on
the ultimate consequences of physical love.

9   DAICHES, DAVID. "The Poetry of Dylan Thomas." In Two
     Studies. London: Shenval Press, pp. 5-16.
     Reprint of 1954.25.

10   _____. The Present Age in British Literature. Bloomington:
     Indiana University Press, pp. 57-65 passim.
     Objects to the view that Thomas represented a "new romanti-
cism" whose goal was to "overthrow" T.S. Eliot's school. He was
"neither a whirling romantic nor a metaphysical imagist, but a
poet who used pattern and metaphor in a complex craftsmanship in
order to create a ritual of celebration."

11   DEUTSCH, BABETTE. "Friends and Fellow-Poets." New York
     Herald Tribune Book Review 34 (26 January):3.
     Reviews Letters to Vernon Watkins, calling the letters to
his friend and fellow-poet "of durable interest," primarily
because they provide important evidence of just how hard Thomas
worked to make theme and expression "indivisible." "What is
evident throughout is the instinct for workmanship and a wit un-
quenched by the ugliness of circumstances."

12   ESSIG, ERHARDT H. "Thomas' 'Sonnet I (Altarwise by owl-
     light).'" Explicator 16 (June): item 53.
     Explicates the first sonnet of the "Altarwise by owl-light"
sequence as depicting a religious experience. "It deals with
Christ's death, resurrection, and eternal session in heaven."

13   FORBES-BOYD, ERIC. "From One Poet to Another." Christian
     Science Monitor, 30 January, p. 5.
     Finds the letters in Letters to Vernon Watkins not to be
very illuminating as far as Thomas's "difficult" poetry is concerned, but considers them to be a real "delight" from a human
angle.

14   GILLETT, ERIC. "War over London." National and English
     Review 150 (January):30-31.
     Discovers that the Thomas who comes out of Letters to
Vernon Watkins is a "lively, likeable, amusing and very human
character."

15   HORNICK, LITA R. "The Intricate Image: A Study of Dylan
     Thomas." Ph.D. dissertation, Columbia University, 258 pp.
     Discusses the structure and meaning of Thomas's poetry by
focusing on the use of imagery, specifically by analyzing individual images and their natures and looking at their function in
the poetic organization as a whole. Two appendixes provide
archival information and a consideration of Thomas's surrealistic
use of hair imagery. See Dissertation Abstracts International 19
(1958):327.

16   JEPSEN, LAURA. Review of Dylan Thomas: Letters to Vernon
      Watkins. English Journal 47 (March):175.
         Discovers that the letters reveal two important aspects of
      Thomas--his "painstaking craftsmanship" and his "gift for fan-
      tastic comedy."

17   JOHN, AUGUSTUS. "Dylan Thomas and Company." Sunday Times
      (London), 28 September, p. 17.
         Remembers his experience with Thomas when he was a
      "cherubic young fellow." States that whereas some of Thomas's
      poetry impressed him greatly, Under Milk Wood struck him as
      "false and sentimental." Revised and reprinted: 1960.5.

18   JONES, GLYN. "Dylan Thomas--The Other Man." Western Mail,
      21 April, p. 4.
         Offers a personal reminiscence. Other installments fol-
      lowed in the Western Mail during the next four days.

19   KANN, NINA N. Review of Leftover Life to Kill. American
      Mercury, January, pp. 147-48.
         Complains that Caitlin Thomas has written an "unreadable"
      confession that "charges back and forth like an angry bull"
      without telling us very much about her husband.

20   LANDER, CLARA. "With Welsh and Reverend Rook: The Biblical
      Element in Dylan Thomas." Queen's Quarterly 65 (Autumn):
      437-47.
         Points out the influence of the Bible on Thomas's poetry.
      Emphasis is placed on his recurrent use of certain biblical
      figures (especially Adam, Gabriel, Jonah, and Jacob) and his com-
      plex identification with Christ (and at times with the Anti-
      Christ).

21   LEHMANN, JOHN. "The Wain--Larkin Myth: A Reply to John
      Wain." Sewanee Review 66 (Autumn):578-87.
         Disagrees with John Wain's assertion (see Wain, 1957.67)
      that the Thomas "myth" replaced the Auden "myth." The situation
      of contemporary English poetry is presented as being more complex
      than the one imagined by Wain.

*22   McBRIEN, WILLIAM AUGUSTINE. "Likeness in the Themes and
      Prosody of Gerard Manley Hopkins and Dylan Thomas." Ph.D.
      dissertation, St. John's University.
         Source: Maud, 1970.14, p. 30.

23   McDONNELL, THOMAS P. "Who Killed Dylan?" Catholic World 187
      (July):285-89.
         Considers the various theories concerned with explaining
      Thomas's premature death. They include Thomas's refusal to grow
      up.

*24   MAUD, RALPH N. "Language and Meaning in the Poetry of Dylan
      Thomas." Ph.D. dissertation, Harvard University.
         Source: Maud, 1970.14, p. 30.

25   MERCIER, VIVIAN. "What I Mean Is. . . ." Nation 186
      (26 April):369-70.
          Reviews Letters to Vernon Watkins. Compares these letters
      to Keats's, finding that although they fail to match the other
      poet's propensity for philosophizing about poetry in general, in
      two other ways they are "equal or superior to Keats's: their
      intense, exaggerated awareness of life and their quasi-religious
      devotion to the 'craft or sullen art' of poetry."

26   MORGAN, W. JOHN. "Under Milk Wood under Milk Wood."
      Twentieth Century 164 (September):275-76.
          Gives an account of the preparations for and the production
      of the play-for-voices in Laugharne's Dragon's Park.

27   MOSS, HOWARD. "Dylan Thomas." Transcript of Radio Broadcast,
      New York's WBAI (November).
          Remembers Thomas as a rebel who dared to be himself, a
      perpetual adolescent, and a writer of some great poems. Re-
      printed: 1960.5.

28   MOYNIHAN, WILLIAM TRUMBULL. "Thomas' 'Light breaks where no
      sun shines.'" Explicator 16 (February): item 28.
          Explicates the poem as one dealing primarily with the sub-
      ject of "intercourse-and-conception."

29   PETERS, ROBERT L. "The Uneasy Faith of Dylan Thomas: A Study
      of the Last Poems." Fresco 9:25-29.
          Examines the apparent conflicts and ambiguities behind
      Thomas's search for faith. He was a poet of "unresolved con-
      flict" who could "within the confines of a single poem" convince
      himself of the "soundness of contrary views" by allowing himself
      to be caught up "in the sweep of his own rhetoric and imagina-
      tion."

30   PORTER, KATHERINE ANNE. "In the Morning of the Poet." New
      York Times Book Review, 2 February, p. 4.
          Reviews Letters to Vernon Watkins, recommending the collec-
      tion for the "good long look" provided of Thomas "in the morning
      of his energies and gifts." The letters record the development
      of the poetry to the point of mastery, showing at the same time
      the simple excitement of the poet working "with his sleeves
      rolled up."

31   PRESS, JOHN. The Chequer'd Shade: Reflections on Obscurity
      in Poetry. London: Oxford University Press, pp. 1-2 passim.
          Refers to Thomas in the course of a general discussion of
      obscurity in (especially modern) poetry.

32   Review of Letters to Vernon Watkins. Listener 59 (9 January):
      71.
          Notes the "pathos" of some of the letters, particularly
      where Thomas "begs" for money.

33   Review of <u>Letters to Vernon Watkins</u>. <u>New Yorker</u> 34
     (12 April):163–64.
         Remarks on both the charming and serious sides of Thomas
     revealed in these letters. Watkins's introduction portrays the
     "more genial" side of Thomas.

34   SCHARPER, PHILIP. Review of <u>Letters to Vernon Watkins</u>.
     <u>America</u> 99 (12 April):78–79.
         Recommends the collection highly because it's a "valuable
     commentary" by the poet on his craft.

35   SITWELL, EDITH, ed. "Dylan Thomas." In <u>The Atlantic Book of</u>
     <u>British and American Poetry</u>. Boston: Atlantic, Little,
     Brown, pp. 982–84.
         Praises the "religious fervor and animal heat" of Thomas's
     poetry, adding that here was a unique voice whose "spirit is that
     of the beginning of created things." Reprinted: 1960.5.

36   SLOTE, BERNICE. Review of <u>Letters to Vernon Watkins</u>. <u>Prairie</u>
     <u>Schooner</u> 32 (Summer):85–86.
         Finds the letters of great value to a true understanding of
     the poet's achievement. They reveal just how exacting Thomas was
     when he was working. The "glory" of the letters is the history
     they provide of some of the best poems.

37   STONESIFER, R.J. "Thomas' <u>Adventures in the Skin Trade</u>."
     <u>Explicator</u> 17 (November): item 10.
         Offers the possibility that Thomas's fragmentary story was
     meant both as farcical autobiography and satirical parody of
     Samuel Butler's <u>The Way of All Flesh</u>.

38   TELLIER, A.R. Review of <u>Letters to Vernon Watkins</u>. <u>Études</u>
     <u>anglaises</u> 11 (July–September):271–72.
         Foresees the usefulness of the letters for readers of
     Thomas's difficult poetry.

39   THOMAS, WYNFORD VAUGHAN. "Dylan Thomas and Nellie Wallace."
     <u>Listener</u> 59 (16 January):94.
         Reminisces about a visit from Thomas.

40   THWAITE, ANTHONY. Review of <u>Letters to Vernon Watkins</u>.
     <u>London Magazine</u> 5 (April):61–63.
         Notes that the letters Thomas wrote to Watkins are first
     about poetry and second about money.

41   VARNEY, HAROLD LORD. Review of <u>Dylan Thomas in America</u>.
     <u>American Mercury</u>, January, pp. 146–47.
         Finds John Malcolm Brinnin's account of Thomas's final
     years "compellingly interesting"; so interesting, in fact, that
     the story will be read a long time after Thomas's "uneven verse
     has been dropped from anthologies."

42   WHITE, WILLIAM. "Dylan Thomas and A.E. Housman." Papers of
      the Bibliographical Society of America 52:309-10.
         Speculates on the significance of Thomas's at one time
      having copied out Housman's "Infant Innocence."

43   WILLIAMS, RAYMOND. "Dylan Thomas's Play for Voices."
      Critical Quarterly 1 (Spring):18-26.
         Notes the developing stages of Under Milk Wood and dis-
      tinguishes the three levels of writing employed, namely narra-
      tive, dialogue, and song. Williams also points out the possi-
      bility that Joyce's Ulysses and King Lear served as sources.
      Reprinted: 1966.8.

                                 1959

1   BALLIETT, WHITNEY. "The Burning Bush." New Yorker 35
      (13 June):127-29.
         Refers to a part in Muriel Spark's Memento Mori where
      Thomas is the subject. One of the "grotesques" appearing in the
      novel, he ultimately comes out looking "something of a saint."

2   BLÖCKER, GÜNTER. "Zu Dylan Thomas' Unter dem milchwald."
      Akzente 6 (February):89-95.
         Discusses Under Milk Wood as a new kind of dramatic crea-
      tion. Ends by pointing out that the play-for-voices was an
      effective vehicle for Thomas's desire to celebrate life. If the
      world could be changed, it would be by means of such stories
      "sung" by poets.

3   CASEY, BILL. "Thomas' 'To-day, this insect.'" Explicator 17
      (March): item 43.
         Explicates the poem as one in which Thomas attempts to
      link his own creations with man's primary fables.

4   CORIN, FERNAND. "En traduisant Dylan Thomas." Revue des
      langues vivantes 25:286-99.
         Discusses the distinctions of Thomas's craft. Then takes
      a close look at how Under Milk Wood works.

5   COX, C.B. "Dylan Thomas's 'Fern Hill.'" Critical Quarterly 1
      (Summer):134-38.
         Finds "Fern Hill" to be an outstanding poem, one that
      employs "highly original ways" to describe the "joyful exhilara-
      tion of a child." Primarily through evocative imagery and
      "ecstatic" rhythms, he approaches the communication of romantic
      emotions "almost beyond expression." Reprinted: 1963.5.

6   "Craftsmanship in Poetry." Times (London), 23 May, p. 10.
         Reports on a lecture by Bonamy Dobrée in which he talked
      about the essentially lyrical quality of Thomas's poetry. Two
      points emphasized were the fact that Thomas always celebrated the
      universal theme of the "generative process" and that his lines
      could defy ordinary syntax because "they were formed of images."

7 DREW, ELIZABETH. Poetry: A Modern Guide to Its Understanding and Enjoyment. New York: W.W. Norton & Co., pp. 21, 181–83, 215.
   Points out that Thomas is the only modern poet who felt the kind of "oneness" the romantics experienced with nature; however, his identification is based on the knowledge of the "life–death cycle" rather than on spiritual or moral inspiration.

8 GARRINGUE, JEAN. "Dark Is a Way and Light Is a Place." Poetry 94 (May):111–14.
   Reviews the augmented edition of Collected Poems. Calls Thomas the "heir" of Rimbaud, Blake, Hopkins, and the Bible, praising him for creating a new visionary language.

9 HILL, JANE. "A Look Back on Anger." Prairie Schooner 33 (Spring):100–103.
   Looks at the "thundering impact" left by Caitlin Thomas's Leftover Life to Kill. In the end the book raises without satisfactorily answering the question of why Thomas's widow "so ruthlessly laid bare" herself.

10 HOFFMAN, FREDERICK J. Freudianism and the Literary Mind. New York: Grove Press; London: Calder, pp. 286–90.
   Reprint of 1945.1.

11 "Inspired Clown." Times (London), 6 February, p. 5.
   Praises Emlyn Williams's performance on "The Fight" for the B.B.C. More than anyone, Williams gives the "inspired clown" side of the poet its "due."

12 JENKINS, DAVID CLAY. "Dylan Thomas and Wales Magazine." Trace, February–March, pp. 1–8.
   Discusses the relationship between Thomas and Wales Magazine.

13 JONES, ROBERT C. "Thomas' 'The Conversation of Prayer.'" Explicator 17 (April): item 49.
   Explicates the poem while focusing on how rhyming patterns carry much of the meaning.

14 KNIEGER, BERNARD. "Thomas' 'Sonnet II.'" Explicator 18 (November): item 14.
   Gives the second sonnet of the "Altarwise by owl-light" sequence a line-by-line reading, stressing its "to be born is to die" theme.

15 LOUGÉE, DAVID. "An Open Window." Poetry 94 (May):114–17.
   Welcomes the publication of the letters of Thomas to his friend and fellow-poet in Letters to Vernon Watkins. Points to the "frequent disparity between the man and his work" found in the letters, but also to the fact that they manage to give us a "touching" and "human portrait."

16   MAUD, RALPH N. "Dylan Thomas' First Published Poem." <u>Modern Language Notes</u> 74 (February):117-18.
      Establishes the fact that "And death shall have no dominion" was the first poem published by Thomas outside Swansea and refers to the minor differences between its early and final versions.

17   MOYNIHAN, WILLIAM TRUMBULL. "Thomas' 'In the white giant's thigh.'" <u>Explicator</u> 17 (May): item 59.
      Explicates the poem as one whose central concern involves the meaning of death.

18   MUECKE, D.C. "Come Back! Come Back!--A Theme in Dylan Thomas's Prose." <u>Meanjin</u> 18 (April):67-76.
      Finds that lost love is a theme that recurs in Thomas's prose (as it does in his play-for-voices and poetry). Argues that Thomas at the end was approaching the development of a transcendental vision that reconciled life and death.

19   PARK, B.A. Review of <u>Letters to Vernon Watkins</u>. <u>Books Abroad</u> 33 (Autumn):417.
      Notes that the letters give evidence of the fact that Thomas's "arbitrary and intoxicated" style was the result of a carefully conscious effort.

20   SLOTE, BERNICE, and MILLER, JAMES E., Jr. "Of Monkeys, Nudes and the Good Grey: Dylan Thomas and Walt Whitman." <u>Western Humanities Review</u> 13 (Autumn):339-53.
      Examines the links between Whitman and Thomas, particularly the fact that both took part in the "affirmative, physical, intuitive, incantatory" tradition. Reprinted: 1960.26.

21   SPACKS, PATRICIA MEYER. "Thomas' 'In my Craft or Sullen Art.'" <u>Explicator</u> 18 (December): item 21.
      Shows the fresh, ironic meaning of lines 6-9 of the poem.

22   "Thomas' Script Acted." <u>New York Times</u>, 21 January, p. 27.
      Notes the opening of Joseph Everingham's adaptation of <u>The Doctor and the Devils</u> at MIT's Little Theatre.

23   TODD, RUTHVEN. "Dylan Thomas in London." <u>Listener</u> 62 (17 December):1065-66.
      Reminisces about the Thomas the writer knew in London.

24   UNTERMEYER, LOUIS. "Dylan Thomas." In <u>Lives of the Poets</u>. New York: Simon & Schuster, pp. 716-22.
      Provides a biographical essay that stresses Thomas's "tumultuous" nature. His intoxicated, original poetry reflects the fact that he "reeled through the world with tragic innocence and took a child's irresponsible delight in all its turmoil."

1960

1   BEARDSLEY, MONROE C., and HYNES, SAM. "Misunderstanding
    Poetry: Notes on Some Readings of Dylan Thomas." College
    English 21 (March):315-22.
        Uses Thomas's "Altarwise by owl-light" sequence to illus-
    trate ways in which criticism can go wrong when faced with poetry
    of great obscurity.

2   BLOOM, EDWARD A. "Dylan Thomas' 'Naked Vision.'" Western
    Humanities Review 14 (Autumn):389-400.
        Establishes the fact that Thomas's grand ambition was to
    discover and reveal a transcendental vision that surpasses mate-
    rial truth. For him, truth came to reside in life's paradoxes,
    which he tried desperately and obsessively to express.

3   BLOOM, EDWARD A., and BLOOM, LILLIAN D. "Dylan Thomas: His
    Intimations of Mortality." Boston University Studies in
    English 4 (Autumn):138-52.
        Depicts Thomas as a serious existential thinker. His
    primary intellectual obsessions were concerned with the existence
    of loneliness and death.

4   BRADBURY, MALCOLM. "Poet and Speaking Tree." Manchester
    Guardian Weekly, 1 December, p. 11.
        Reviews E.W. Tedlock's Dylan Thomas: The Legend and the
    Poet. Complains that the collection of essays leans too much
    toward Thomas's legend-makers even though "some very good criti-
    cal essays" (namely those by Elder Olson, Cid Corman, Marshall
    Stearns, and Geoffrey Moore) are included.

5   BRINNIN, JOHN MALCOLM, ed. A Casebook on Dylan Thomas. New
    York: Thomas Y. Crowell, 325 pp.
        Collects the most important reminiscences, critical essays,
    and selections from books by both friends and critics. Some of
    the pieces are basically personal observations, but most are
    concerned primarily with the poetry. Ten of Thomas's most
    important poems are reprinted and an extended bibliography is
    appended. Contains reprints of 1942.1; 1946.14; 1947.7;
    1948.4, 11; 1949.8, 11; 1950.5; 1952.2; 1953.19, 26, 33, 47;
    1954.5, 18, 36, 53, 69, 78, 85, 94; 1955.11, 30-31, 77;
    1956.18-19, 22; 1957.17, 23, 27, 52, 60; 1958.17, 27, 35.

6   BROOKS, CLEANTH, and WARREN, ROBERT PENN, eds. Understanding
    Poetry. 3d ed. New York: Holt, Rinehart & Winston,
    pp. 195-96, 385-86.
        Anthologizes "A Refusal to Mourn" and "The force that
    through the green fuse," with analytical questions and brief
    commentary attached.

7   CHAMBERS, MARLENE. "Thomas' 'In the white giant's thigh.'"
    Explicator 19 (October): item 1.
        Explicates the poem as an unconventional descriptive
    affirmation of the death-and-conception process.

8   COLLINGE, PATRICIA. "Once More unto the Breach." New Yorker
     36 (5 November):48–49.
     Parodies Under Milk Wood, entitling the piece Under
Silkwood.

9   CORAN, ANTHONY. "The English Poet in Wales II: Boys of
     Summer in Their Ruin." Anglo-Welsh Review 10:11–21.
     Looks at the situation and scene of Anglo-Welsh poetry.
Thomas is said to represent the special predicament of these
writers: "the poet is caught between two fires. He is neither
English nor Welsh; neither a member of the anglicized middle-
class, nor of the Welsh-speaking peasantry."

10   DAICHES, DAVID. "The Poetry of Dylan Thomas." College
     English 22 (November):123–28.
     Reprint of 1954.25.

11   ENRIGHT, D.J. "Once Below a Time." Spectator, 21 October,
     pp. 607–8.
     Reviews E.W. Tedlock's Dylan Thomas: The Legend and the
Poet. Criticizes the collection for focusing on the legendary
aspects of Thomas at the expense of a serious consideration of
his poetry.

12   "Four Just Men." Times Literary Supplement, 2 September,
     p. 555.
     Reviews Rayner Heppenstall's Four Absentees. The best
thing about the book is the "extraordinary fidelity" of the
backdrop against which Thomas and the other "absentees" (Eric
Gill, J. Middleton Murry, and George Orwell) are seen. Thomas
appears in some "typical" drinking bouts.

13   FRASER, GEORGE SUTHERLAND. "Dylan Thomas." In Vision and
     Rhetoric. New York: Barnes & Noble, pp. 211–41.
     Reprint of 1957.17.

14   GASSNER, JOHN. Theatre at the Crossroads: Plays and Play-
     wrights of the Mid-Century American Stage. New York: Holt,
     Rinehart & Winston, pp. 286–88.
     Comments on Emlyn Williams's "A Boy Growing Up" presenta-
tion. It was a "superb reading," but the literary sources
appeared to be "put together with virtually no dramaturgy at
all."

15   HAWKES, TERENCE. "Dylan Thomas's Welsh." College English 21
     (March):345–47.
     Notes Thomas's use of the Welsh language, particularly in
Under Milk Wood.

16   HEPPENSTALL, RAYNER. Four Absentees. London: Barrie &
     Rockcliff, pp. 42–47 passim.
     Reminisces about encounters with Thomas and other famous
dead friends. The first meeting with Thomas took place when the
latter was "a chuckling cherubic twenty-year-old."

17   HEWES, HENRY. "Father Courage." Saturday Review 43
      (4 June):30.
         Finds the production of Under Milk Wood at the experi-
mentally conscious Dallas Theater Center surprisingly successful
and applauds the direction of Burgess Meredith for some "bold,
imaginative touches."

18   HIGHET, GILBERT. "The Great Welsh Poet: Dylan Thomas."
      Vogue 135 (15 March):111, 152-54.
         Reprint of 1960.19.

19   _____. The Powers of Poetry. New York: Oxford University
      Press, pp. 151-57.
         Submits that in order to understand Thomas's poetry, we
must appreciate his Welsh character and background. He is
"emphatically a Celtic poet." Reprinted: 1960.18.

20   HUGH-JONES, STEPHEN. "A Little Set of Facts." Manchester
      Guardian Weekly, 13 October, p. 10.
         Reviews Rayner Heppenstall's Four Absentees. It's a "dis-
agreeable" book despite the fact that it does have some good
stories about Orwell, Eric Gill, Middleton Murry, and Thomas. It
confirms the "extraordinary pettiness of the literary world."

21   KNIEGER, BERNARD. "Thomas' 'Sonnet III.'" Explicator 18
      (January): item 25.
         Gives the third sonnet of the "Altarwise by owl-light"
sequence a line-by-line reading, showing that it dramatizes
Christ's birth, Crucifixion, and Resurrection.

22   "Kritische Rückschau." Forum 6 (December):145.
         Criticizes the stage version of The Doctor and the Devils
for lacking dramatic power. It does have Thomas's characteristic
magical touch in other ways.

23   LOGAN, JOHN. "Dylan Thomas and the Ark of Art." Renascence
      12 (Winter):59-66.
         Concludes that for Thomas the "Christian images find their
unity not only in the liturgical year and in the life of the Holy
Family but also in every event of art."

24   MANDER, JOHN. "Lives of the Prophets." New Statesman 60
      (3 September):316-17.
         Reviews Rayner Heppenstall's Four Absentees. As an example
of "literary gossip," it has limited critical value; but the
"truth" about Thomas seems to be revealed--that he had a
"curiously infantile 'denial of the idea of death.'"

25   MAUD, RALPH N. "Obsolete and Dialect Words as Serious Puns in
      Dylan Thomas." English Studies 41 (February):28-30.
         Looks at Thomas's penchant for puns. His use of them in-
volves their usual, connotative, and thematic possibilities.
They are especially expressive of his obsessive themes of birth,
death, and marriage.

26   MILLER, JAMES E., Jr.; SHAPIRO, KARL; and SLOTE, BERNICE.
     Start with the Sun: Studies in Cosmic Poetry. Lincoln:
     University of Nebraska Press, pp. 169-90 passim.
        Reveals the striking similarities between Thomas's and
     Whitman's poetry.   With reference to dominant ideas, themes, and
     images, Thomas belongs to Whitman's poetic tradition even though
     at the same time he was "at home in the movement of modern
     English poetry toward syntactical disintegration." Expansion
     and reprint of 1959.20.

27   MILLS, RALPH J., Jr. "Dylan Thomas: The Endless Monologue."
     Accent 20 (Spring):114-36.
        Shows Thomas's developing tendency to write poetry that
     attempts to include more and more of the great plurality of
     existence until he reached the point where he depended on an
     inclusive creative language providing its own reality independent
     of the exterior world.   Thomas believed that human existence was
     "determined from within by the unalterable governance of time,"
     but that the poet's imagination could create order and value
     through the "stillness of art."

28   MONTAGUE, GENE. "Thomas' 'To-day, this insect.'" Explicator
     19 (December): item 15.
        Explicates the poem as an argument that "in our search for
     'truth' we have destroyed mystery and with it the techniques of
     art."

29   PORTEUS, HUGH GORDON. "Nights Out in the Thirties."
     Spectator 205 (2 September):342, 344.
        Reviews Rayner Heppenstall's Four Absentees, adding his own
     reminiscences about Thomas.   He was "very good company."

30   ROSENTHAL, M.L. "Exquisite Chaos: Thomas and Others." In
     The Modern Poets: A Critical Introduction. New York: Oxford
     University Press, pp. 203-19 passim.
        Emphasizes certain qualities that Thomas had in common with
     Hart Crane, particularly the romantic, bardic, primitivistic, and
     mystical strains.   His "modernity" derives from the way he "pours
     his amazing psychic energy into the manipulation of sound, syntax,
     and metaphor" in the service of his obsessive themes.   His poetry
     is ultimately a "reaction away from the topical, the 'social,'
     and the ratiocinative to a realm of introspective personalism
     which is at the same time inclusively human."

31   SHAPIRO, KARL. "Dylan Thomas." In In Defense of Ignorance.
     New York: Random House, pp. 171-86.
        Reprint of 1955.77.

32   STANFORD, DEREK. "The Image of God in the Work of Dylan
     Thomas." Visvabharati Quarterly 25 (August):304-14.
        Notes how Thomas's God often is marked by a personal, in-
     formal quality characteristic of Celts.   His pantheism is marked
     more by guilt than celebration, except when he can imagine life
     divinely transformed into a glorious existence.

33 TEDLOCK, E.W., ed. Dylan Thomas: The Legend and the Poet.
London: William Heinemann, 287 pp.
Divides this collection of articles into two parts—one
focusing on the man and the other on the poet. Claims that the
main hope is to "restore the focus" so that the legend can begin
to disappear into the background and the poetry to the fore-
ground. Contains reprints of 1944.3; 1945.2; 1946.8; 1948.4,7;
1950.1; 1952.22; 1953.9, 19, 25-26, 33; 1954.18, 53, 70, 78;
1955.24, 60, 77; 1957.15.

34 "Through Cadaver's Country." Times Literary Supplement,
23 December, p. 826.
Reviews E.W. Tedlock's Dylan Thomas: The Legend and the
Poet and Roberto Sanesi's Dylan Thomas. Finds Tedlock's collection of biographical and critical essays to be thoroughly disappointing, with the obvious exception of Karl Shapiro's clear
and sensitive discussion of Thomas's poetry. Sanesi's "straight-
forward" account lacks originality.

35 WATKINS, VERNON. Afterword to Adventures in the Skin Trade
and Other Stories. New York: New American Library,
pp. 184-90.
Sees Thomas as a religious poet who "sought the company of
unbelievers," someone who was always "remaking himself" in his
creative act. He was always "assailing his own established position lest it should hinder or obstruct the vision when the ground
was broken for a new poem."

36 ZIGERELL, JAMES. "Thomas' 'When all my five and country
senses see.'" Explicator 19 (November): item 11.
Explicates the poem as a manifesto of the poet's belief
that the heart "is sacred and in touch with the truth."

1961

1 BALLIETT, WHITNEY. "Off Broadway." New Yorker 37 (8 April):
132, 134.
Reviews a revival of Under Milk Wood. Assumes that this
"bewitching pure-cream poem" continues to undergo attempts at
staging it due to a "genuine hunger" for verse drama. Finds,
however, that it's an "irrationality" to try to bend this play-
for-voices to the theater stage.

2 BAUMGART, WOLFGANG. "Die Gegenwart des Barocktheaters."
Archiv für das Studium der neueren Sprachen und Literaturen
113/198:65-76.
Draws connections between baroque and modern theater,
emphasizing such similar elements as allegory, passive heroes,
and resistance to reality, elements that appear in Thomas as
well as in several other modern dramatists.

3   BEVINGTON, HELEN. "A Meeting with Dylan Thomas." In When
     Found, Make a Verse. New York: Simon & Schuster, pp. 58-60.
        Recalls a public reading by Thomas and his expressed hatred
     of reading his own poems under such circumstances and his reluc-
     tance to talk about their meaning with others.

4   BLACKBURN, THOMAS. "Dylan Thomas." In The Price of an Eye.
     London: Longmans, Green, pp. 111-23.
        Suggests that the complete link between Thomas's poetry and
     life was a tragic flaw that affected painfully both his art and
     his existence. Thomas "could never obtain the degree of self-
     consciousness which would have enabled him to separate himself
     from his great gift, to become its medium . . . instead of its
     creature." Reprinted: 1974.3.

5   BUTLER, FRANK A. "On the Beat Nature of Beat." American
     Scholar 30 (Winter):83-84.
        Points to Thomas's poetic control as the essential quality
     missing in "beat" art.

6   CHAMBERS, MARLENE. "Thomas' 'In the white giant's thigh.'"
     Explicator 19 (March): item 39.
        Comments on the possible legendary source of the "barren
     women" of the poem.

7   CIARDI, JOHN. "Discs for the Library." Saturday Review 44
     (13 May):58.
        Recommends Richard Burton's recorded reading (for Spoken
     Arts) of Under Milk Wood, but finds Burton's recording of fifteen
     selected poems by Thomas (also for Spoken Arts) to be inferior to
     the poet's own readings for Caedmon.

8   COMMON, JACK. Review of Four Absentees. Twentieth Century
     169 (January):92, 94.
        Reviews Rayner Heppenstall's autobiographical reminiscence
     focusing on four famous friends, including Thomas. The author's
     account is "successful in presenting his friends vividly and
     naturally."

9   "Dylan Thomas Ms. for Display." Times (London), 21 June,
     p. 8.
        Marks the acquisition of the original manuscript of Under
     Milk Wood by the Times Bookshop and gives a brief history of how
     it got there.

10   "Dylan Thomas Well Served." Times (London), 9 August, p. 11.
        Reviews the performance of Under Milk Wood at the Lyric,
     Hammersmith, finding it to be surprisingly successful because it
     is presented "much nearer a concert performance than a play
     proper."

11   EMERY, CLARK. "Two-Gunned Gabriel in London." <u>Carrell</u> 2
     (June):16–22.
          Ranges over the life and personality of Thomas, using
     <u>Adventures in the Skin Trade</u> as a springboard.

12   GELLERT, ROGER. "Youth Week." <u>New Statesman</u> 62 (18 August):
     226.
          Reviews R.A.D.A.'s performance of <u>Under Milk Wood</u>. Sug-
     gests that the less visual aids or other marginalia are added to
     the text, the better.

13   GREENSBERG, CLEMENT. "The Jackson Pollock Market Soars."
     <u>New York Times Magazine</u>, 16 April, pp. 42, 132, 135.
          Draws a comparison between Thomas and Jackson Pollock,
     especially as far as the misunderstanding concerning their con-
     scious craft is concerned.

14   HOLBROOK, DAVID. "Two Welsh Writers: T.F. Powys and Dylan
     Thomas." In <u>The Modern Age</u>. Pelican Guide to English Liter-
     ature, edited by Boris Ford, 7. Harmondsworth: Penguin
     Books, pp. 415–28.
          Discusses (comparatively) the achievements of Thomas and
     T.F. Powys. While Powys is praised, especially for his "moral
     seriousness," Thomas is denigrated. His reputation is said to
     rest "on his abrogation of the artist's responsibility, and even
     his consequent inarticulateness."

15   JONES, RICHARD. "The Dylan Thomas Country." <u>Texas Quarterly</u>
     4 (Winter):34–42.
          Believes that one must understand Thomas's homeland to have
     a full understanding of his poetry because the "character" of the
     country "penetrated" his work. Provides a particularly detailed
     view of Laugharne. Speculates that Thomas "inhaled" the beauty
     of his homeland's language.

16   _____. "Introductory Note to Dylan Thomas's 'Poetic
     Manifesto.'" <u>Texas Quarterly</u> 4 (Winter):44.
          Records the story behind Thomas's written description of
     his attitude toward poetry. Approached by a student working on
     a thesis, Thomas commented "frankly" on the following issues:
     the impetus to write poetry, the major influences on his work,
     the degree of spontaneity in his use of poetic devices, the rela-
     tion with surrealism, and his definition of poetry. A facsimile
     of this document of "incomparable value" follows the note
     (pp. 45–53).

17   KNIEGER, BERNARD. "Thomas' 'Love in the Asylum.'" <u>Explicator</u>
     20 (October): item 13.
          Explicates the poem as one dealing with the madness of love
     in a mad world.

18   _____. "Thomas' 'On the Marriage of a Virgin.'" <u>Explicator</u>
     19 (May): item 61.
          Explicates the poem as a depiction of the conception and
     birth of Christ.

19 ____. "Thomas' 'Twenty-four years.'" Explicator 20
(September): item 4.
Explicates the poem as one of Thomas's creations dealing
with the "life predicates death" theme.

20 LEACH, ELSIE. "Dylan Thomas' 'Ballad of the Long-legged
Bait.'" Modern Language Notes 76 (December):724-28.
Offers a reading of "Ballad of the Long-legged Bait" that
contrasts with the conclusions of Elder Olson (a poem about the
possibility of salvation through sensual mortification) and
Richard Condon (a poem affirming the human condition's necessary
surrender to the flesh). The poem is actually a "narrative of
Christ's salvation of mankind through the Incarnation," with the
sexual act representing not the poem's subject but its key
metaphor.

21 LEHMANN, JOHN. "English Letters in the Doldrums? An Editor's
View." Texas Quarterly 4 (Autumn):58-59, 63.
Looks back to the post-World War II writing scene and re-
fers to Thomas as one of the figures who made the time "excep-
tionally full of excitement and promise."

22 LOESCH, KATHARINE TAYLOR. "Prosodic Patterns in the Poetry of
Dylan Thomas." Ph.D. dissertation, Northwestern University,
363 pp.
Using the Trager and Smith analytical method and focusing
on selected poems phonemically transcribed from his recorded
readings, attempts to describe the prosodic patterns found in
Thomas's poetry. The distinct and common patterns are system-
atically collected and a phonemic transcription of the poems is
included. See Dissertation Abstracts International 22 (1961):
3295.

23 McCORD, HOWARD L. "Dylan Thomas and Bhartrihari." Notes and
Queries 8 (March):110.
Proposes that Thomas may have gotten the central fishing
image used in "Ballad of the Long-legged Bait" from an Indian
poet writing in the seventh century.

24 MAUD, RALPH N. "Dylan Thomas' Collected Poems: Chronology of
Composition." PMLA 76 (June):292-97.
Provides the evidence that the order in which Thomas's
poems were published is very different from the order in which
they were written. The value of establishing an authentic
chronology lies in isolating the "main line" of his creativity.

25 NIST, JOHN. "Dylan Thomas: Perfection of the Work."
Arizona Quarterly 17 (Summer):101-6.
Argues that Thomas's work is marked by an interesting in-
version, whereby an understanding of life's imperfection inspires
artistic perfection. This inversion is especially at work in
"Vision and Prayer."

26   OPPEL, HORST. Review of Dylan Thomas: The Legend and the
      Poet. Die neueren Sprachen, July, pp. 340–41.
          Welcomes E.W. Tedlock's volume as a useful early step in
      the direction of discovering Thomas's place in his literary
      generation.

27   PESCHMANN, HERMANN. Review of Dylan Thomas: The Legend and
      the Poet and Four Absentees. English 13 (Summer):198–99.
          Finds E.W. Tedlock's Dylan Thomas a mixed bag and Rayner
      Heppenstall's Four Absentees a reminiscence that amounts to
      "very small beer."

28   RODWAY, ALLAN. "A Note on Contemporary English Poetry."
      Texas Quarterly 4 (Autumn):66–68.
          Provides a look at the causes and ambitions of the 1950s
      New Movement. It was sparked by a reaction against the "Anglo-
      Catholic wing" that followed T.S. Eliot and the "Dionysiac or
      neoromantic wing" represented by Thomas.

29   SLOCOMBE, MARIE, and SAUL, PATRICK. "Dylan Thomas
      Discography." Recorded Sound 1 (Summer):80–95.
          Catalogs and indexes the Thomas reading records. Support-
      ive participants are also indexed.

30   SPILKA, MARK. Review of Start with the Sun: Studies in
      Cosmic Poetry. Modern Language Notes 76 (December):892–96.
          Dismisses Start with the Sun as a book written by "intel-
      ligent cranks." The attempt to categorize Thomas as one of the
      pagan poets who "believe in body as well as soul" ignores the
      fact that this poet's work was filled with a "modern sense of
      reality" reflected by verbal and mental flexibility and com-
      plexity.

31   TAUBMAN, HOWARD. "Innocence of Spirit." New York Times,
      9 April, sec. 2, p. 1.
          Compares Thomas and Tagore. Both Under Milk Wood and
      Tagore's The King of the Dark Chamber are "delightful examples"
      of nonrealistic drama, and both are pointed in the same direc-
      tion: the expression of the "innocence of the human spirit."

32   . "Theatre: Images of Wales." New York Times,
      30 March, p. 25.
          Praises the Circle in the Square production of Under Milk
      Wood. It brought the "earthy and rapturous incantation" to life
      by being true to the unconventional qualities of Thomas's dra-
      matic creation.

33   TELLIER, A.R. Review of Dylan Thomas: The Legend and the
      Poet. Études anglaises 14 (July-September):261–62.
          Recommends E.W. Tedlock's volume for its balancing selec-
      tions between those about the man and those about the work.

34   "Thomas Screen Play on the Stage." <u>Times</u> (London),
      14 February, p. 6.
      Faults Judith Gick's stage adaptation of <u>The Doctor and the</u>
      <u>Devils</u> for lacking form, but responds to the vitality of the
      dialogue, which "reverberates like laughter."

35   THWAITE, ANTHONY. "Dylan Thomas and George Barker." In
      <u>Contemporary English Poetry: An Introduction</u>. Philadelphia:
      Dufour, pp. 93–109.
      Revision and reprint of 1957.62.

36   "Two Off-Broadway Closings." <u>New York Times</u>, 18 October,
      p. 48.
      Gives notice of the closing of the Circle in the Square
      production of <u>Under Milk Wood</u> after 202 performances.

37   "Verse on the Record." <u>Times Literary Supplement</u>, 14 July,
      p. 434.
      Reviews the Argo recordings of <u>Homage to Dylan Thomas</u>.
      What is most obviously missed is Thomas's own voice, and Richard
      Burton's attempt to take the place is "gallant" but not success-
      ful.

38   WAIN, JOHN. "One Book Too Many." <u>Encounter</u> 16 (March):81–82.
      Dismisses E.W. Tedlock's <u>Dylan Thomas: The Legend and the</u>
      <u>Poet</u> as a "silly, unuseful, dreary little book" that fails in the
      two essential ways a book like this should have satisfied. It
      fails to settle any critical issues, and it fails to speculate
      about what Thomas might have gone on to accomplish had he lived.

39   WATKINS, VERNON. "A Painter's Studio." <u>Texas Quarterly</u> 4
      (Winter):54.
      Provides an introductory note on Thomas's role in <u>A</u>
      <u>Painter's Studio</u>, a television program designed to depict the
      artistic life of Swansea as revealed through Alfred Janes's
      paintings.

40   _____. "Review: Behind the Fabulous Curtain." <u>Poetry</u> 98
      (May):124–25.
      Reviews E.W. Tedlock's <u>Dylan Thomas: The Legend and the</u>
      <u>Poet</u>, emphasizing the difficulty of explaining Thomas because the
      quality he happened to prize the most was "seriousness" even
      though he was "a born clown."

41   _____. "Swansea." <u>Texas Quarterly</u> 4 (Winter):59–64.
      Remembers Swansea as a "hidden place," without "sophisti-
      cation" or "cultural props." The "stubborn oddity" of the place
      remains; the park where Thomas wrote "The Hunchback in the Park,"
      for example, hasn't changed much. On second thought, he laments
      the fact that with the coming of the war the iconoclasm of
      Thomas's early years disappeared.

42   WOOD, FREDERICK T. Review of Dylan Thomas: The Legend and
     the Poet. English Studies 42 (December):407.
         Finds E.W. Tedlock's volume to fail in providing a solid
     estimate of Thomas's achievement. It lacks critical sobriety,
     detachment, and balance.

                                1962

1   "At Edinburgh Tragedy." Times (London), 22 August, p. 5.
        Reviews the stage adaptation of The Doctor and the Devils.
    It turned out to be a surprisingly successful version of Thomas's
    "not very remarkable text" in great part because the staging was
    properly suggestive and the actors delivered the poet's words
    with cumulative effectiveness.

2   BERGONZI, BERNARD. "Maturitocracy." Spectator 208
    (6 April):452.
        Reviews David Holbrook's Llareggub Revisited. As a critic,
    Holbrook represents Dr. Leavis's thinking "stripped down to a
    crude and fanatical simplicity."

3   COMBECHER, HANS. "Interpretationen zu drei Gedichten von
    Dylan Thomas." Die Neueren Sprachen, March, pp. 130–42.
        Focuses on the fact that Thomas's posthumous influence
    continues to grow. To assess Thomas's true ability, the critic
    selects "The Conversation of Prayer" and "Fern Hill" for espe-
    cially close analysis.

4   COOK, BRUCE A. "A Literary Gent." Commonweal 75
    (23 February):560–62.
        Reviews Rayner Heppenstall's Four Absentees. In what is
    basically an autobiography, the stories and impressions having
    to do with Thomas are "no more than filler material."

5   DAVENPORT, JOHN. "Black Sheep." Harper's Bazaar, June,
    pp. 88–89, 97.
        Reminisces about the Thomas he knew as a friend.

6   DAVIES, ANEIRIN TALFAN. "William Barnes, Gerard Manley
    Hopkins, Dylan Thomas: The Influence of Welsh Prosody on
    Modern English Poetry." In Proceedings of the IIIrd Congress
    of the International Comparative Literature Association. The
    Hague: Mouton, pp. 90–122.
        Traces the influence of Welsh versification on Thomas's
    poetry. William Barnes influenced Hopkins, who in turn influ-
    enced Thomas. Hopkins, in fact, was the "one great and deciding"
    influence on Thomas's poetry, an influence that becomes increas-
    ingly apparent as the religious theme develops.

7   DAVIES, M. BRYN. "Dylan Thomas--An Appraisal." Literary
    Half-Yearly 3 (July):53-56.
        Looks at Thomas's achievement, concluding that much of his
    popularity depends on his being so different. Under Milk Wood
    must be seen as a tour de force.

8   EMERY, CLARK. The World of Dylan Thomas. Coral Gables:
    University of Miami Press, 318 pp.
        Explicates the poems, organizing the study into six com-
    partments with the aim that the selections within each group
    comment on each other. These groups are as follows: those that
    reveal Thomas as a human being, as an observer of human rela-
    tions, as a craftsman, and as a man concerned with the issues of
    war, religion, and philosophical understanding. An introduction
    focuses on the various prominent aspects of his life and art.

9   ENRIGHT, D.J. "Llareggub and Erewhon." New Statesman 62
    (30 March):453, 456.
        Reviews David Holbrook's Llareggub Revisited. Doesn't deny
    the critic's sincerity in finding fault with Thomas, but counters
    that the apparent foundation of the attack (namely that litera-
    ture precedes life) is nonsense.

10 HALPEREN, MAX. "Thomas' 'If I were tickled by the rub of
    love.'" Explicator 21 (November): item 25.
        Explicates the poem by concentrating on the "grim accep-
    tance" of man's fatal existence found in the conclusion.

11 "Himself a Poet." Times Literary Supplement, 13 April,
    p. 250.
        Reviews David Holbrook's Llareggub Revisited, satirizing
    the critic's smug, obsessive attack on Thomas. Holbrook fails
    to appreciate the fact that perhaps precisely because Thomas
    wasn't "normal" and "mature" he managed to create some poems that
    will last." "Any work of art has a cost in human suffering."

12 "Idiom and Style." Times Literary Supplement, 21 December,
    p. 987.
        Doubts the ultimate value of the kind of expository, para-
    phrastic criticism found in William York Tindall's A Reader's
    Guide to Dylan Thomas. It's a useful "tool" for readers new to
    this poetry, but it "will not settle the critical argument about
    Thomas one way or the other."

13 KAZIN, ALFRED. Contemporaries. Boston: Little, Brown,
    pp. 192-202.
        Reprint of 1957.32.

14 KEOWN, ERIC. "At the Festival." Punch 243 (29 August):
    317-18.
        Reviews the Edinburgh Festival stage production of The
    Doctor and the Devils, a play that leaves a powerful impression
    even if it uses a "clumsy" narrator device and "suffers" from
    its film script origin.

15   KNIEGER, BERNARD. "Dylan Thomas: The Christianity of the
      'Altarwise by owl-light' Sequence." College English 23 (May):
      623-28.
          Gives the sonnets a Christian reading. The Christian theme
      follows after a "positive Christian note is struck" in the first
      sonnet of the sequence.

16   LARKIN, PHILIP. "Master' Voices." New Statesman 62
      (2 February):170-71.
          Surveys contemporary recording practitioners and fashions.
      Notes that Thomas's voice "has a rich fraudulence that sets you
      chuckling."

17   LEVY, MERVYN. "A Womb with a View." John O'London's Weekly,
      29 November, pp. 484-85.
          Remembers his friend as someone different from the legend.
      For example, Thomas was not the womanizer of the myth. Points
      out that his childhood room inspired the ways of his poetry as a
      whole.

18   MAUD, RALPH N. "Letter from Wales." Nation 195 (1 Septem-
      ber):98-100.
          Writing from Wales, gives an impression of the kind of
      "benign nationalism" from which Thomas sprang.

19   MILLS, RALPH J., Jr. Poets in Progress. Evanston, Ill.:
      Northwestern University Press, p. 4.
          Compares Thomas and Theodore Roethke.

20   MORTON, RICHARD. "Notes on the Imagery of Dylan Thomas."
      English Studies 43 (June):155-64.
          Shows that Thomas's imagery moves from the general use of
      archetypal imagery to artificial imagery (that is, imagery en-
      dowed with personal meaning). The "essential feature" of his
      poetry is "warring imagery." "The development of the poetry
      shows a growing tendency to use an argument or narrative." While
      the earlier poems used a "host of archetypal images aimed at pro-
      ducing in the reader . . . the author's own sensations," the
      later poems acquired their effect "through the tensions arising
      between carefully worked out extended images."

21   MOYNIHAN, WILLIAM TRUMBULL. "The Poetry of Dylan Thomas: A
      Study of Its Meaning and Unity." Ph.D. dissertation, Brown
      University, 236 pp.
          Discusses Collected Poems with an eye toward Thomas's
      feelings about poetry in general, the techniques and artifices he
      tended to employ, the general argument of his writing, and the
      symbolic vision of the poems as a whole. Although his ultimate
      vision is ambivalent about the theme of regeneration, it is clear
      in its depiction of creative love. See Dissertation Abstracts
      International 23 (1962):2531.

22 MURDY, THELMA LOUISE BAUGHAN. "Sound and Meaning in Dylan
    Thomas's Poetry." Ph.D. dissertation, University of Florida,
    226 pp.
        Analyzes some of the habitual auditory and semantic charac-
    teristics found in Thomas's poetry. The study begins by con-
    sidering the importance of oral reading, the connection between
    sound and meaning, and Thomas's unusual compositional method. In
    the end, Thomas learned that meaning and sound should strengthen
    each other and impress the reader in a simultaneous way. See
    Dissertation Abstracts International 23 (1962):3382.

23 NIST, JOHN. "No Reason for Mourning: A Reading of the Later
    Poems of Dylan Thomas." Approach 42 (Winter):3-7.
        Traces Thomas's turn to Christianity and its myth. In "A
    Refusal to Mourn the Death, by Fire, of a Child in London" he
    reaches the point where he confronts death as a "religious
    promise." He now believes mourning the child's death would
    amount to blaspheming his belief in resurrection.

24 OLIVER, EDITH. "Next Stop, New Hampshire." New Yorker 38
    (15 December):130, 132.
        Reviews a revival of Under Milk Wood, declaring that it was
    a work with "many witty bull's eyes" in the middle of "all that
    lush and ribald imagery."

25 PERRINE, LAURENCE. "Thomas' 'Especially when the October
    wind.'" Explicator 21 (September): item 1.
        Explicates the poem as one that deals not only with the
    process of "making" a poem but also with the theme of death and
    time.

26 _____. "Thomas' 'The Hunchback in the Park.'" Explicator 20
    (January): item 45.
        Focuses on the meaning of some key participles in the poem.

27 "Poetry in English: 1945-62." Time 79 (9 March):92-95.
        Surveys the English poetry scene since World War II, point-
    ing to Thomas as one of the two forces (the other being the war)
    that shattered the "self-sealing vacuum" of the thirties, a time
    when poets wrote for other poets and their approval instead of a
    general reading public. Thomas managed to remind the art that
    its origins were in "ritual and chant."

28 RAWSON, CLAUDE. "Dylan Thomas." In Talks to Teachers of
    English. Vol. 2. Newcastle upon Tyne: Department of Educa-
    tion, King's College, pp. 30-56.
        Offers a general introduction to Thomas and his art.

29 ROBIE, BURTON A. Review of A Casebook on Dylan Thomas.
    Library Journal 87 (1 January):98-99.
        Praises John Malcolm Brinnin's volume for providing a col-
    lection of "contradictory viewpoints" offering the "key" to the
    poet's work and personality.

30 _____. Review of A Reader's Guide to Dylan Thomas. Library Journal 87 (15 March):1137-38.
Recommends William York Tindall's volume for its "precise, detailed analysis" of the poet's writing.

31 ROGERS, TIMOTHY. Review of Llareggub Revisited. English 14 (Summer):67-68.
Criticizes David Holbrook's study for being based on the false assumption that Thomas's influence was pervasive. His attack on Thomas ironically works to arouse sympathetic interest for the poet and his work.

32 SERGEANT, HOWARD. "The Religious Development of Dylan Thomas." Review of English Literature 3 (April):59-67.
Regards Thomas as a "naturally religious poet" whose faith was apparently "firmly implanted" by the Welsh Bethel. Tracing the evidence through the successive volumes of poetry leads to the necessary conclusion that "at the centre of his vision was an awareness of the spiritual nature of man." The ambiguity surrounding the question of his religious side is due to his partiality for paradoxical style, not to any religious doubt.

33 SEYMORE, WILLIAM KEAN. "Dylan Under Fire." Contemporary Review 202 (July):53.
Reviews David Holbrook's Llareggub Revisited, noting the critic's objection to Thomas's "infantile sense of being of cosmic importance."

34 SMITH, A.J. "Ambiguity as Poetic Shift." Critical Quarterly 4 (Spring):68-74.
Using "Our Eunuch Dreams" as a sample poem, argues that Thomas employed ambiguity because he was concerned with "the ideas of which words and images are complex vehicles." The result of the young poet's "calculated indirection," his "clotting" of images, and his "conscious confusion of syntax" is strange but pregnant poetry.

35 TAYLOR, DONALD. "The Story of the Film." In The Doctor and the Devils. London: J.M. Dent, pp. 135-38.
Tells about the development of the Thomas screenplay based on a story by Donald Taylor himself.

36 THOMAS, GEORGE R. "Bard on a Raised Hearth: Dylan Thomas and His Craft." Anglo-Welsh Review 12:11-20.
Looks at the development of Thomas's poetic art. He largely fails to communicate his meaning in the first three volumes, mainly because he hasn't found a successful way to express a variety of simultaneous experiences in a clear and unified way. After much structural experimentation, he perfected a style that basically joined periodic sentences to complex stanzaic patterns, a method uniquely appropriate for his declamatory poetry.

37   TINDALL, WILLIAM YORK. A Reader's Guide to Dylan Thomas.
     London: Thames & Hudson; New York: Farrar, Straus, & Giroux,
     Noonday Press, 306 pp.
          Explicates the poems in Collected Poems in sequence. Notes
     that thematic and aesthetic development from Thomas's "dark early
     poems of womb and tomb" to the subsequent brighter poems of
     "childhood and Laugharne" can be discovered. But cautions
     against any final conclusions about the poetry's development
     because Thomas "took one step back for every step forward--and
     one step sideways." The introductory essay surveys Thomas's
     volatile reputation and touches on political, religious, sur-
     realistic, Freudian, and Welsh factors found in his work.

38   TREWIN, J.C. "Dr. Knox and Mr. Boswell." Illustrated London
     News, 15 September, p. 414.
          Reviews the stage performance of The Doctor and the Devils
     at the Edinburgh Festival. Finds that, with the exception of an
     "occasional gust" of Thomas's language, it's a monotonous drama.

39   WEATHERBY, A.J. "Guinness for Dylan." Manchester Guardian
     Weekly, 27 December, p. 14.
          Tells the story of how one of Thomas's Greenwich Village
     friends was bound to react to the news that Alec Guinness was
     going to play the poet on stage.

40   WHITE, WILLIAM. "The Poet as Critic: Unpublished Letters of
     Dylan Thomas." Orient/West 7 (September):63-73.
          Includes letters to Glyn Jones and Harry Klopper that deal
     with Thomas's reactions to some of the experimentations with
     language then being tried by various writers.

                              1963

1   BERGONZI, BERNARD. Review of A Reader's Guide to Dylan
     Thomas. Listener 69 (3 January):37-38.
          Objects to William York Tindall's microscopic explications,
     which fail to assess the value of the poems as a whole.

2   BOKANOWSKI, HÉLÈNE, and ALYN, MARK. Dylan Thomas. Paris:
     Pierre Seghers, 222 pp.
          Stresses the legendary romanticism of the poet, especially
     those aspects that led to a popularity consisting of a mixture
     of love and hate. Suggests that, primarily because of Vernon
     Watkins, Thomas was familiar with such European poets as
     Laforgue, Rilke, and Rimbaud, and that he came to resemble the
     latter in particular. Though not belonging to the surrealist
     movement, he shared some of the tendencies (a pronounced taste
     for paradox, sex, and scandal). Rounding out the study are
     textual presentations and a bibliography.

3   CHRISTIENSEN, NAOMI. "Dylan Thomas and the Doublecross of
    Death." Ball State Teachers College Forum 4 (Autumn):49–53.
        Investigates the recurring concern and imagery of the
    "double cross" of death. The doublecross image comes to stand
    for Thomas's combined feelings about physical death, the hope of
    Christian immortality, and Christ's crucifixion.

4   COMBECHER, HANS. "Tod und Transzendenz in zwei Gedichten von
    Dylan Thomas." Die Neueren Sprachen, December, pp. 554–62.
        Takes a close look at "A Refusal to Mourn the Death, by
    Fire, of a Child" and "When all my five and country senses" and
    decides that one must agree with William Empson's conclusion that
    the poems essentially express a "pantheistic pessimism."

5   COX, C.B., and DYSON, A.E., eds. Modern Poetry: Studies in
    Practical Criticism. London: Edward Arnold, pp. 122–27.
        Reprint of 1959.5.

6   DEUTSCH, BABETTE. Poetry in Our Time: A Critical Survey of
    Poetry in the English-speaking World, 1900 to 1960. 2d ed.
    New York: Doubleday & Co., pp. 369–84 passim.
        Reprint of 1952.5.

7   FAULK, CAROLYN SUE. "The Apollonian and Dionysian Modes in
    Lyric Poetry and Their Development in the Poetry of W.B. Yeats
    and Dylan Thomas." Ph.D. dissertation, University of Illinois,
    377 pp.
        Applies Nietzsche's thoughts on the Apollonian-Dionysian
    modes to the works of Thomas and Yeats. Mostly consisting of
    explications employing Nietzsche's key concepts, the study even-
    tually goes on to consider the value of such poetry to the work
    of other modern poets having the same scope. Ultimately, the
    combined explications (including a few centered on lyric poetry
    taken from periods stretching back to the Renaissance) are meant
    to show the overall relevance of Nietzsche's findings to the
    genre of lyric poetry as a whole. See Dissertation Abstracts
    International 24 (1964):4173.

8   FIRMAGE, GEORGE, ed. A Garland for Dylan Thomas. New York:
    Clarke & Way, 177 pp.
        Contains a collection of poems dedicated to or concerned
    with Thomas.

9   FRANKEL, HASKEL. "On the Fringe." Saturday Review 46
    (3 August):18.
        Tells the story behind the publication of The Beach of
    Falesá.

10 FUSON, BEN W. Review of The World of Dylan Thomas. Library
    Journal 88 (1 March):1014.
        Recommends Clark Emery's study especially for its "deft"
    and "sympathetic but nonsycophantic" interpretations of Thomas's
    collected poems.

11   "Ghosts Fly Backwards." <u>Time</u> 82 (27 September):47.
      Gives an account of the development of Thomas's "stagy"
      script of <u>The Beach of Falesá</u> and of Richard Burton's plans for
      filming it.

12   GOLDSTEIN, MELVIN. "A Source for Faulkner's 'Nobel Prize
      Speech of Acceptance': Or, Two Versions of a Single
      Manifesto." <u>Ball State Teachers College Forum</u> 4 (Spring):
      78-80.
      Finds "startling" correspondences between Thomas's "In my
      Craft or Sullen Art" and Faulkner's Nobel Prize acceptance
      speech.

13   GRIGSON, GEOFFREY, ed. <u>The Concise Encyclopedia of Modern</u>
      <u>World Literature</u>. London: Hutchinson; New York: Hawthorne,
      pp. 439-40.
      Objects to the "curiously agglutinative" quality of
      Thomas's early poetry and believes that few of his poems will
      prove to be "acceptable" to readers "sensitively educated in the
      words or rhythms of English or American verse."

14   HOLZHAUER, JEAN. "Tigress, Not Suburban Mamma." <u>Commonweal</u>
      79 (6 December):330-31.
      Reviews <u>Not Quite Posthumous Letters to My Daughter</u>, noting
      that Caitlin Thomas "shares her late husband's personal talent
      for arousing mixed emotions."

15   JANEWAY, ELIZABETH. "A Mother's Advice: Do." <u>New York Times</u>
      <u>Book Review</u>, 24 November, pp. 66-67.
      Reviews Caitlin Thomas's <u>Not Quite Posthumous Letters to My</u>
      <u>Daughter</u>, calling it a sad "harangue" that is "haunted" by the
      memory of her late husband.

16   JENKINS, DAVID CLAY. "Dylan Thomas' <u>Under Milk Wood</u>: The
      American Element." <u>Trace</u> 51 (Winter):325-35.
      Makes the case that Thomas's experiences in the United
      States inspired his employment of Welsh material in the play-
      for-voices. The play aspires to celebrate love despite the
      reality of death.

17   JONES, T.H. <u>Dylan Thomas</u>. New York: Grove Press, 119 pp.
      Declares that Thomas was perhaps the "most sensational
      poet of our time." Goes on to survey the Thomas "story." The
      "true" Thomas was the author of several great poems, "not the
      anti-hero of a thousand sniggered tales, nor the retching wreck
      eventually passing into oblivion in a New York hospital."

18   KERR, WALTER. <u>The Theatre in Spite of Itself</u>. New York:
      Simon & Schuster, pp. 78-82.
      Sets up <u>Under Milk Wood</u> as an example of what is needed in
      the contemporary theater--splendid language.

19 KLEINMAN, HYMAN H. The Religious Sonnets of Dylan Thomas: A
    Study in Imagery and Meaning. Berkeley: University of
    California Press, 158 pp.
       Analyzes Thomas's religious sonnets as an extended poem.
    The sequence is ultimately seen as a "deeply moving statement of
    religious perplexity concluding in spiritual certainty," with
    the first of the ten poems "mocking the descent of the Word" and
    the last revealing a "spiraling ascent of faith." The conclu-
    sions are based on detailed textual explications that are
    grounded on close anlysis of the far-ranging imagery. The
    imagery draws on such varied sources as medieval pageant plays,
    seventeenth-century sermons, English poetry, mythical lore,
    marine biology, and movies.

20 LONGCORE, CHRIS. "A Possible Echo of Jonathan Swift in Dylan
    Thomas." Notes and Queries 10 (April):153.
       Notes some similarities between Swift's "The Hand that
    sign'd the Mortgage paid the Shot" and Thomas's "The hand that
    signed the paper."

21 MANDEL, OSCAR. "Artists Without Masters." Virginia Quarterly
    Review 39 (Summer):401-19.
       Discusses the position of artists with relation to the
    contemporary public, pointing to Thomas as a prime example of
    someone who, because of the difficulties of his style, is bound
    to remain at "arm's length" from the reading public, especially
    as far as his "best" poems are concerned.

22 MAUD, RALPH N. Entrance to Dylan Thomas' Poetry. Pittsburgh:
    University of Pittsburgh Press, 177 pp.
       Analyzes Thomas's poems in a carefully systematic way,
    employing at times the evidence of the original worksheets to
    reveal valuable new insights. Maud's ultimate conclusion is that
    Thomas, "supposedly the lyric poet, the singer of the self," re-
    veals himself in his final poems to be a writer who, conscious of
    contemporary problems, was concerned with "what it is to live
    well and die well." Reprinted in part: 1966.8.

23 _____. "Holbrook vs. Thomas." Essays in Criticism 13
    (January):86-88.
       Reviews David Holbrook's Llareggub Revisited, finding the
    attack on Thomas to amount basically to the point that the
    author/poet "does not like poetry that differs much from his
    own."

24 MAUD, RALPH N., and DAVIES, ANEIRIN TALFAN, eds. The Colour
    of Saying: An Anthology of Verse Spoken by Dylan Thomas.
    London: J.M. Dent; Dylan Thomas's Choice: An Anthology of
    Verse Spoken by Dylan Thomas. New York: New Directions,
    198 pp.
       Collects the poems Thomas chose as a public reader. An
    introduction by the authors traces his route to public readings,
    comments on his "astounding" ability to make his audiences re-
    spond to a large variety of poems, and concludes that Thomas's

experience as a reader was in large part behind the greater
clarity and simplification found in his later poetry.

25   MILLS, RALPH J., Jr. "The Development of Apocalyptic Vision
      in Five Modern Poets." Ph.D. dissertation, Northwestern
      University, 220 pp.
          Looks at selected modern poets in the context of apocalyp-
      tic writing. Thomas is shown to move from poetry obsessed with
      process to the ultimate concern with pastoral innocence. His
      final vision, like that of the other poets discussed, was in-
      tended to discover meaning for human existence. See Dissertation
      Abstracts International 24 (1964):3753.

26   _____. Theodore Roethke. Minneapolis: University of
      Minnesota Press, pp. 7, 14, 18.
          Indicates some points of comparison between Thomas and
      Theodore Roethke.

27   MITCHISON, LOIS. "The Spoken Word." Listener 70
      (14 November):806.
          Reviews "Behind the Dylan Legend," a documentary program
      offered on the Third Program. Notes that everyone agreed that
      Thomas was always professional about his work.

28   "Modern Love." Times Literary Supplement, 28 June, p. 475.
          Reviews Caitlin Thomas's Not Quite Posthumous Letters to
      My Daughter. Compared to Mrs. Thomas's first book, this one is
      "more carefully written" but less successful because less sin-
      cere. In her prose, there is a "quality not at all like anything
      in her husband's, a peculiar unappeasable Irish bitterness."

29   MOYNIHAN, WILLIAM TRUMBULL. "Boily Boy and Bard." New York
      Times Book Review, 3 November, pp. 6, 48.
          Surveys Thomas's fluctuating reputation and growing
      legend. Speculates that he will be eventually remembered as the
      "first in modern literature to be both a maker and a speaker of
      poetry." In retrospect, Thomas's career "had an esthetic com-
      pleteness," for he "moved surely through surrealistic, symbolic,
      and romantic influences, developing and perfecting his poetry at
      each stage."

30   NYREN, DOROTHY. "Review: Not Quite Posthumous Letters to My
      Daughter." Library Journal 88 (15 October):3847.
          Describes Caitlin Thomas's second book as a "bitter and
      humorous" work.

31   _____. Review of The Beach of Falesá. Library Journal 88
      (1 December):4659-60.
          Dismisses this posthumously released book as a "very minor
      work" that is short on characterization and realistic detail.

32   "Poetry and the Film: A Symposium." Film Culture 29
     (Summer):55-63.
        Transcribes a discussion that took place on 28 October 1953,
     at Cinema 16 among Thomas, Maya Deren, Arthur Miller, and Parker
     Taylor on the subject of the connection between film and poetry.

33   POORE, CHARLES. "Books of the Times." New York Times,
     7 November, p. 35.
        Describes Caitlin Thomas's Not Quite Posthumous Letters to
     My Daughter as a kind of "totting up" of accounts, particularly
     with the dreary lot of "seething intellectuals" who surrounded
     her husband. The aim of the book is "both maternal and
     infernal."

34   Review of The Beach of Falesá. New Yorker 39 (5 October):191.
        Calls the script based on a Robert Louis Stevenson story
     "utterly banal."

35   RHYS, KEIDRYCH. "A BBC Version." Spectator 211 (13 Decem-
     ber):796, 798.
        Reviews The Colour of Saying. Thinks that this anthology
     of poetry read by Thomas is rather presumptuous and ultimately of
     little critical value.

36   SIMON, JOHN. Acid Test. New York: Stein & Day, pp. 68
     passim.
        Makes various admiring references to Thomas.

37   _____. "Godlessness and Godawfulness." New Leader 46
     (27 May):31.
        Dismisses Jack Howell's film Dylan Thomas as a serious
     attempt to "glorify" the poet which "comes out only as a show-
     case" for Richard Burton.

38   SMITH, STEVIE. "Suitors." New Statesman 65 (21 June):941.
        Dismisses Caitlin Thomas's Not Quite Posthumous Letters to
     My Daughter as an affected, melancholy, and trite account that
     "puts one in a vile temper."

39   "Thomas & the Legacy." New York Times Book Review,
     3 November, p. 6.
        Remarks that a decade after his death, Thomas had appar-
     ently become the most widely read English poet.

40   THOMAS, CAITLIN. Not Quite Posthumous Letters to My Daughter.
     London: Putnam; Boston: Little, Brown & Co., 174 pp.
        Following up Leftover Life to Kill, this emotional out-
     pouring by Thomas's widow contains less about the poet than the
     previous confessional. Addressing her daughter in epistolary
     form, Caitlin admits that "there was no limit to my daftness;
     nor Dylan's either, for that matter, in those days."

41   THOMAS, GEORGE R. "Dylan Thomas: A Poet of Wales?" English
     14 (Spring):140–45.
     Disagrees with the conception of Thomas as a Welsh poet.
     One should keep in mind that he didn't know the Welsh language or
     literature and that he was raised in an atmosphere cut off from
     the authentic Welsh culture. Instead, one should recognize that
     he was mostly concerned with discovering a form that would
     appropriately express his private mythology.

42   TRITSCHLER, DONALD. "The Metamorphic Stop of Time in 'A
     Winter's Tale.'" PMLA 78 (September):422–30.
     Examines the "dialectic of images" working "through a
     series of metamorphoses to the small stop" in "A Winter's Tale."
     In the end, the poem "defeats" time and, in a manner of speaking,
     "thrusts" death on man. While the central paradox of Thomas's
     vision has life consuming itself, the main metamorphic movement
     is from blindness to "naked vision."

43   VANDERBILT, GLORIA. "Peripatetic Nellie Bly." Saturday
     Review 46 (30 November):42–43.
     Describes Caitlin Thomas's Not Quite Posthumous Letters to
     My Daughter as a record of hatred, particularly self-hatred.

44   WHITE, WILLIAM. "Presenting an Unknown Dylan Thomas Piece."
     Prairie Schooner 37 (Summer):126–28.
     Comments on the background of a recently discovered piece
     in which Thomas gives his proposal for a critical column in the
     Swansea & West Wales Guardian. The article provides a revealing
     glimpse of the young writer's "lively personality."

                              1964

1   ACKERMAN, JOHN. Dylan Thomas: His Life and Work. London:
     Oxford University Press, 203 pp.
     Establishes the fact that, to understand why Thomas acted
     and wrote the way he did, one has to focus on his Welsh back-
     ground. The study illustrates the significance of such Welsh
     factors as the tradition of nonconformity, the idea of the bard,
     and the influence of the Anglo-Welsh community of writers. Above
     all, Ackerman tries to show that Thomas's poetry moved from a
     "clinical" to a "religious" nature and that the great artistry of
     the later poems is in the tradition of Welsh verse. Reprinted in
     part: 1966.8.

2   BERGONZI, BERNARD. "Book Reviews." Listener 72 (16 July):98.
     Reviews Ralph Maud's Entrances to Dylan Thomas and Aneirin
     Talfan Davies's Dylan: Druid of the Broken Body. Both of these
     "dedicated Dylanists" fail to confront the essential question of
     whether or not Thomas is doubtless a major poet.

3   BRAHMS, CARYL. "Marilyn, Dolly and Dylan." Spectator 212
(14 February):213.
      Believes that the appearance of Alec Guinness in the stage
production Dylan was a "masterly triumph of miscasting."

4   BROYARD, ANATOLE. "A Fling with Dylan." Cavalier, September,
pp. 20-22, 33.
      Reminisces about experiences with Thomas.

5   BRUMMELL, O.B. "Do Not Go Gentle Into That Good Night." High
Fidelity 14 (June):65.
      Comments on Caedmon's recordings of Thomas reading in his
own "golden voice" and on the Columbia recording of Alec
Guinness's performance in Sidney Michaels's Dylan (see Michaels,
1964.30). Praises in particular Thomas's memorable reading
ability and Guinness's ability to weave the loose ends of a
"dramatically diffuse" play "into a stunning whole."

6   BURDETTE, ROBERT KENLEY. "Dylan Thomas and the Gnostic
Religion." Ph.D. dissertation, University of Michigan,
200 pp.
      Sets out to discover the nature of the religion found in
Thomas's poetry and to investigate the way in which it is expressed in the writing. Concentrates on Gnosticism, showing how
it differs from other religions, how it appears in Thomas's
poetry, and how it relates to other modern poets. Thomas's
religious experience is finally defined as a pre-Christian
mystical one. See Dissertation Abstracts International 25
(1965):7262.

7   "Change of Emphasis." Times Literary Supplement, 30 July,
p. 670.
      Reviews The Beach of Falesá, finding it to be a "thoroughly
professional script" which nevertheless is "embarrassing" because
Thomas's adaptation of Stevenson's story is adjusted for the box
office. Thomas has "bowdlerized" the source story in "just the
right way" for it to be made into a cost-effective film feature.

8   DAVIES, ANEIRIN TALFAN. Dylan: Druid of the Broken Body.
London: J.M. Dent, 77 pp.
      Attempts to "sketch an outline" for appreciating and
approaching the Collected Poems. "It is the remarkable con-
sistency of his probing into the nature of man, and his place in
the economy of God's creation, which gives to the Collected Poems
a feeling of unity."

9   DAVIES, M. BRYN. "A Few Thoughts About Milk Wood." Literary
Half-Yearly 5 (January):41-44.
      Disagrees with the view that Under Milk Wood was essen-
tially a celebration of life. It was instead a work expressive
of Thomas's obsession with death.

10   DAVIES, WALFORD D. "Owl-Light." Essays in Criticism 14
      (July):318-23.
          Reviews H.H. Kleinman's The Religious Sonnets of Dylan
      Thomas, finding the study essentially flawed because the critic
      fails to recognize in the sonnet sequence the autobiographical
      narrative.

11   "Dealing with Thomist Memories." Times Literary Supplement,
      22 October, p. 960.
          Comments on Thomas's "singularly intimate" yet "impersonal"
      poetry, then reviews recent publications concerning him. Sidney
      Michaels's Dylan is attacked as an overly theatrical, sentimental
      play that fails to confront the "real man." Aneirin Talfan
      Davies's Dylan: Druid of the Broken Body fails to appreciate
      sufficiently the effects that both Christian and "Mediterranean
      dying-god" mythology had on Thomas. John Ackerman's Dylan Thomas
      is recommended mainly for its emphasis on Thomas's Welsh back-
      ground. Thomas's Twenty Years A-Growing is another of his pro-
      fessionally slick film scripts.

*12   DUGDALE, J.S., ed. Dylan Thomas: "Under Milk Wood." Bath:
      James Brodie.
          Makes notes on the chosen English texts. See Maud,
      1970.14, p. 37.

13   "Dying Days." Newsweek 63 (27 January):58.
          Reviews Sidney Michaels's play Dylan, praising in particu-
      lar the performance of Alec Guinness in the role of the poet.
      The briskly moving play depicts Thomas's "disintegration, playing
      down the harrowing in favor of the hilarious."

14   "Dylan Thomas Bust for Museum" Times (London), 20 May, p. 14.
          Describes how two sculptors made a secret death mask of
      Thomas and reports that a bronze bust developed from the mask
      was being acquired by the National Museum of Wales.

15   "Dylan Thomas on the Stage." Times (London), 6 January, p. 6.
          Reviews the Toronto presentation of Sidney Michaels's
      Dylan, complaining that the play treats an innately dramatic
      subject as "little more than a series of flippant jokes inter-
      spersed with pathos." Alec Guinness, however, gives "one of his
      finest performances" in the role of the poet.

16   "Dylan Thomas Play a Thriller." Times (London), 17 September,
      p. 15.
          Reviews the stage performance of The Doctor and the Devils
      at the Queen's Theatre, Hornchurch, finding it to be a "faltering
      triumph of language over melodrama." Thomas's language is
      lively, but in the end it fails to impart "conviction."

17   FITZGIBBON, CONSTANTINE. "The Posthumous Life of Dylan
      Thomas." Spectator 213 (27 November):704, 707.
          Voices his thoughts on the reaction that set in after
      Thomas's death and what his posthumous future might hold.

18   FRASER, GEORGE SUTHERLAND. "The Legend and the Puzzle."
     Times Literary Supplement, 5 March, pp. 185–86.
     Surveys the reaction that followed Thomas's sudden death
     and comments on the value of recent books concerned with the
     poet. The collection of elegies entitled A Garland for Dylan
     Thomas is dismissed for too often striking a "falsetto voice" and
     being "pastiches" of the poet's method. The Colour of Saying is
     more useful because it provides important evidence of how impor-
     tant poetic tone and feeling were to Thomas. The expositional
     guides (by William York Tindall, Clarke Emery, and Elder Olson)
     tend to "dilute" the essence of the poems. H.H. Kleinman's The
     Religious Sonnets of Dylan Thomas strains with "ingenuity."
     Ralph Maud's Entrances to Dylan Thomas' Poetry comes highly
     recommended, though, because this critic understands that Thomas
     tried to create images and concepts that were "new and original
     within the poem" instead of attempting to refer to things
     outside.

19   GRIGSON, GEOFFREY. "Dylan and the Dragon." New Statesman 68
     (18 December):968–69.
     Reacts to the "gush" of "nonsense" recently written about
     the poet and his poetry, particularly by American "Dylanists."
     Believes that, once the legend and life are discounted, Thomas
     proves to have been a "provincial of poetry, smoozing, if with
     the best hopes and intentions, a masticated old manner with pop
     modernism."

20   GROSS, HARVEY. "Dylan Thomas." In Form in Modern Poetry: A
     Study of Prosody from Thomas Hardy to Robert Lowell. London:
     Cresset Press; Ann Arbor: University of Michigan Press,
     pp. 265–71.
     Points out that Thomas's kind of poetry required "severe
     prosodic regulation." His poems move not by carefully grammati-
     cal expression but by extremely rigorous rhythmic forms. His
     best writing contains "spacious stanzas where the long-breathed
     rhythms can rise and fall, move up to a climax, and dwindle to
     silence."

21   HOLBROOK, DAVID. Dylan Thomas and Poetic Dissociation.
     Crosscurrents: Modern Critiques, edited by Harry T. Moore,
     Carbondale, Ill.: University of Southern Illinois Press,
     185 pp.
     Reconsiders Thomas's reputation, concluding that his major
     flaw was a lack of moral capacity, so that the vitality of the
     writing derives mainly from its self-conscious verbal display.
     The lack of an "essential compassion" is especially obvious when
     the work is compared with that of such directly influential
     writers as Joyce. Contains a preface by Harry T. Moore lauding
     the importance of this reprint of the previously entitled
     Llareggub Revisited: Dylan Thomas and the State of Modern
     Poetry (London: Bowes & Bowes, 1962). Reprinted in part:
     1966.8.

22 HUGH-JONES, STEPHEN. "Thomas the Film." New Statesman 67
    (26 June):999-1000.
    Dismisses The Beach of Falesá as a screenplay made of
    "purest hundred-proof corn."

23 JOHNSON, GEOFFREY. "Louis MacNeice, 1907-1963." Literary
    Half-Yearly 5 (January):15-17.
    Indicates how Louis MacNeice influenced Thomas and was
    influenced by him in turn.

24 JOSELYN, Sister M. "Green and Dying: The Drama of 'Fern
    Hill.'" Renascence 16 (Summer):219-21.
    Argues that "Fern Hill" has two levels of meaning, the
    first dealing with the magical pleasure of childhood and the
    second with destructive time. The latter dominates, so that the
    poem is ultimately about the process of dying rather than the
    joys of the "green" time of youth.

25 LEVERTOV, DENISE. "Rhythms of Speech." New York Times Book
    Review, 21 June, pp. 10, 12.
    Reviews A Garland for Dylan Thomas, an "unpleasing" col-
    lection of poems on Thomas.

26 MacLAREN-ROSS, J. "The Polestar Neighbor." London Magazine
    4 (November):102-12.
    Reminisces about the Thomas known to the writer. He did
    not much resemble the "cherub" of popular imagination.

27 MANLEY, FRANK. "The Text of Dylan Thomas' Under Milk Wood."
    Emory University Quarterly 20 (Summer):131-44.
    Brings in Thomas's handwritten (and previously unpublished)
    final revisions of the play-for-voices for a consideration of the
    final direction it was taking. Based on this evidence, Thomas
    was moving toward a more consciously dramatic and organically
    musical work.

28 MARTIN, J.H. "Dylan Thomas." Times Literary Supplement,
    19 March, p. 235.
    Reminisces in a lengthy letter to the editor about the
    Thomas he knew in Cornwall. Concludes that the man he was
    acquainted with was "always a great joker" and that if he were
    alive to see some of the "solemn examination" of his work by
    certain critics, he would have thought this "the funniest joke
    of all."

29 MARTIN, RICHARD. "For the Love of Man and in Praise of God:
    An Evaluation of Dylan Thomas' Poem 'This bread I break.'"
    Die Neueren Sprachen, March, pp. 133-36.
    Offers "This bread I break" as an example of Thomas's
    often ignored intellectual (or "reasoned-emotional") ability.
    There is an "intensive poetical activity" sustained on several
    levels at once.

30   MICHAELS, SIDNEY. Dylan. London: Andre Deutsch, 119 pp.
     Based on John Malcolm Brinnin's Dylan Thomas in America and
     Caitlin Thomas's Leftover Life to Kill, the play imagines the
     turmoil of Thomas's American experience, ending with his wife's
     accompanying the body of the poet back home.

31   MOYNIHAN, WILLIAM TRUMBULL. "Dylan Thomas and the 'Biblical
     Rhythm.'" PMLA 79 (December):631-47.
     Finds Thomas's body of poetry unified by cohesive imagery,
     related themes, and the "subsuming source" of the Bible. The
     major symbolism comes from "an imaginative re-creation" of the
     Bible, and various figures of the poetry can be seen to derive
     from Jehovah, Satan, Adam, Abraham, Cain, Jacob, Samson, Christ,
     and Noah. In the end, the body of poetry is further unified by
     Thomas's regeneration vision.

32   NAULT, CLIFFORD A., Jr. Review of The Religious Sonnets of
     Dylan Thomas. College English 26 (October):65.
     Finds H.H. Kleinman's study to be an ingenious piece of
     work but ultimately not significant criticism but instead "simply
     another man's opinion."

33   "New Fiction." Times (London), 25 June, p. 13.
     Reviews The Beach of Falesá, finding Thomas's screenplay
     version of Robert Louis Stevenson's story to be very successful
     in replacing the "oblique manner" of the original with "clean"
     dramatic lines.

34   NICHOLS, LEWIS. "Alec Guinness as 'Dylan.'" New York Times,
     12 January, sec. 2, pp. 1, 3.
     Describes how Guinness was drawn into performing in Dylan
     and his opinion of the play as a "tragic-farce."

35   OHMAN, RICHARD M. "Criticism, 1963 (Part II)." Wisconsin
     Studies in Contemporary Literature 5 (Autumn):282-84.
     Recommends Ralph Maud's Entrances to Dylan Thomas as a
     genuinely helpful primer on how best to approach Thomas's diffi-
     cult poetry. Accepts Maud's argument that the best clues to
     meaning reside in the poems themselves. Finds H.H. Kleinman's
     The Religious Sonnets of Dylan Thomas to be impressive in the
     scholarship but finally confusing in the attempt to trace down
     all the possible sources for the images employed.

36   ORMEROD, DAVID. "Thomas' 'Twenty-four years.'" Explicator
     22 (May): item 76.
     Explicates the poem as one primarily amounting to a state-
     ment of Thomas's horror of death's permanence.

37   PHILLIPS, ROBERT S. "Death and Resurrection: Tradition in
     Thomas's 'After the Funeral.'" McNeese Review 15:3-10.
     Argues that Thomas's "After the funeral" belongs to the
     same elegiac tradition as Dryden's "To the Memory of Mrs. Anne
     Killigrew" because of the appearance of certain elements that

are characteristic of that type of poem. Certain types of
motifs, conceits, conventions, and orthodoxy occur in both poems.

38 PRESS, JOHN. "Joy and Terror." Punch 247 (18 November):783.
    Reviews John Ackerman's Dylan Thomas: His Life and Work.
The study is "careful, scholarly" in its description of Thomas's
life and work but isn't satisfactory as a "critical evaluation"
of the poetry.

39 REA, J. "A Topographical Guide to Under Milk Wood." College
    English 25 (April):535-42.
    Provides a topographical outline of the play-for-voices,
with the purpose of revealing the possible creative connection
between the place described and the play.

40 READ, BILL, and McKENNA, ROLLIE. The Days of Dylan Thomas.
    New York: McGraw-Hill; London: Weidenfeld & Nicolson,
    189 pp.
    Gives an affectionate account of Thomas's life and career
and provides many illustrative photographs. Tries to tell the
"real" story by laying it out in a chronologically factual way
without dwelling on the sensational aspects of the Thomas legend.

41 REES, DAVID. "Windy Boy and a Bit." Spectator, 21 August,
    pp. 246-47.
    Reviews H.H. Kleinman's The Religious Sonnets of Dylan
Thomas, Ralph Maud's Entrances to Dylan Thomas' Poetry, and A.T.
Davies's Dylan: Druid of the Broken Body, coming to the conclusion that Thomas was not a major poet. Still, he employed his
lyrical gifts to great effect, succeeding impressively in expressing his personal life through a new poetic language.

42 REVELL, PETER. "'Altarwise by owl-light.'" Alphabet 8
    (June):42-61.
    Studies the sonnet sequence and discovers it to be the
exhaustive artistic and thematic expression of young Thomas's
death-in-life obsession. The sequence revolves around autobiographical, biblical, Freudian, astrological, and literary
points. The sequence ends by Thomas's joining together certain
repeated tensions existing in the previous sonnets: Adam and
the poet, Christ and Mary, Hercules and the sun, and the sexes.

43 Review of The Beach of Falesá. Virginia Quarterly Review 40
    (Spring):lxi.
    Complains that the script based on Robert Louis Stevenson's
story doesn't give a clear enough idea of what a film based on
it would actually be like.

44 ROSS, J. ETHEL. "We Had Evidence and No Doubt." Gower 16:
    47-50.
    Remembers Thomas by drawing on the recollections of his
mother and the midwife.

45   RUBENSTEIN, J.S. "Dylan Thomas as Poet." Commonweal 79
     (21 February):642-43.
         Welcomes the books by H.H. Kleinman (The Religious Sonnets
     of Dylan Thomas) and Clark Emery (The World of Dylan Thomas) be-
     cause they are concerned with the poetry itself rather than
     "anecdotal drivel" about the man.

46   SAROYAN, WILLIAM. "The Wild Boy." Books and Bookmen, July,
     pp. 5-7.
         Remembers Thomas with pleasure, particularly his awe-
     inspiring pub presence.

47   SIMON, JOHN. "Theatre Chronicle." Hudson Review 17 (Summer):
     233-34.
         Finds Sidney Michaels's play Dylan to be a failure as drama
     and gossip column.

48   SMITH, RAY. Review of A Garland for Dylan Thomas. Library
     Journal 89 (1 March):1095.
         Dismisses this "garland" of selected poetic tributes to
     Thomas as being of dubious value.

49   _____. Review of The Religious Sonnets of Dylan Thomas.
     Library Journal 89 (1 February):632.
         Finds H.H. Kleinman's study to be "earnest" and "exhaus-
     tive" yet finally not totally successful in dealing with Thomas's
     "extreme allusiveness."

50   SMITH, TIMOTHY d'ARCH. "Note 227. The Second Edition of
     Dylan Thomas's 18 Poems." Book Collector 13 (Autumn):351-52.
         Provides a bibliographical note on the Fortune Press edi-
     tion of 18 Poems.

51   STANFORD, DEREK. "Dylan Thomas: A Literary Post-Mortem."
     Queen's Quarterly 71 (Autumn):405-18.
         Thomas is seen to celebrate the energy of life in a dis-
     tinct way. He had a "naturally religious," romantic imagination
     despite being an agnostic.

52   TAUBMAN, HOWARD. "Theatre: Alec Guinness as 'Dylan.'" New
     York Times, 20 January, p. 18.
         Finds that Guinness's performance provides the depth of
     character that Sidney Michaels's play Dylan actually lacks. The
     play ultimately doesn't measure up to the ambition of dramatiz-
     ing Thomas's "furious, tormented existence."

53   TINDALL, WILLIAM YORK. "The Poetry of Dylan Thomas." In On
     Contemporary Literature. Edited by Richard Kostelanetz. New
     York: Avon Books, pp. 607-15.
         Reprint of 1948.9.

54   YERBURY, GRACE D.   "Of a City Beside a River: Whitman, Eliot,
     Thomas, Miller."   Walt Whitman Review 10 (September):67-73.
     Points out the apparent influence of Walt Whitman's "Cross-
     ing Brooklyn Ferry" on Thomas's "Prologue to an Adventure" as
     well as on works by T.S. Eliot and Henry Miller.

                            1965

1   "Bard Reborn."   Newsweek 66 (1 November):96.
     Praises Constantine FitzGibbon's The Life of Dylan Thomas
     for bringing the poet's story and legend "into focus."   It's an
     "authoritative, fond" biography that succeeds in re-creating the
     "romance of tragedy" that was the poet's life.

2   BARKER, GEORGE.   "A Pond-Green Corpse."   Listener 74
     (4 November):714-15.
     Reviews Constantine FitzGibbon's The Life of Dylan Thomas.
     The "failure" of the biography is "an intellectual failure: the
     author is not . . . quite sophisticated enough to appreciate the
     irony inherent in any process of self-destruction."

3   BITTNER, WILLIAM.   "A Poet's Days of Grace."   Saturday Review
     48 (30 October):44-45.
     Praises Constantine FitzGibbon's biography, The Life of
     Dylan Thomas, for its objectivity, quiet eloquence, and honesty.

4   BOX, SIDNEY.   Foreword to Rebecca's Daughters.   Boston:
     Little, Brown; London: Triton, 144 pp.
     Provides factual introductory commentary.

5   BROY, EVELYN J.   "The Enigma of Dylan Thomas."   Dalhousie
     Review 45 (Winter):499-507.
     Examines the characteristic tension residing between sex
     and religion in Thomas's work.   His best poems contain this
     mixture.

6   BURTON, RICHARD.   "Genius Agonistes."   Book Week 3
     (24 October):1, 43.
     Praises Constantine FitzGibbon's The Life of Dylan Thomas
     and remembers some of his own experiences as one of Thomas's
     "bewitched hanger-ons."   Declares that Thomas was a rare actor
     of great, "crude" force.

7   CAMPBELL, COLIN.   "Other Face of a Legend."   Christian Science
     Monitor, 9 December, p. 19.
     Discovers several virtues in Constantine FitzGibbon's The
     Life of Dylan Thomas, including those of objectivity, scholar-
     ship, and wit.

8   CLINTON-BADDELEY, V.C.   "The Written and the Spoken Word."
     Essays and Studies 18:73-82.
     Recalls working with Thomas in the course of discussing
     various experiences of recording poetry.

9   COOK, RODERICK. Review of The Life of Dylan Thomas. Harper's
     Magazine 231 (November):132–33.
        Finds Constantine FitzGibbon's biography to be a dis-
     appointing account because it's "so conscientiously restrained."

10   DAVENPORT, JOHN. "Dylan Thomas: A Green Man from the Sea."
     Spectator, 15 October, pp. 487–88.
        Reviews Constantine FitzGibbon's The Life of Dylan Thomas.
     The biographer is especially praised for separating fact and
     legend. After a survey of the poet's life is given, the conclu-
     sion drawn is that Thomas had "ephemeral" faults and "permanent"
     virtues.

11   _____. "Face of the Bard." Spectator, 25 June, pp. 826–27.
        Reviews Bill Read's The Days of Dylan Thomas. This "latest
     necrology" has some valuable photographs, but the text is
     "worthless."

12   "Dylan Thomas Manuscript for Museum." Times (London),
     15 June, p. 6.
        Describes the British Museum's acquisition of the
     "Prologue" for its contemporary poets manuscripts collection.

13   EMPSON, WILLIAM. "Dylan Thomas in Maturity." New Statesman
     70 (29 October):647–48.
        Reviews Constantine FitzGibbon's The Life of Dylan Thomas
     as a fine biography that "makes the legend shine all the
     brighter." The account is largely a sad one, the sadder because
     toward the end of his life Thomas almost escaped the pressures
     that were destroying him.

14   FITZGIBBON, CONSTANTINE. The Life of Dylan Thomas. London:
     J.M. Dent; Boston: Little, Brown & Co., 374 pp.
        Attempts to give a complete, balanced, chronological
     account of the man and poet he knew. Approved by Thomas's
     trustees, the biographer uses various sources (personal acquaint-
     ances, letters, documents, published and unpublished material) in
     an exhaustive effort to portray the objective truth. "The trivia
     of life bored him, his failures to deal with them distressed him,
     his own dishonesty and partial compromise with the outside world
     disgusted him, and therefore he looked back to the golden age
     before women and publishers and tax gatherers, when birth and a
     child's vision of fresh beauty and death were the realities." He
     found his "purest and deepest inspiration" in those earlier days.
     Provides three informed lists in an appendix section: of
     Thomas's broadcasts, film scripts, and lectures in America.

15   _____. "Young Dylan Thomas: The Escape to London." Atlantic
     Monthly 216 (October):63–70.
        Previews part of the author's forthcoming The Life of Dylan
     Thomas (see 1965.14). The selection focuses on the poet's early
     years.

16   _____. "Young Dylan Thomas: The Poet in Love." Atlantic
        Monthly 216 (November):66-72.
            Follows a preview published in the October issue (see
        1965.15) with another selected part of the author's The Life of
        Dylan Thomas. The selection focuses on his affair with Pamela
        Hansford Johnson.

17   FRASER, GEORGE SUTHERLAND. "Dylan Thomas." In British
        Writers and Their Work. British Writers and Their Work,
        edited by Bonamy Dobrée, no. 5. Lincoln: University of
        Nebraska Press, pp. 123-58.
            Reprint of 1957.17.

18   _____. The Modern Writer and His World. New York: Frederick
        A. Praeger, pp. 45 passim.
            Reprint of 1953.16.

19   "Golden Tongued." Economist 217 (4 December):1084.
            Reviews Constantine FitzGibbon's The Life of Dylan Thomas.
        The biography is praised for telling an essentially "sad" story
        about a man with "ruinous weaknesses" with "remarkable balance of
        clear-sightedness and compassion." The "excellent" sections on
        Thomas's adolescent years are especially helpful to students of
        his poetry.

20   GREIFF, LOUIS K. "Image and Theme in Dylan Thomas' 'A
        Winter's Tale.'" Thoth 6 (Winter):35-41.
            Shows that "A Winter's Tale" manages perfectly to achieve
        a "poetic trinity" simultaneously religious, sexual, and visual
        by means of a network of key metaphorical images--those of
        physical and sexual hunger and religious awe.

21   GRIGSON, GEOFFREY. "Croquet at the Watkins'." New Statesman
        69 (18 June):963, 966.
            Reviews Me and My Bike and Bill Read's The Days of Dylan
        Thomas. Smirks at the unfinished film script as some "sludge"
        from the Thomas "barrel" and at Read's book as a fawning "guide-
        book." Offers the suggestion that Thomas's success with many
        critics of poetry "derives from its High Victorian rhythms and
        its distortion of a High Victorian vocabulary.

22   GRUBB, FREDERICK. "Worm's Eye: Dylan Thomas." In A Vision
        of Reality: A Study of Liberalism in Twentieth-Century Verse.
        New York: Barnes & Noble; London: Chatto & Windus,
        pp. 179-87.
            Surveys Thomas's achievement and finds it disappointingly
        shallow. Once his "obscurity" is penetrated it's "found to har-
        bour either a very private truth, or a truth which . . . is
        commonplace but would gain if expressed in starker and less
        verbose terms." Thomas's Collected Poems strike one "like a box
        of cunningly cut jigsaw-puzzle pieces which throw up the same
        glorious colours again and again" without ever falling into an
        overall pattern "which we may live with." Compares Thomas and
        Auden on several points.

23   HALPERN, MAX.   "Thomas' 'How soon the servant sun.'"
     Explicator 23 (April): item 65.
         Explicates the poem as one showing how Thomas contrasts
     opposing views of reality and death.

24   HAWKES, TERENCE.   "Playboys of the Western World." *Listener*
     74 (16 December):991-93.
         Argues that Thomas in *Under Milk Wood* (like Synge in
     Playboy of the Western World) tried (unsuccessfully) to depict a
     culture by means of a foreign language. Thomas's play only con-
     tains a Welsh "veneer." He also fails to resolve effectively the
     sanity-insanity theme.

25   _____. "Some 'Sources' of *Under Milk Wood*." *Notes and
     Queries* 12 (July):273-75.
         Shows Thomas to have consciously tried for Welshness in
     Under Milk Wood. The proof lies in looking at Thomas's use of
     Welsh tales and guide books. Also suggests that there is some
     self-parody in the character of Eli Jenkins.

26   HIGGINS, BRIAN.   "Now a Thirst Is Not Enough." *Twentieth
     Century* 174 (Summer):37-39.
         Looks at some famous literary drunks in the shadow of
     Thomas's death. Claims that the poet died of "diabetes exacer-
     bated by alcoholism."

27   KORG, JACOB. *Dylan Thomas*. Twayne's English Authors Series,
     edited by Sylvia E. Bowman. New York: Twayne Publishers,
     205 pp.
         Opens with a biographical sketch and follows with an ana-
     lytical survey of Thomas's poetry, fiction, and dramatic works.
     Shows that Thomas was essentially a mystic with mythic propensi-
     ties and a romantic egoism. Concludes that the distinctive
     nature of his art was a "union of barbaric subject with an
     arcane, sophisticated style."

28   KUNITZ, STANLEY.   "The Tumult of Dylan." *New York Times Book
     Review*, 31 October, pp. 1, 86.
         Reviews Constantine FitzGibbon's *The Life of Dylan Thomas*,
     arriving at the conclusion that his life "belongs as much to
     legend as to literary history." Written with objective,
     thoroughly professional authority, the biography is certainly
     the best study of the poet. Thomas's ultimate "disintegration"
     is explained by the fact that he didn't have the strength of
     character required "to support his genius."

29   LEECH, GEOFFREY.   "'This bread I break'--Language and Inter-
     pretation." *Review of English Literature* 6 (April):66-75.
         Approaches a critical interpretation of "This bread I
     break" by means of linguistic description. Concludes that ulti-
     mately there may be "room for disagreement" as to whether all
     aspects of a poem must be interpreted or whether the choice to
     allow obscurities stay obscurities should be allowed in critical
     explications.

30 LEIBOWITZ, HERBERT. "Paradise of Words." New Leader 48 (6 December):24-26.
Reviews Constantine FitzGibbon's The Life of Dylan Thomas. The poet's "untidy, tragic, barmy life" has been described with "fine sympathy and disinterestedness."

31 LEWIS, MIN. "Where Dylan Met Captain Cat." Country Quest, Summer, pp. 21-22.
Suggests one Johnny Thomas as the real-life model of Captain Cat.

32 McDONALD, GERALD D. Review of The Life of Dylan Thomas. Library Journal 90 (1 December):5262.
Recommends Constantine FitzGibbon's account as a "trust-worthy, candid, and compassionate" biography.

33 MacLAREN-ROSS, J. Memoirs of the Forties. London: Alan Ross, pp. 157 passim.
Reminisces about the Thomas he knew during the forties.

34 MILLS, RALPH J. "Dylan Thomas: Poetry and Process." In Four Ways of Modern Poetry. Edited by Nathan A. Scott. Richmond, Va.: John Knox Press, pp. 51-69.
Examines the religious nature of Thomas's poetry. Claims he was a religious poet from the beginning, even when his thoughts seem to spring from the biological aspect of existence in the early poems. Eventually, though always of an unconventional kind, his religious vision is reflected in writing where the "ritual pattern" of existence "supplies a religious resonance" that suggests a growing "mythic vision." After showing how his essential view of the life cycle "shifted from one of pessimism, anxiety, and obsessiveness about biological determinacy to one of religious exaltation, faith in the value and sanctity of life," places Thomas in the ranks of England's great religious poets.

35 MOYNIHAN, WILLIAM TRUMBULL. "Dylan Thomas's Conception of Poetry." Forum 4 (Fall-Winter):10-16.
Examines Thomas's thoughts on the art of poetry found both in his poems and prose writings. Demanding hard work but capable of prophecy, this art is meant above all to give expression to the issues of time and spirit.

36 NEUVILLE, A. RICHMOND. "Thomas' 'Ballad of the Long-legged Bait.'" Explicator 23 (February): item 43.
Explicates the poem as one that tells about the "epic struggle of all men against the assaults of the flesh."

37 O'BRIEN, CONOR CRUISE. "The Dylan Cult." New York Review of Books 5 (9 December):12, 14, 16.
Complains that Constantine FitzGibbon's The Life of Dylan Thomas, while carefully written, fails to relate successfully the writing with the life of the poet. Turning to David Holbrook's Dylan Thomas and Poetic Dissociation is a "relief" because, while

"priggish and pedantic," this book does concentrate on Thomas's
work, even if in a hostile way. Holbrook's book, though "un-
couth," is also "honest and courageous" in challenging the Thomas
cult.

38   OHMAN, RICHARD M. "Criticism, 1964 (Part II)." Wisconsin
     Studies in Contemporary Literature 6 (Autumn):379-80.
         Recommends T.H. Jones's Dylan Thomas primarily because the
     study succeeds in bringing together a consensus of the poet's
     critical estimates and pointing out the growing note of celebra-
     tion in the work. Aneirin Talfan Davies's Dylan: Druid of the
     Broken Body is found useful for the evidence it provides that
     Thomas's vision grew increasingly sacramental.

39   O'NEILL, DAN. "Letter from Wales." Saturday Night 80
     (January):8-9.
         Reports from Laugharne on what the place is like and what
     the people think about the famous poet who lived there.

40   "Pinpot Pan." Time 86 (29 October):102, 104.
         Reviews Constantine FitzGibbon's The Life of Dylan Thomas.
     It's a "careful and eloquent" account that shows in "vivid
     detail" the real and the legendary poet with both great character
     flaws and many admirable qualities who "failed to become a great
     poet only because he became a great clown." Thomas always in-
     voked the "fundamental experiences: birth, copulation and
     death." Thomas was "a matriarchal mystic who delivered verse
     from the tyranny of the intellect and created a modern poetry of
     the heart."

41   "Poet off the Wagon." Times (London), 14 October, p. 15.
         Reviews Constantine FitzGibbon's The Life of Dylan Thomas,
     complimenting the biographer for successfully making plain "where
     the poet ended" and the "Bohemian took over."

42   PRATT, ANNIS VILAS. "The Early Prose of Dylan Thomas." Ph.D.
     dissertation, Columbia University, 179 pp.
         Shows that in his early stories Thomas creates lyric fables
     involving private symbols and mythological sources. After a
     biographical section the study goes on to an examination of the
     mythological, theological, and occult underpinnings of the tales.
     Finally suggests that the development of the lyric narratives
     anticipates Thomas's lyric poetry and points toward a unity in
     the total work previously not appreciated. See Dissertation
     Abstracts International 28 (1967):2260A. Revised and reprinted
     in part: 1966.8.

43   RAY, PAUL C. "Dylan Thomas and the Surrealists." Notes and
     Queries 12 (July):275.
         Draws parallels between two of Thomas's "surrealistic"
     lines and items appearing in works by André Breton and Buñuel.

44   Review of Dylan Thomas's Choice: An Anthology of Verse Spoken
      by Dylan Thomas. Choice 2 (June):230.
          Recommends the volume because this anthology is marked by
      the poet's "imprint" of taste for selections that express "wisdom
      to the human heart."

45   Review of The Life of Dylan Thomas. Newsweek 66 (27 Decem-
      ber):73.
          Recommends Constantine FitzGibbon's biography as one of the
      year's best books. It "doggedly" proves that the poet famous
      for his roistering excesses surpassed his legend.

46   RICHMOND, LEE J. "Thomas' 'Ballad of the Long-legged Bait.'"
      Explicator 23 (February): item 43.
          Explicates the poem, noting how Thomas employs the Wander-
      ing Jew story to express man's doomed quest for ideal love.

47   ROBINSON, THEODORE R. "Dylan Thomas's 'On the Marriage of a
      Virgin." English Studies in Africa 8 (September):157–65.
          Reveals how Thomas used the story of the Virgin Mary's
      "sexual" experience as the central point in "On the Marriage of
      a Virgin." Argues that a knowledge of Thomas's tendency to com-
      bine biblical lore and sexual imagery is the key to an under-
      standing of his obscure poems.

48   ROGERS, TIMOTHY. Review of Dylan Thomas: His Life and Work
      and Dylan: Druid of the Broken Body. English 15 (Spring):
      148–49.
          Criticizes John Ackerman's Dylan Thomas for falling into
      discussions that are "too summary" and applauds A.T. Davies's
      Dylan: Druid of the Broken Body for raising the issue that it
      was time to judge Thomas's accomplishments by his oeuvre.

49   SAUNDERS, THOMAS. "Religious Elements in the Poetry of Dylan
      Thomas." Dalhousie Review 45 (Winter):492–97.
          Debates Thomas's Christianity. Having been classified
      variously as a follower of Swinburne, a bard, a writer obsessed
      with sex, and a celebrator of nature, Thomas was now being criti-
      cally examined as a religious poet.

50   SUSS, IRVING D. Review of Dylan Thomas: His Life and Work.
      Commonweal 82 (14 May):262–64.
          Pans John Ackerman's study. Using a "peculiarly subjec-
      tive" approach, Ackerman "elaborates a myth" that the key to
      Thomas's work is his Welsh blood.

51   _____. Review of The Life of Dylan Thomas. Commonweal 83
      (17 December):350–51.
          Praises Constantine FitzGibbon's biography for its "com-
      passionate" but honest description of an "essential poet who was
      an incomplete man."

52   SYMONS, JULIAN. "Cwmdonkin Blues." Punch 249 (10 November):
     705.
        Faults Constantine FitzGibbon's The Life of Dylan Thomas
     for providing "all the facts" without looking beneath them very
     far.

53   TALBOT, NORMAN. "Polly's Milk Wood and Abraham's Bosom."
     Southern Review 1:33–43.
        Disagrees with David Holbrook's harsh criticism of Under
     Milk Wood, seeing it instead as a successful dramatic creation
     concerned with the complex nature of love.

54   TELLIER, A.R. "Comptes rendus." Études anglaises 18
     (October–December):427–29.
        Reviews T.H. Jones's Dylan Thomas, Ralph Maud's Entrance to
     Dylan Thomas' Poetry, and John Ackerman's Dylan Thomas, His Life
     and Work. All three writers are commended for showing the
     development of Thomas's genius.

55   THOMPSON, KENT E. "An Approach to the Early Poems of Dylan
     Thomas." Anglo-Welsh Review 14 (Winter):81–88.
        Suggests that recognizing the narrative line of the poem is
     the key to their understanding. When the line is disrupted or
     broken, it is meant to draw an imaginative response from the
     reader. Another key element of his style is his method of
     extreme compassion designed to lead to expanded meaning.

*56 _____. "Dylan Thomas in Swansea." Ph.D. dissertation,
     University College of Swansea.
        See Maud, 1970.14, p. 38.

57   "Top of the Second Eleven." Times Literary Supplement,
     21 October, p. 940.
        Reviews Bill Read's The Days of Dylan Thomas and Constantine
     FitzGibbon's The Life of Dylan Thomas. Read's book is a "useful
     pictorial biography" that suffers from a lack of deep understand-
     ing of the English scene. FitzGibbon's biography is praised for
     its "astringent honesty" and for its presentation of a great deal
     of new information about the poet's life and character.

58   TOWNER, ANNEMARIE EWING. "Welsh Bardic Meters and English
     Poetry." Massachusetts Review 6 (Spring–Summer):614–24.
        Describes the growing influence of the Welsh poetic tra-
     dition, with poets such as Thomas in effect "rescuing" poetry that
     is meant to be not just read but heard.

59   "Versatility in a Double Bill." Times (London), 4 February,
     p. 16.
        Looks at the performance of Return Journey, a lament
     imagining the dead poet returning to Swansea to hear his
     obituaries. It's "so faithful as to be parody."

60   WAIN, JOHN. "Dylan Thomas Today." New York Review of Books
     4 (25 February):12, 14-15.
     Believes that Thomas's Welshness lies "very near the
     heart" of his poetry. His work was marked by such character-
     istically Welsh qualities as "open emotionalism," broad "verbal
     gestures," and "rapt pleasure" in craftsmanship. Most important,
     his poetry was marked by the "bardic tone" typical of Welsh
     bards. Also finds Thomas to be an "archetype" of modern exis-
     tence because of the essential, paradoxical divisions that can be
     discovered in his character and writing. Recommends John
     Ackerman's Dylan Thomas as the "most helpful general study" of
     the poet and Bill Read's The Days of Dylan Thomas as a helpful
     aid for those wishing to picture the Welsh life that surrounded
     him. David Holbrook's Dylan Thomas and Poetic Dissociation is
     dismissed as a "sour little book."

61   WILLINGHAM, JOHN R. Review of Dylan Thomas: His Life and
     Work. Library Journal 90 (1 April):1720.
     Praises John Ackerman's study as a "thorough, lucid" work
     that succeeds in relating "meaningfully" Thomas's background and
     his writing.

                              1966

1   ADAMS, PHOEBE. Review of Rebecca's Daughters. Atlantic
     Monthly 217 (May):132.
     Believes the script is a fine example of "how to tell a
     story purely in terms of what can be seen and heard."

2   BLIVEN, NAOMI. "Out of This World and in It." New Yorker 41
     (22 January):100-102.
     Reviews Constantine FitzGibbon's biography, The Life of
     Dylan Thomas. The writer is praised for the "undogmatic
     restraint" with which he tells the story of the many-sided
     poet--a baby, a family man, a charmer, an actor, a wastrel, and
     a dedicated poet.

3   BROWN, ARTHUR W. "Requiem." Social Education 30 (April):
     299.
     Reviews Constantine FitzGibbon's The Life of Dylan Thomas,
     praising its success in deflating the various exaggerated myths
     and false legends surrounding the working poet.

4   BURGESS, ANTHONY. "Man and Artist." Spectator, 25 November,
     pp. 693-94.
     Looks at recently published Thomas books and concludes that
     it's a mistake to think of some kind of Thomas revival happening
     since this poet "goes on all the time." Thomas's "devotion to
     language was absolute."

5   _____. "The Writer as Drunk." Spectator, 4 November, p. 588.
     Comments on the significant role pub-drinking played in the
poetic careers of Thomas and Brendan Behan. The pub was a setting for creative social action.

6   COCKERILL, DONALD J. Review of Dylan: Druid of the Broken
     Body. University of Denver Quarterly 1 (Autumn):154-55.
     Praises Aneirin Talfan Davies's work for reminding us that
Thomas's importance lies strictly in his poetry. Davies tries
"neither to make Thomas out as a Catholic or a Welsh Protes-
tant . . . but he does see a highly Catholic awareness in the
poet's imagistic struggles in his poems."

7   COHEN, JOHN MICHAEL. Poetry of This Age: 1908-1965. New
     York: Harper & Row, pp. 167-71.
     Looks at Thomas's intellectual limitations. "A naturally
unintellectual poet, he allowed a dream-like association of
images . . . to form the connecting thread on which a poem was
to be hung."

8   COX, C.B., ed. Dylan Thomas: A Collection of Critical
     Essays. Twentieth Century Views, edited by Maynard Mack.
     Englewood Cliffs, N.J.: Prentice-Hall, 186 pp.
     Collects what the editor considers to be the most note-
worthy essays written during the decade after Thomas's death to
demonstrate the changes and developments in critical opinion surrounding the poet. In his introductory comments, Cox concludes
that, based on the evidence, the critical debate is bound to
continue for a long time. Reprints of 1954.25, 36, 69; 1955.1,
77; 1957.5, 66; 1958.43; 1963.22; 1964.1, 21; 1965.42. Also see
Nowottny, 1981.7.

9   DUBUQUE, REMI G. "Dylan Thomas." Jubilee 13 (March):53-55.
     Compares John Malcolm Brinnin's and Constantine Fitz-
Gibbon's biographical accounts of Thomas. Though FitzGibbon's
work has more substance, Brinnin's provides more excitement.

10   "Dylan Thomas Fantasy of Soho." Times (London), 8 March,
     p. 15.
     Reviews Andrew Sinclair's dramatized version of Adventures
in the Skin Trade, finding it to be a failure mainly because the
playwright "seems to be operating on a different wavelength" from
the Welsh poet.

11   "Dylan Thomas's Widow Sues for Milk Wood Ms." New York Times,
     9 March, p. 38.
     Reports on Caitlin Thomas's suing Douglas Cleverdon to
recover the original manuscript of Under Milk Wood.

12   FITZGIBBON, CONSTANTINE, ed. Selected Letters of Dylan
     Thomas. London: J.M. Dent, pp. vii-ix.
     Gives introductory remarks on the decisions involved in
the selection process.

13   GEIGER, DON. "New Books in Review." Quarterly Journal of
     Speech 52 (December):400-401.
        Reviews Constantine FitzGibbon's The Life of Dylan Thomas,
     William Moynihan's The Craft and Art of Dylan Thomas, and C.B.
     Cox's Dylan Thomas: A Collection of Critical Essays. Praises
     FitzGibbon's biography in particular for the "well-grounded
     interpretations of Thomas's character and actions, which stimu-
     late, without dictation, further interpretation." Moynihan
     succeeds in revealing the principles of the poet's art by care-
     fully analyzing his use of images, symbols, auditory devices,
     structural techniques, and visionary themes. Cox's collection of
     essays is an important contribution to the posthumous reevaluation
     of the poet's reputation.

14   GERSH, GABRIEL. "Thomas in Full View." Prairie Schooner 40
     (Spring):82-83.
        Praises Constantine FitzGibbon's The Life of Dylan Thomas
     for its comprehensive and objective qualities. Notes that the
     biographer establishes four significant points about the poet:
     Thomas felt from early age he was doomed to die young; he wrote
     the first drafts of most of his poems between the ages of fifteen
     and twenty; he was naturally inclined toward acting; and he was
     basically a shy and timid person.

15   "Golden Bard or Brassy Orator." Library Review 20 (Spring):
     358-59.
        Reviews Constantine FitzGibbon's The Life of Dylan Thomas.
     Praises the writer especially for showing Thomas's "poetic inno-
     cence and integrity."

16   "Half-Ironic Self-portrait." Times (London), 10 November,
     p. 14.
        Reviews three new books concerning Thomas. Constantine
     FitzGibbon's edition of Selected Letters proves valuable because
     through this volume Thomas's total devotion to poetry and con-
     stant worry about money are revealed. A Garland for Dylan Thomas
     is called a "fine testimony," but William Moynihan's The Craft
     and Art of Dylan Thomas is dismissed as a "somewhat woodenly"
     attempt to analyze the poet's art.

17   HAMILTON, IAN. "Nothing or Me." Listener 76 (24 November):
     779.
        Welcomes Constantine FitzGibbon's edition of Selected
     Letters but dismisses two other recent publications: the
     "drooling" A Garland for Dylan Thomas and the "plodding" The
     Craft and Art of Dylan Thomas.

18   "High Court Action Over Under Milk Wood Manuscript." Times
     (London), 9 March, p. 5.
        Reports on the initial court hearing held to decide the
     legal ownership of Under Milk Wood. Douglas Cleverdon claimed
     Thomas had given him the manuscript; Caitlin Thomas held that,
     as the personal representative of her husband's estate, she was
     entitled to what Thomas once referred to as his "life's work."

Daily reports of the progress of case follow--on 10 March, p. 6;
11 March, p. 8; 12 March, p. 12; and 19 March, p. 5. The latter
two reports tell about the court's finding against Mrs. Thomas
and ordering her to pay all the court costs.

19   "How Green Was His Valley." Economist 221 (12 November):687.
     Reviews Selected Letters and William Moynihan's The Craft
and Art of Dylan Thomas. Recommends the letters edited by
Constantine FitzGibbon primarily because they give an illuminating "judicious" picture of the poet's creative development.
Moynihan's study is also an "illuminating" volume, especially in
its illustration of Thomas's poetic craft, themes, symbols, and
unified vision.

20   HUGHES, TED. "Dylan Thomas's Letters." New Statesman 72
     (25 November):783.
     Reviews Constantine FitzGibbon's edition of Selected
Letters. Finds the letters to be exceedingly interesting and
pleasurable. A number represent Thomas's "best comic work,"
many of them wonderful "prose poems in comic vein." But the
"crucifixion of his last years makes for painful reading."

21   JENKINS, JACK L. "How Green Is 'Fern Hill'?" English Journal
     55 (December):1180-82.
     Analyzes the "green" imagery in "Fern Hill," discovering
during the course of the explication that these color images
prove to be central to the poem's concern with time and death.

22   JONES, Sister M. ROBERTA. "The Wellspring of Dylan." English
     Journal 55 (January):78-82.
     Offers readings of "Poem in October," "A Winter's Tale,"
and "Vision and Prayer" to illustrate Thomas's vitality, music,
and figurative eloquence working together to reveal universal
truths.

23   JOST, EDWARD F. Review of The Life of Dylan Thomas. America
     114 (8 January):51.
     Gives Constantine FitzGibbon credit for a balanced,
graceful and honest biography of this poet who became a
"performer."

24   KORG, JACOB. "Perceptions of Dylan Thomas." Antioch Review
     26 (Summer):281-88.
     Reviews recent books dealing with the poet. Taken together,
these books (Constantine FitzGibbon's The Life of Dylan Thomas,
John Ackerman's Dylan Thomas: His Life and Work, William
Moynihan's The Craft and Art of Dylan Thomas, and J. Hillis
Miller's Poets of Reality) "show that the rebelliousness with
which Thomas is often associated is only a part of the whole
attitude expressed in his poetry."

25   LENTRICCHIA, FRANK. "Some Coordinates of Modern Literature."
      Poetry 108 (April):65-67.
      Reviews four books on poetry, pointing to the failure of
David Holbrook's "debunking" work, Dylan Thomas and Poetic Dissociation. Accuses the critic of a "narrow positivistic stance."

26   LINDSAY, JACK. "Memories of Dylan Thomas." Meanjin 25
      (Autumn):48-75.
      Remembers the Thomas he knew between 1943 and 1950. Makes
some critical observations of his poetry.

27   MARSHALL, PERCY. Masters of English Poetry. London: Dennis
      Dobson, pp. 214-28.
      Describes Thomas as the one British-born poet of this cen-
tury who can be seen to have "possessed genius."

28   McDONALD, GERALD D. Review of The Doctor and the Devils and
      Other Scripts. Library Journal 91 (August):3732.
      Recognizes Thomas's film scripts as the work of a "highly
professional writer and one of considerable range."

29   _____. Review of Dylan Thomas: A Collection of Critical
      Essays. Library Journal 91 (15 May):2495.
      Describes the variety of essays contained in the C.B. Cox
edited collection.

30   _____. Review of Rebecca's Daughters. Library Journal 91
      (1 June):2870.
      Says that Thomas's film script is so effectively written
that the romantic melodrama can be "clearly" seen.

31   MAUD, RALPH N. "The London Model for Dylan Thomas' Under Milk
      Wood. In The Doctor and the Devils and Other Scripts. New
      York: New Directions, pp. 209-11.
      Provides the complicated history of the development of
Under Milk Wood. The idea for the play-for-voices originated and
was "fashioned once and for all" in New Quay, where Thomas
stayed while writing "Quite Early One Morning" for the B.B.C.

32   MELLER, HORST. "Zum literarischen Hintergrund von Dylan
      Thomas' Under Milk Wood." Die Neueren Sprachen 15 (February):
      49-58.
      Traces Under Milk Wood back to Wilder's Our Town, Master's
Spoon River Anthology, and Joyce's Ulysses; but insists nevertheless that Thomas has written something original in intent and
design. Not precisely a radio play, it's instead a series of
mono-dramas linked by narrative voices.

33   MILLER, J. HILLIS. "Dylan Thomas." In Poets of Reality: Six
      Twentieth-Century Writers. Cambridge, Mass.: Belknap Press,
      Harvard University, pp. 190-216 passim.
      Shows that Thomas's poems attempt to contain the self, the
world, and God all at once, and that they're constructed in such

a way that the reader must make a "single leap" to arrive at the full meaning. To appreciate his most difficult poems, the reader must also understand that his use of the microcosm and macrocosm relation is not so much a metaphorical manipulation as the means of revealing the "literal fact" of his envisioned universe.

34   MOYNIHAN, WILLIAM TRUMBULL. The Craft and Art of Dylan Thomas. London: Oxford University Press; Ithaca, N.Y.: Cornell University Press, 311 pp.
     Traces the development of Thomas's imagination and poetic craft. A close examination of his auditory and rhetorical practices precedes a consideration of thematic issues, which is followed by an analysis of the symbolic meaning of his work. Logically, his work "may be mired in confusions and contradictions, but, symbolically, it reveals a mythic unity."

35   MURDY, LOUISE BAUGHAN. Sound and Sense in Dylan Thomas's Poetry. The Hague: Mouton, 172 pp.
     Argues that while Thomas's poetry isn't marked by the kind of intellectualism found in T.S. Eliot's work, it contains serious meaning. But this meaning is fully apprehended more by "mood" and "feeling" than by concentrated thinking. A close analysis of Thomas's use of sound reveals that he moved from a "staccato" auditory method in the early poems to a "legato" method in the later ones. His unique orchestration generally resulted from stress-arrangement, sound choice, and sound arrangement.

36   OHMANN, RICHARD. "Literature as Sentences." College English 27 (January):261-67.
     Brings the first sentence of "A Winter's Tale" into the discussion of what certain kinds of sentence structures can reveal about a writer's "habits of meaning."

37   PRESS, JOHN. The Fire and the Fountain: An Essay on Poetry. 2d ed. New York: Barnes & Noble, 151-54 passim.
     Complains that in Thomas's poetry there is usually such a jumble of language that instead of enjoying the verses as harmonious units "we are alternately worried and fascinated by a succession of dismembered images."

38   Review of Dylan: Druid of the Broken Body. Library Journal 91 (1 May):2344.
     Recommends Aneirin Talfan Davies's work as an "insightful" study on the subject of Thomas as a religious poet.

39   Review of The Life of Dylan Thomas. Choice 2 (January):770.
     Recommends Constantine FitzGibbon's biography as the "indispensable," "definitive" account that succeeds in distinguishing the "poseur from the person."

40 Review of Me and My Bike. Choice 3 (April):137.
    Recommends the work for showing an additional creative side
    of Thomas. This fragment of a projected operetta reveals his
    gift for lyrical music, entertaining story, and effective pacing.

41 SCHMIDT, DANA ADAMS. "Dylan Thomas's Widow Loses Suit for
    Under Milk Wood MS." New York Times, 12 March, p. 22.
    Reports Caitlin Thomas's losing her suit to gain possession
    of the original manuscript of Under Milk Wood. The court found
    for Douglas Cleverdon, believing his story that Thomas had
    promised him the manuscript "if he could find it."

42 SCHOFF, GRETCHEN HOLSTEIN. "The Major Prose of Dylan Thomas."
    Ph.D. dissertation, University of Wisconsin, 338 pp.
    Surveys in more or less chronological order Thomas's work
    in short stories, novelette, radio, drama, and film writing. The
    conclusion reached is that Thomas's prose moved steadily away
    from subjective and experimental writing toward a more objective,
    public, and dramatically controlled art. See Dissertaion
    Abstracts International 28 (1967):1086A.

43 SERGEANT, HOWARD. "Religion in Modern British Poetry: The
    Ambiguities of Dylan Thomas." Aryan Path 37 (August):354-60.
    Traces the development of Thomas's religion, which finally
    consisted of a mixture of Christianity, pantheism, and mysticism.
    Always granting man's spiritual character, he tended to obscure
    the issue through a penchant for paradox.

44 SEYMORE, WILLIAM KEAN. "Seeing Dylan Plain." Contemporary
    Review 208 (January):49-50.
    Reviews Constantine FitzGibbon's The Life of Dylan Thomas.
    Praises it for its unbiased, balanced analysis of the poet's
    character. Believes that the part of the biography dealing with
    Thomas's national and family background is the most valuable.
    Agrees with T.S. Eliot's assessment that it was a "peculiarity"
    of Thomas's "type of genius that he either wrote a great poem or
    something approaching nonsense and one ought to have accepted the
    inferior with the first-rate."

45 SYMONS, JULIAN. "Dylan Plain." Punch 251 (23 November):787.
    Recommends Selected Letters as a very useful aid in under-
    standing the difficult person. "The course of the letters shows
    clearly his retreat from life to infantilism."

46 TEMPLE, RUTH Z., and TUCKER, MARTIN, eds. A Library of
    Literary Criticism: Modern British Literature. Vol. 3. New
    York: Frederick Ungar, pp. 218-24.
    Starting with Edith Sitwell's praise in 1936, gives samples
    of various critical opinions on Thomas. Arranged chronologi-
    cally, the excerpts provide a look at the development of his
    reputation and critical appreciation of his work up to 1963.

47   TRICK, BERT. "The Young Dylan Thomas." Texas Quarterly 9
     (Summer):36-49.
          Recalls Thomas as a young poet in Swansea. Highlights the
     first meeting and other revealing events. Struck immediately by
     the "sonorous" voice of the precocious young man, Trick grew
     close to Thomas after discovering they both felt rebellious
     toward traditionalism, they both loved invective, and they both
     were intoxicated by words. Describes Swansea in the thirties to
     offer a picture of the environment that helped form the poet.
     Defends Thomas against the popular "roistering" image, insisting
     that his friend was a compassionate and "deeply religious" person
     who hated any kind of cruelty. Includes a brief introduction by
     Bill Read.

48   VENDLER, HELEN HENNESSY. "Thomas and Lowell." Yale Review 55
     (Spring):439-42.
          Finds Constantine FitzGibbon's The Life of Dylan Thomas to
     be an unsatisfactory biography because, while it gives an ex-
     tended summary of what was "visible to the naked eye or camera,"
     it doesn't give the "sufficient human instances" that are re-
     quired to reveal the "hidden" man.

49   WHITE, WILLIAM. "Dylan Thomas, Mr. Rolph, and 'John
     O'London's Weekly.'" Papers of the Bibliographical Society
     of America 60 (Third Quarter):370-72.
          Points out the absence of a poem in J.A. Rolph's bibliog-
     raphy of Thomas's works. This poem, "Dare I," appeared in John
     O'London's Weekly.

50   WOOD, FREDERICK T. Review of The Life of Dylan Thomas.
     English Studies 47 (December):472.
          Finds that, despite Constantine FitzGibbon's attempts to
     the contrary in his biography, Thomas comes out as perhaps a
     genius but a "not very admirable person."

51   YEOMANS, W.E. "Dylan Thomas: The Literal Vision." Bucknell
     Review 14 (March):103-15.
          Suggests that a literal reading of Thomas's poems should
     precede an investigation of their symbolic significance.
     Thomas's vision was based on an understanding of nature follow-
     ing the laws of imagination, and he imagined man's experience
     extending into cosmic truth.

                              1967

1   ADAMS, PHOEBE. Review of Selected Letters. Atlantic Monthly
     220 (July):114.
          Finds the letters to be both fascinating and painful.
     They were written with "something of the concentrated intention
     that went into his poetry."

2   BUCKLEY, VINCENT. "The Persistence of God." Critical Review
    10:74-87.
        Looks at how modern poets confront the idea that God is
    dead. Thomas addresses a primitive, sensual god.

3   de HART, OLGA HARVILL. "Thomas' 'O make me a mask.'"
    Explicator 26 (October): item 12.
        Gives the poem a religious reading, submitting that it
    expresses a paradoxical yearning for a return to "prelapsarian
    innocence."

4   DEVAS, NICOLETTE. Two Flamboyant Fathers. New York: William
    Morrow, pp. 192-208 passim.
        Recollects the Thomas she knew, especially during the early
    years of his marriage to Caitlin.

5   FRENCH, WARREN. "Two Portraits of the Artist: James Joyce's
    Young Man; Dylan Thomas's Young Dog." University of Kansas
    City Review 33 (June):261-66.
        Compares Thomas's Portrait of the Artist with Joyce's
    Portrait. Differences do exist, namely in structure and literary
    disposition. The various similarities in subject matter and
    organizational strategies suggest, however, that Thomas had
    Joyce's work on his mind and may even have been consciously
    burlesquing the master.

6   FULLER, EDMUND. "An Odd Little Person." Wall Street Journal,
    8 June, p. 14.
        Finds the Selected Letters volume edited by Constantine
    FitzGibbon to be "nakedly revealing." The most "appealing"
    letters are those written by Pamela Hansford Johnson. The most
    valuable ones focus on his various creative efforts. Prominent
    among these is a long letter about Under Milk Wood.

7   GINGERICH, MARTIN E. "Time and Persona in the Poetry of Dylan
    Thomas." Ph.D. dissertation, Ohio University, 165 pp.
        Describes Thomas's stylistic and thematic use of time and
    persona. Such an approach helps to point out the development of
    Thomas's art and aids in the understanding of his most compli-
    cated poetry. Ultimately, his invention of persona free of time
    leads to the poet's appreciation and acceptance of man's tempo-
    rality. See Dissertation Abstracts International 28 (1967):2246A.

8   GREGORY, HORACE. "A Piece of Earth of the Earth." New York
    Times Book Review, 25 June, pp. 5, 26, 28.
        Finds Selected Letters to be important for revealing the
    "tensions and dynamics" of the poet's creative career. High-
    lights the fact that Thomas was a poet of "minute particulars"
    who believed in a sort of "invested pantheism." At its best,
    his poetry works to fuse perfectly the essential opposites of
    existence.

9   GRIGSON, GEOFFREY. "Alas, Poor Dylan: Letters from
Llareggub." <u>Times Literary Supplement</u>, 2 March, pp. 157-58.
     Reviews <u>Selected Letters</u>, admitting that they explain a
great deal about the man and his poetry. But faults the "slat-
ternly and inconsistent" editing of Constantine FitzGibbon and
believes too many of the selections are simply "irrelevancies."
In the course of the mostly negative review Grigson criticizes
three other volumes. William Moynihan's <u>The Craft and Art of
Dylan Thomas</u> is criticized especially for its wrong-headed
attempt to establish Hopkins's influence on Thomas. Louise
Baughan Murdy's <u>Sound and Sense in Dylan Thomas's Poetry</u> takes
the subject of the poet as dramatic reader too seriously. <u>A
Garland for Dylan Thomas</u> is dismissed as a collection of "pre-
dominantly insipid and exclamatory" elegies.

10   HANSEN, KURT HEINRICH. "Vorbemerkungen zu Dylan Thomas'
Gedichten 'Poem in October' und 'Fern Hill.'" <u>Sprache im
Technischen Zeitalter</u> 21 (January):17-20.
     Considers the special problems of translating the meaning
and sensual nature of Thomas's poetry. The translator must take
into account Thomas's celebration of the mystical character of
language and his Welsh background.

11   HODGART, MATTHEW. "Old Pup." <u>New York Review of Books</u> 9
(3 August):19-22.
     Reviews <u>Selected Letters</u> and R.C. Williams's <u>A Concordance
to the Collected Poems of Dylan Thomas</u>. Complains that the
editor of <u>Selected Letters</u> is responsible for some "odd" omis-
sions (certain letters to Caitlin Thomas, for example) and that
he fails to help answer the key question of how "this boy turned
into the finest lyrical poet of his age." Praises the <u>Concordance</u>
for being compiled with the sort of "scrupulous care and accuracy"
that should be especially helpful in "decoding" Thomas's most
difficult poems.

12   KROLL, JACK. "Whirligig." <u>Newsweek</u> 69 (22 May):106.
     Reviews <u>Selected Letters</u>, finding them to be as full of
life as was Thomas, that "noisy creature." The letters provide
vivid highlights of Thomas's existence.

13   LEWIS, MIN. <u>Laugharne and Dylan Thomas</u>. London: Dennis
Dobson, 128 pp.
     Provides an affectionate look at Thomas and Laugharne, the
place so important in his life and work.

14   MADDOCKS, MELVIN. "Giving "a bit of oneself.'" <u>Christian
Science Monitor</u>, 18 May, p. 11.
     Reviews <u>Selected Letters</u>, finding them useful in redress-
ing the Thomas legend. Thomas "was an original both in his
strengths and weaknesses," and the letters reveal that he was
"usually clear about himself."

15 MAUD, RALPH N. "Dylan Thomas." Wisconsin Studies in Con-
    temporary Literature 8 (Summer):450-53.
        Reviews William T. Moynihan's The Craft and Art of Dylan
    Thomas against the backdrop of other recent studies of the poet.
    Though "useful for reference," this like many other studies on
    Thomas suffers from scholarship apparently done in isolation.

16 _____. "That Terrible United States." Anglo-Welsh Review 16
    (Spring):149-51.
        Argues that Thomas shouldn't be compared to Bob Dylan but
    to D.H. Lawrence. The poet "was brutally torn: seeing more
    possibilities than the average person, he could also see the
    enormity of his failure to respond."

17 _____, ed. The Notebooks of Dylan Thomas. New York: New
    Directions, 364 pp.
        Explains in an introduction the critical value of having
    the evidence of Thomas's work in the notebooks at hand. Offers
    a "reading text" of Thomas's four exercise books containing the
    poems written during the "crucial" years between 1930 and 1934.
    Tries to inform the reader of Thomas's second thoughts about his
    compositions "without obliterating his first." Provides evidence
    of just how creatively energetic he was between his fifteenth and
    nineteenth years and also reveals how much of the work published
    up to his twenty-sixth year was a "reworking" of the earlier
    poetry. Printed as Poet in the Making by J.M. Dent in 1968.

18 MORGAN, EDWIN. "Scalped by a Bourbon." Review 17 (April):
    41-44.
        Reviews Constantine FitzGibbon's edition of Selected
    Letters. While providing little new information about Thomas's
    views on his craft, they do reveal the process of self-
    destruction.

19 MOSS, HOWARD. "A Thin, Curly Little Person." New Yorker 43
    (7 October):185-89.
        Reviews Selected Letters. They reveal that Thomas "re-
    mained whole as a poet without compromise, though he may have had
    to compromise almost everything else to do it." Thomas's
    "second-greatest claim to genius," the letters finally give us
    the "history of a wildly gifted and brilliant child, not only
    stumbling and bumbling his way to the grave but digging it for
    himself in the process."

20 MOSS, STANLEY. "Fallen Angel." New Republic 156 (10 June):
    19-20.
        Looking at Constantine FitzGibbon's biography (The Life of
    Dylan Thomas) and Selected Letters, the necessary conclusion to
    be drawn is that "no great writer of this century fell from such
    innocence to such disarray." Thomas had a "special kick for
    death."

21 OPPEL, HORST. "Entwicklungsphasen der englischen Lyrik im
    20. Jahrhundert." Neueren Sprachen 16 (January):1-16.
    Shows that English poetry, withdrawing from the influence
of the powerful poets of the postwar era (Eliot, Auden, Empson,
and Thomas), indicates a move back to local and formal emphases.

22 PRYCE-JONES, ALAN. "Letters from a Stranger." Book Week 4
    (18 June):8, 11.
    Reviews Selected Letters, noting that they effectively
reveal both the good and the bad Dylan, and his "protean capacity
for change." Feels that Thomas began to "fade" several years
before his death.

23 READ, BILL. "His Beloved Words." Saturday Review 50
    (22 July):39.
    Finds the Selected Letters to be "magnificent" in the way
they reveal the life of the poet falling from the great exuberance of the early years to the painful times that eventually
followed. The highlights are the artistically illuminating
letters he wrote to Henry Treece and the personal letters to
Pamela Hansford Johnson.

24 ROSENTHAL, M.L. "Poems in Embryo." Saturday Review 50
    (30 December):24-25.
    Finds the publication of The Notebooks of Dylan Thomas to
be an important event mainly because these notebooks reveal the
"precocious" and profligate nature of the young poet and because
they allow the reader to discover some of the significant variations in the developing poems and a number of "secret" poems that
were left unpublished or incomplete.

25 SEYMORE, WILLIAM KEAN. "Dylan Thomas Letters." Contemporary
    Review 210 (April):221-22.
    Reviews Constantine FitzGibbon's edition of Selected
Letters. These letters provide us with a "convincing, conscious
self-portrait of one of the most complex creative writers of our
century."

26 SINCLAIR, ANDREW. Adventures in the Skin Trade: An Adapta-
    tion for the Stage by Andrew Sinclair. London: J.M. Dent,
    94 pp.
    Dramatizes Thomas's uncompleted novel. Includes an intro-
duction by James Roose-Evans.

27 STRAVINSKY, IGOR. In Memoriam Dylan Thomas. Columbia
    MS 6992.
    Columbia record of mass, performed by the Gregg Smith
Singers, includes the composer's program notes.

28 "That Prodigal." Time 89 (30 June):74-76.
    Reviews Selected Letters, complimenting Constantine
FitzGibbon for a careful editing job that provides a convincing
psychological revelation. The letters to Pamela Hansford Johnson
are especially valuable in revealing his complex character.

29   WEST, PAUL. "Dylan Thomas: The Position in Calamity."
      Southern Review, Autumn, pp. 922-43.
          Attempts to assess Thomas's achievement. After glancing at
      various works by and about Thomas, the critic concludes that this
      poet "wanted to know how the universe runs itself on earth, both
      before and beyond an ordinary life-span; he wanted . . . a sense
      of the all, rather than everything making sense." Because he is
      more interested in how than in why life works, his poetry essen-
      tially provides information rather than wisdom.

30   WILLIAMS, ROBERT COLEMAN, ed. A Concordance to the Collected
      Poems of Dylan Thomas. Lincoln: University of Nebraska
      Press, 582 pp.
          Bases the concordance on J.M. Dent's 1954 reprinting of
      Collected Poems. Following every word that is indexed is the
      line of poetry where the word is used.

31   WOODCOCK, GEORGE. "Dylan Thomas: Flavor of the Man." New
      Leader 50 (5 June):18-20.
          Reviews Selected Letters. This collection gives us the
      "best chart yet" of the poet's life and accomplishments.

32   "Worm Beneath the Nail." Time 90 (22 December):82.
          Recommends Ralph Maud's The Notebooks of Dylan Thomas to
      anyone interested in tracing the development of the poet and in
      discovering just how methodical he was in his work.

                              1968

1   AIKEN, CONRAD. "Dylan Thomas." In Collected Criticism.
      London: Oxford University Press, pp. 370-71.
          Reprint of 1940.1.

2   AYERS, JAMES R. "Dylan Thomas in the Aural Dimension."
      Computer Studies in the Humanities and Verbal Behavior 1
      (January):6-9.
          Describes an attempt to use the advantages of a computer to
      deal with the difficulties of Thomas's poetry. Concludes that
      the computer can be especially helpful in dealing with the
      stylistics of the verse.

3   CLEVERDON, DOUGLAS. "Under Milk Wood." Times Literary
      Supplement, 18 July, p. 761.
          Lists eleven versions of Under Milk Wood and asks for in-
      formation concerning any other possible versions.

4   DAVIES, WALFORD. "An Allusion to Hardy's 'A Broken Appoint-
      ment' in Dylan Thomas's 'In country sleep.'" Notes and
      Queries 15 (February):61-62.
          Discusses Hardy's influence on Thomas, particularly with
      reference to tone and content. Concentrates on allusive connec-
      tions between "A Broken Appointment" and "In country sleep."

                              131

5 _____. "Imitation and Invention: The Use of Borrowed Material in Dylan Thomas's Prose." Essays in Criticism 18 (July): 275-95.
    Discusses Thomas's tendency to use borrowed material in his short stories. This tendency is a "good indication of the nature of Thomas's imagination." Such stories as "The Dress" and "Who Do You Wish Was with Us" show the "quality of fresh creativity" transforming inherited plots.

6 FRANKENBERG, LLOYD. "Dylan Thomas." In Pleasure Dome: On Reading Modern Poetry. New York: Gordian Press, pp. 316-23. Reprint of 1949.5.

7 HALLIBURTON, DAVID G. Review of Sound and Sense in Dylan Thomas's Poetry. Journal of Aesthetics and Art Criticism 27 (Fall):104-5.
    Reviews Louise Baughan Murdy's study, finding it to be fatally flawed in assuming that criticism is a question of gathering data. The work collects facts that are mostly sterile because they fail to illuminate in any essential way Thomas's work.

8 HAPPEL, NIKOLAUS. "Dylan Thomas: 'The force that through the green fuse.'" Die Neueren Sprachen 67 (September):433-38.
    Attempts to develop a "scholarly" interpretation of "The force that through the green fuse" by means of a systematic, analytical reading. Praises the poem in the end for its impressive theme, simplicity, and complexity and mystery aside from the "beauty" of the language.

9 HELMSTETTER, CAROL RUTH. "The Prose Fiction of Dylan Thomas." Ph.D. dissertation, Northwestern University, 198 pp.
    Traces the growth of Thomas's fiction with an eye to his changing aims and the connection between the prose and poetry. His early prose, like his poetry of that time, describes a fearful, frustrated life. His late fiction is more concerned with the complex nature of language than life. See Dissertation Abstracts International 29 (1969):2262A.

10 HOLBROOK, DAVID. "R.D. Laing & the Death Circuit." Encounter 31 (August):35-45.
    Links R.D. Laing's findings about "schizoid madness" with the neurotic nature of Dylan Thomas's and Sylvia Plath's creative lives.

11 JONES, GLYN. The Dragon Has Two Tongues: Essays on Anglo-Welsh Writers and Writing. London: J.M. Dent, pp. 172-203.
    Remembers the Thomas he knew. He was a man "without malice, greed or pettiness."

*12 JONES, T. JAMES. Dan Y Wenallt. Llandysul: Gwasg Gomer. Translates Under Milk Wood into Welsh. See Maud, 1970.14, p. 41.

13 LOESCH, KATHARINE TAYLOR. "The Shape of Sound: Configurational Rime in the Poetry of Dylan Thomas." Speech Monographs 35 (November):407-24.
Illustrates Thomas's use of "configurational rime," particularly in "After the funeral." A "device" used by Thomas throughout his poetry, configurational rime adds to the meaning of the poems through appropriate and cunning use of sound. Considering this aspect of Thomas's poetry "deepens" our appreciation of his achievement. Reprinted: 1972.18.

14 MAUD, RALPH N. "A Clark Lecture Revisited." Essays in Criticism 18 (January):60-62.
Accepts Robert Graves's "mischievous bluff" made ten years ago at a Clark lecture to make sense of a quoted stanza from Thomas's poetry.

15 _____. "Dylan Thomas in Welsh Periodicals." National Library of Wales Journal 15:265-89.
Traces the development of Thomas's reputation in Wales by means of a bibliography of writings on and by Thomas.

16 MONTAGUE, GENE. "Dylan Thomas and Nightwood." Sewanee Review 76 (Summer):420-34.
Compares "How shall my animal" with Djuna Barnes's Nightwood and suggests that, consciously or unconsciously, the latter work was Thomas's source for his complicated poem. An explication of the poem reveals the sexual theme and rhetorical method, and the comparative approach lessens the critical confusion surrounding it.

17 MORGAN, GERALD. "Dylan Thomas." In This World of Wales. Cardiff: University of Wales Press, pp. 159-71.
Anthologizes several poems with an eye toward Thomas's debt to his Welsh background. An introduction focuses on the poet's "Welshness."

18 MURPHY, B.W. "Creation and Destruction--Notes on Dylan Thomas." British Journal of Medical Psychology 41 (June): 149-67.
Applies psychoanalytic analysis to Thomas with the ultimate purpose of understanding the nature of creativity. The discussion is broken down into focal considerations of character, neurosis, psychoanalytical factors, castration anxiety, superego anomalies, origins and vicissitudes of creativity, and illness leading to death. "Although alcohol was a major cause," the poet "died of his neurosis."

19 ORMEROD, DAVID. "The Central Image in Dylan Thomas' 'Over Sir John's hill.'" English Studies 49 (October):449-50.
Analyzes the hawk-hangman image introduced in the first stanza of "Over Sir John's hill." The image finally makes the critic think of the electric chair.

20   RAWSON, C.J. "Some Sources or Parallels to Poems by Ted
Hughes." Notes and Queries 15 (February):62–63.
     Refers to parallels between Ted Hughes's "The Hawk in the
Rain" and Thomas's "Over Sir John's hill."

21   REDDINGTON, ALPHONSUS M. Dylan Thomas: A Journey from Darkness to Light New York: Paulist Press, 100 pp.
     Begins by referring to typical and representative critical
views of Thomas as a poet, then goes on to discuss his way of
creating a "non-conceptional world" in which a religious attitude
becomes increasingly prominent. After an extended experimental,
creative journey, he was "ultimately introduced to the experience
of divine faith and love through his experience of human love."

22   Review of Adventures in the Skin Trade: An Adaptation for the
Stage by Andrew Sinclair. Choice 5 (October):982.
     Recommends Andrew Sinclair's stage adaptation of the un-
finished novel. It's a "truly creative adaptation" that adds a
great deal of new material but retains the spirit of its source.
The ultimate result is a "tighter, funnier play than the original
story."

23   Review of Collected Letters. Choice 5 (May):348.
     Laments the absence of letters to Caitlin Thomas and
Augustus John, but still finds the collection edited by
Constantine FitzGibbon to be "essential" because it provides
many pictures of the poet's "uninhibited" life and casts light
on certain of his poems and aesthetics.

24   Review of The Notebooks of Dylan Thomas. Choice 5 (November):
1134.
     Edited by Ralph Maud, the volume provides an orderly look
at the poet's crucial early work. The introduction and notes are
"excellent" and "full."

25   Review of The Notebooks of Dylan Thomas. New York Times Book
Review, 25 February, pp. 16, 18.
     Finds the main value of this scholarly edition of Thomas's
copybooks to be its revelation of how early Thomas became a
"serious" poet.

26   SYMONS, JULIAN. "Dylan." Punch 254 (17 April):584.
     Reviews Ralph Maud's The Notebooks of Dylan Thomas. From
this "impeccable" editing job one can see "with devastating
clarity" Thomas's lack of development in his poetry. He had
nothing new to say after he reached the age of nineteen. The
notebooks illustrate "an immense word-spinning talent based on a
very few images and ideas."

27   TAIG, THOMAS. "Swansea Between the Wars." Anglo-Welsh
Review 17 (Summer):23–32.
     Describes Swansea between the world wars and mentions its
connection to some of Thomas's writing.

28   VERGHESE, C. PAUL. "Religion in Dylan Thomas's Poetry."
     Literary Criterion 8 (Winter):35-41.
          Considers the question of the kind of religion that can be
     discovered in Thomas's poetry. It's certainly not a conventional
     Christianity. Suggests that instead it "approximates" pantheism.
     "Images and symbols are only an aid to the creation of that per-
     sonal myth which seems to be the real aim of his poetry."

29   "Wunderkind." Economist 227 (27 April):57.
          Reviews Ralph Maud's The Notebooks of Dylan Thomas, recom-
     mending it highly for its "readability" and "meticulous editing."
     The introductory essay is valuable for the biographical informa-
     tion and literary commentary it contains. "No one reading these
     notebooks could doubt that Thomas was a Wunderkind."

30   "The Young Dylan." Times Literary Supplement, 2 May, p. 460.
          Reviews Ralph Maud's The Notebooks of Dylan Thomas. This
     "careful and intelligently introduced" study is valuable for
     several important reasons: it shows that Thomas's first great
     creative phase predated 18 Poems by about four years; it reveals
     the poet moving from free verse experimentation to formal disci-
     pline; it provides evidence of how and when he discovered his
     unique idiom; and it indicates how the "pervasive necrogenic
     physical-process themes" are eventually "consolidated as central,
     almost exclusive issues."

                              1969

1   ASTLEY, RUSSELL. "Stations of the Breath: End Rhyme in the
     Verse of Dylan Thomas." PMLA 84 (October):1595-1605.
          Attempts to establish a suitable language for analyzing the
     radical ideas Thomas developed concerning the sorts of syllabic
     relationships that for "modern ears" could serve to stand for
     the "jingling sound of like endings." Speculates that, although
     a general drift toward a more conservative style can be traced in
     Collected Poems, Thomas's interest in experimental prosody is
     something he would never have abandoned had he lived to write
     more poetry.

2   BREMER, R. "An Analysis and Interpretation of 'Over Sir
     John's hill.'" Neophilologus 53 (July):307-20.
          Analyzes the craft and meaning of "Over Sir John's hill."
     Suggests four "interpenetrating approximations to the full mean-
     ing" of the poem--on the literal, story telling, allegorical, and
     symbolic levels.

3   CLEVERDON, DOUGLAS. The Growth of "Milk Wood." New York:
     New Directions, 126 pp.
          Offers the eleven text versions of Under Milk Wood, with a
     section that gives the history of the work, followed by a section
     that attempts to explain the possible reasons for the succeeding
     changes.

                              135

4   COX, J.S. "Under Milk Wood: Account of an Action to Recover
the Original Manuscript." Guernsey: Toucan, 17 pp.
    Tells the story of the recovery of the "lost" manuscript
of Under Milk Wood.

5   DAVIDON, MARY C. "Journey from Apple Orchard to Swallow
Thronged Loft: 'Fern Hill.'" English Journal 58 (January):
78-81.
    Offers a plan for teaching "Fern Hill" to the "uninitiated,"
including a stanza-by-stanza interpretation and a list of ques-
tions for discussion.

6   DAVIS, WILLIAM VIRGIL. "Several Comments on 'A Refusal to
Mourn the Death, by Fire, of a Child in London.'" Concerning
Poetry 2 (Fall):45-48.
    Comments on the "deceptively simple" quality of "A Refusal
to Mourn," emphasizing in particular the fact that the poem is
"a celebration of both death and life and of the eternal cycle
of becoming—in both the religious and aesthetic senses."

7   DAY-LEWIS, SEAN. "Radio Drama." Drama: The Quarterly
Theatre Review 94 (Autumn):58-59.
    Reviews Douglas Cleverdon's The Growth of Milk Wood, find-
ing this study of the genesis and textual variations of the radio
play valuable both for the general and academic reader. The
radio medium was "ideally suited" for Thomas's "free ranging
imagination."

8   FITZGIBBON, CONSTANTINE, ed. Twelve More Letters. London:
Turret, 23 pp.
    Supplements Selected Letters, also edited and introduced by
FitzGibbon.

9   FRIEDMAN, STANLEY. "Whitman and Laugharne: Dylan Thomas's
'Poem in October.'" Anglo-Welsh Review 18 (Summer):81-82.
    Compares "Poem in October" to Whitman's "There Was a Child
Went Forth." The two poems employ similar language, focus on a
child's link with nature, and end by purposefully condensing
aspects of time.

10   GILL, STEPHEN M. "A Consideration of Thomas's Poems in In
Country Sleep." Literary Criterion 9 (Winter):29-34.
    Discusses the Welsh poet's Welsh background and the dis-
tinct attitudes toward religion, nature, and human existence as
they are revealed in In Country Sleep. Comments on Thomas's
meticulous craft, especially with reference to his use of diction, imagery, and lyrical technique.

11   KANNEL, GREGORY JOSEPH. "Word, Structure, and Meaning in the
Poetry of Dylan Thomas." Ph.D. dissertation, Kent State
University, 116 pp.
    Examines Thomas's poetry by treating the individual poems
as organized symbolic collections that can be interpreted free of
biographical, historical, or artistic influences. The overall

intention is to discover the poetry's meaning in the context of
the world suggested by the poems themselves. In this poetic
world, the poet represents a special case in the life of man.
See Dissertation Abstracts International 30 (1970):5412A.

12   KELLY, RICHARD. "The Lost Vision of Dylan Thomas' 'One Warm
     Saturday.'" Studies in Short Fiction 6 (Winter):205-9.
        Compares the last story in A Portrait of the Artist as a
     Young Dog with Joyce's Portrait. Concludes that, like Joyce's
     protagonist, the "autobiographical" protagonist of Thomas's story
     "undergoes a strikingly similar process of maturing with one
     important difference—whereas Joyce's wading girl provides
     Stephen with aesthetic and emotional autonomy," the girl in
     Thomas's story fills the protagonist "with anguish and frustra-
     tion and returns him to an ugly, hostile world." The story ulti-
     mately centers on the "loss of innocence" theme and depicts a
     "hero whose fate is the tragedy of youth and the comedy of
     experience."

13   KIDDER, RUSHWORTH MOULTON. "Religious Imagery in the Poetry
     of Dylan Thomas." Ph.D. dissertation, Columbia University,
     265 pp.
        Tries to establish terms that can help to elucidate the
     religious import of Thomas's poetry. After developing an appro-
     priate critical approach for analyzing the religious quality of
     the poetry, the study moves on to a systematic analysis of
     Collected Poems. Finally, the conclusion is reached that, while
     in the early poems referential and allusive imagery are common,
     in the later poems thematic imagery takes over, ultimately lead-
     ing in the last poems to a style that more directly expresses his
     Christian thought. See Dissertation Abstracts International 33
     (1972):316A.

14   KOHAK, FRANCES MacPHERSON. "Concepts of Time in the Poetry
     of Dylan Thomas." Ph.D. dissertation, Boston University,
     176 pp.
        Looks at Thomas's use of time in his poetry. Thomas tried
     to join natural time and the physical life of man with man's
     understanding of present, past, and future time. In the end,
     he failed to resolve the paradox intellectually but he did suc-
     ceed in joining the conflicting dimensions by means of affirma-
     tive lyricism. See Dissertation Abstracts International 30
     (1969):2028A.

15   McKAY, DON. "Dot, Line and Circle: A Structural Approach to
     Dylan Thomas's Imagery." Anglo-Welsh Review 18 (Summer):
     69-80.
        Provides evidence that Thomas's poems can be seen as a
     "continuous narrative" using metaphors that are shaped like dots,
     line, or circles. Basically, these metaphors have sexual values:
     the dots are sexual seeds, the lines are phallic factors, and the
     circles are wombs, all suggestive in turn of Thomas's natural,
     cosmic vision.

16   MOSHER, HAROLD F., Jr. "The Structure of Dylan Thomas's 'The
     Peaches.'" Studies in Short Fiction 6 (Fall):536–47.
        Shows that, while autobiographical in certain subjective
     ways, "The Peaches" has Thomas actually employing dramatic juxta-
     position, imagery, and pacing as structural devices for express-
     ing the story's initiation theme. Through these structural
     techniques, Thomas "unifies the story and clarifies the conflict
     between imaginative life and dull existence."

17   O'HARA, J.D. "Dylan Thomas' Notebooks and Letters."
     Massachusetts Review 10 (Spring):397–401.
        Reviews Ralph Maud's The Notebooks of Dylan Thomas and
     Constantine FitzGibbon's edition of Selected Letters. Finds the
     primary interest of Maud's work to be the revelation of "how
     slowly Thomas achieved a satisfactory sound and then how quickly,
     that step taken, he achieved the sound of meaning." FitzGibbon's
     editing is faulted; the letters themselves are "painful" ex-
     hibits of Thomas's "increasingly desperate end-game."

18   ORMEROD, DAVID. "The Central Image in Dylan Thomas' 'Over
     Sir John's hill.'" English Studies 49 (October):449–50.
        Analyzes the significance of the extended comparison of
     hawk and hangman that appears in "Over Sir John's hill." Con-
     cludes that in the end this key image "perhaps" stands for
     "execution by burning at the stake" and, with the addition of
     the word "fuse," ultimately the modern equivalent of the electric
     chair.

19   PERRINE, LAURENCE. "Thomas' 'Poem in October,' Stanza I."
     Explicator 27 (February): item 43.
        Explains that the reason why the syntax of the first stanza
     of "Poem in October" has caused some interpretative difficulty is
     because of grammatical spacing. The distance between a gerund
     and an infinitive and their objects is extraordinary.

20   PORTER, PETER. "Spring in Llareggyb." New Statesman 77
     (27 June):911.
        Reviews Douglas Cleverdon's The Growth of "Milk Wood."
     Finds the introductory comments about Thomas as radio writer and
     actor full of insights, although the part of the study tracing
     the growth and variations of the texts is useful too. Concludes
     that the play is "a successful comedy and not an awe-inspiring
     swan song."

21   PRESS, JOHN. "Dylan Thomas." In A Map of Modern English
     Verse. London: Oxford University Press, pp. 218–29 passim.
        Points out that the "crucial question" about Thomas is the
     "extent to which he was able to make valid poetry out of his
     aberrations." In the course of reaching the conclusion that
     Thomas was a "flawed and tragic figure," Press compares him with
     the writers who seemed to influence him most. Though Thomas
     admired Yeats and Hardy, he was a very different kind of poet,
     sharing important characteristics instead with Rimbaud, Beddoes,

and Hart Crane, particularly the "committal of the self to
death."

22   PRICE, CECIL. Review of Poet in the Making: The Notebooks of
     Dylan Thomas. Anglo-Welsh Review 17 (Winter):202-3.
        Praises Ralph Maud's scholarship and "illuminating" notes
     and introductory commentary.

23   STAFFORD, JEAN. Review of A Child's Christmas in Wales. New
     Yorker 45 (13 December):197.
        Recommends New Direction's publication of Thomas's
     Christmas story for the season because of the tale's "haunting,
     wry evocation of boyhood Christmases."

24   THEISEN, Sister LOIS. "Dylan Thomas: A Bibliography of
     Secondary Criticism." Bulletin of Bibliography 26:9-28, 32,
     36, 59-60.
        Offers a bibliography of "general and specific critical
     studies" of Thomas. Designed to be of aid to students and
     scholars, it attempts to cover thirty years of secondary criti-
     cism starting with the year 1935.

25   THOMPSON, THOMAS NORMAN. "Patterns of Imagery in the Poetry
     of Dylan Thomas." Ph.D. dissertation, University of Pennsyl-
     vania, 259 pp.
        Examines systematically the recurring imagery in Thomas's
     poetry, analyzing in detail the kinds of images used and tracing
     their chronological development. Showing the progression of
     imagery patterns finally leads to an elucidation of Thomas's
     creative consciousness and obsessive thoughts. See Dissertation
     Abstracts International 30 (1970):3026A.

26   "Two Swansea Poets: Dylan Thomas and Vernon Watkins."
     Exhibition Catalog. Swansea: Public Libraries Committee,
     30 pp.
        Provides the notes accompanying a public exhibition of the
     achievements of Thomas and Vernon Watkins.

27   WHITTINGTON-EGAN, RICHARD. "Under Milk Wood." Contemporary
     Review 215 (September):164-65.
        Reviews Douglas Cleverdon's The Growth of Milk Wood,
     applauding the "prodigious industry" of tracing the complex
     development of the play. In the end, the main value of the study
     lies in its revealing how the mind of a "remarkable" poet worked.

28   WITTREICH, JOSEPH ANTHONY, Jr. "Dylan Thomas' Conception of
     Poetry: A Debt to Blake." English Language Notes 6 (March):
     197-200.
        Presents evidence of Blake's influence on Thomas. Con-
     cludes that Thomas appeared to "borrow" Blake's idea of "con-
     traries" and then applied it to his own theory of poetry.
     Thomas also learned from Blake how to employ form "to define"
     the "discovery" of a poem.

1970

1   AMIS, KINGSLEY. "'Thomas the Rhymer' and 'An Evening with
    Dylan Thomas.'" In What Became of Jane Austen? And Other
    Questions. New York: Harcourt, Brace, Jovanovich, pp. 54–62.
        Reviews A Prospect of the Sea and recalls an evening spent
    at a pub with Thomas prior to a planned talk by the poet at
    University College of Swansea. Thomas's book is mildly praised,
    particularly where it brings to mind the "comparatively disci-
    plined, responsible" writer of Portrait of the Artist. The most
    striking thing remarked about Thomas's personality was his good-
    natured shyness. Second item a reprint of 1957.1.

2   BRAND, J. "Structure Signals in 'The Hunchback in the Park.'"
    English Journal 59 (February):195–200.
        Analyzes "The Hunchback in the Park" by focusing on
    Thomas's complex use of grammar. The poem's expression of theme
    depends on the grammatical structure of its three declarative
    sentences.

3   CHANDLER, PATRICIA GAIL. "Gerard Manley Hopkins and Dylan
    Thomas: A Study in Computational Stylistics." Ph.D. disser-
    tation, Louisiana State University, 151 pp.
        Compares "the incidence of certain linguistic features"
    found in ten sonnets each by Thomas and Hopkins. Fifteen addi-
    tional sonnets by various late nineteenth-century writers serve
    as a third source of study. The statistical information garnered
    is used to provide specific observations about poetic style.
    See Dissertation Abstracts International 31 (1971):4747A.

4   CHURCHILL, R.C. "The Age of T.S. Eliot." In The Concise
    History of English Literature. Edited by George Sampson.
    3d ed. Cambridge: Cambridge University Press, pp. 862–64.
        Compares Thomas unfavorably with such poets as Edward
    Thomas.

5   "Dylan's Cell." Times (London), 1 May, p. 10.
        Reports on John Summer's effort to buy the Boathouse and
    set it aside as a haven for writers.

6   FITZGIBBON, CONSTANTINE. "Dylan Thomas: A Letter." Dublin
    Magazine 8 (Spring):56–58.
        Gives a summary in letter form of his acquaintanceship
    with Thomas.

7   JACOBSON, ROBERT. "Williams as Thomas." Saturday Review 53
    (25 April):74.
        Praises Emlyn Williams's portrayal of Thomas in his "A Boy
    Growing Up," particularly his ability to express the poet's
    "childlike innocence" that existed beneath the "surface bravado
    and extravagance."

8   JENKINS, DAVID CLAY. "Shrine of the Boily Boy: The Dylan
Thomas Notebooks at Buffalo." Anglo-Welsh Review 19 (Autumn):
114-29.
     Describes going to see the notebooks of Thomas kept at his
"shrine" at the University of Buffalo. Believes that the notebooks are given too much value, particularly by Ralph Maud.
Thomas "developed a great and broad view" after "the provincial,
self-centered, prurient adolescent" coming out of the notebooks
that he sold for money.

9   KLEINMAN, HYMAN H. "Dylan Thomas: A Work of Words."
Computers and the Humanities 4 (March):275-77.
     Praises R.C. Williams's A Concordance to the Collected Poems
as an "immeasurably important reference work" that provides
scholars with very valuable information concerning Thomas's use
of imagery, vocabulary, and verbal construction.

10   LAFFAL, JULIUS. "Toward a Conceptual Grammar and Lexicon."
Computers and the Humanities 4 (January):173-85.
     Proposes and illustrates conceptual grammar and lexicon by
comparing parts of "Over Sir John's hill" with parts of
Gulliver's Travels.

11   McCORMICK, JANE. "'Sorry, Old Christian.'" Anglo-Welsh
Review 18 (February):78-82.
     Describes the close relationship between Thomas and Vernon
Watkins. Watkins played a highly influential role in the
development of Thomas's craft. He didn't succeed, however, in
passing on his quiet Christian faith to his young friend.

12   McDONALD, GERALD D. Review of Dylan Thomas' Early Prose.
Library Journal 95 (1 May):1746.
     Recommends Annis Pratt's study as an "illuminating guide
for the serious student" already acquainted with Thomas's work.
In his early writing, Thomas joined mythology, religion, and
occultism creatively with imagery, symbolism, and thematic
structure.

*13   MARLAND, MICHAEL, ed. Dylan Thomas. The Times Authors, 3.
London: Times Newspapers.
     See Annual Bibliography of English Language and Literature
45 (1970):649.

14   MAUD, RALPH N., and GLOVER, ALBERT. Dylan Thomas in Print:
A Bibliographical History. Pittsburgh: University of
Pittsburgh Press, 264 pp.
     Lists Thomas's publications and whatever was written about
the poet that "seemed to be of possible interest to the literary
historian or the curious general reader." Comments on Thomas's
fluctuating reputation are found in a preface. Criticism found
in periodicals and newspapers is broken down into Welsh, English,
North American, and foreign publications sections. Contains
reprint of 1956.1.

15   MORTON, RICHARD. An Outline of the Works of Dylan Thomas.
     Toronto: Forum House, 111 pp.
        Provides a reader's aid to the writing (especially the
     poetry) of Thomas. A summary of the life is included.

16   MOYNIHAN, WILLIAM TRUMBULL. "Dylan Thomas." Contemporary
     Literature 11 (Autumn):586–88.
        Reviews Annis Pratt's Dylan Thomas' Early Prose. Primarily
     myth criticism, the study is more successful at accumulating than
     distinguishing meaning. But there is a wealth of important in-
     formation about Thomas's use of mythology, religion, Blake, and
     surrealism.

17   MURPHY, MICHAEL W. "Thomas' 'Do not go gentle into that good
     night.'" Explicator 28 (February): item 55.
        Attempts to explain the references in the poem to "wise
     men," "good men," "wild men," and "grave men." "Taken all to-
     gether, the references . . . suggest that life is always too
     brief and incomplete for everyone, regardless of how he has
     lived."

18   MURTY, G. SRI RAMA. "Dylan Thomas's 'The Hunchback in the
     Park.'" Triveni: Journal of Indian Renaissance 38 (January):
     22–32.
        Emphasizes Thomas's concern with the "vocation" of poetry
     as it is revealed in "The Hunchback in the Park." Thus, in this
     poem he resembles Wallace Stevens, a poet with whom he otherwise
     "has very little in common."

19   NEILL, MICHAEL. "Dylan Thomas's 'Tailor Age.'" Notes and
     Queries 17 (February):59–63.
        Discusses Thomas's use of the tailor as a symbolic figure.
     Frequently found in his prewar poetry, this figure "embodies the
     creation/destruction antinomy" seen by Thomas to be the "dynamic
     principle in all natural processes."

20   "Poet's Fund Wound Up." Times (London), 25 February, p. 4.
        Reports on an unsuccessful effort to raise funds to pur-
     chase and renovate the Boathouse.

21   PRATT, ANNIS VILAS. Dylan Thomas' Early Prose: A Study in
     Creative Mythology. Pittsburgh: University of Pittsburgh
     Press, 229 pp.
        Looks at Thomas's early prose and its connection with his
     poetry. The study of the early lyrical tales (those written
     before 1940) concentrates on analyzing the textual, mythological,
     religious, and magical factors. A discussion of the source of
     literary inspiration (with some reference to surrealism) is in-
     cluded in the attempt to see the overall unity of the writing.
     It becomes clear that the early prose was created "out of the
     inner vision" of an extremely subjective young man and the later,
     "pared of symbolism and mythology," diverged from earlier lyrical
     writing and evolved increasingly toward dramatic objectivity.
     Draws on the author's dissertation (see Pratt, 1965.42).

22   SITWELL, EDITH. <u>Selected Letters, 1919-1964</u>. New York:
     Vanguard Press, pp. 54 passim.
         Writing in a 1935 letter, she offers the prediction that
     Thomas "stands a chance of becoming a great poet, if only he gets
     rid of his complexes." The following year she writes him
     directly to praise "A grief ago" for its strange beauty. Subse-
     quent letters are full of her admiration for the young man who
     "is going to be a great poet."

23   STALKER, JAMES CURTIS. "The Stylistic and Interpretative
     Functions of Relative Clauses in Dylan Thomas's Poetry: A
     Transformational Analysis." Ph.D. dissertation, University
     of Wisconsin, 201 pp.
         Applies transformational analysis to relative clauses found
     in sixteen selected poems. An understanding of this idiosyn-
     cratic device helps in the interpretation of Thomas's poetry.
     The primary stylistic characters that are thus revealed are
     tension, density, and ambiguity. See <u>Dissertation Abstracts
     International</u> 31 (1970):1815A.

24   STRONGIN, THEODORE. "A Dylan Thomas Poem Heard as Chamber
     Work." <u>New York Times</u>, 27 October, p. 54.
         Reviews John Coriglano's commissioned musical version of
     "Poem in October." While it has an "engaging air of fantasy,"
     the rendition fails to suggest the original's "poetic surge."

25   TRITSCHLER, DONALD. "The Basic Texts." <u>Southern Review</u> 6
     (Winter):263-66.
         Praises Ralph Maud's careful, informative editing of <u>The
     Notebooks of Dylan Thomas</u>. We are allowed "fascinating" glimpses
     of how many of the poems developed or came about.

26   WEST, PAUL. <u>Doubt and Dylan Thomas</u>. Toronto: University of
     Toronto Press, 20 pp.
         Considers the issue of belief in Thomas's writing.

27   WHITE, WILLIAM. "Beware the Poet's Widow; or, a Note on a
     Dylan Thomas MS." <u>American Book Collector</u> 20 (May):32.
         Gives the circumstances of the "loss" of the <u>Under Milk
     Wood</u> manuscript.

28   WOLFE, LESLIE ROSENBERG. "The Poems and Poetics of Dylan
     Thomas: The Life of His Art." Ph.D. dissertation, University
     of Florida, 204 pp.
         Examines the connection between the structure and stylis-
     tics of Thomas's poetry and his belief in a life dedicated to
     imagination and creation. His poems represent his celebration of
     the process and multiplicity of creation, and the poetics he
     employs (especially his attempts to establish unity and integrity
     in structure and texture) offer a critical way of interpreting
     the poems dedicated to life. See <u>Dissertation Abstracts Inter-
     national</u> 35 (1974):3778A.

1 ADAMS, ROBERT MARTIN. "Crashaw and Dylan Thomas: Devotional
   Athletes." In Strains of Discord. Freeport, N.Y.: Books for
   Libraries Press, pp. 128–45.
   Reprint of 1955.1.

2 BROWER, BROCK. "Dylan's Boathouse." Esquire 75 (January):
   96, 169.
       Reports on Caitlin Thomas's attempt to sell the Boathouse
   and reminisces about the legendary poet.

3 BROYARD, ANATOLE. "Dirge for Dylan—or for Us?" New York
   Times, 8 October, p. 41.
       Reviews The Poems of Dylan Thomas, complaining that the
   editor, Daniel Jones, has not served Thomas well by including the
   worst along with the best poems. But the most "disheartening"
   impression left by the collection is that Thomas's "iambic
   apocalypses" no longer offer what this age demands to hear.

4 DAVIES, WALFORD D., ed. Dylan Thomas: Early Prose Writings.
   New York: New Directions; London: J.M. Dent, 214 pp.
       Comments in an introduction on Thomas's views about his own
   prose writing.

5 EMPSON, WILLIAM. "Some More Dylan Thomas." Listener 86
   (28 October):588–90.
       Reviews Early Prose Writing and Dylan Thomas: The Poems.
   Welcomes the first book especially because Thomas even in his
   minor work was capable of "glittering" writing. The second (by
   Daniel Jones) fails to provide very much elucidating information
   about Thomas's poetry.

6 FINNEY, BRIAN. "Dylan Thomas's 'A Visit to Grandpa's.'"
   London Review 8 (Winter):31–35.
       Analyzes Thomas's juxtaposition of emotional and natural-
   istic language and the way he consequently can merge childhood
   dreaming and adult fact into an overlapping world of fantasy and
   reality. The technique ultimately manages to give his characters
   an essential personal integrity.

7 FISHLOCK, TREVOR. "Fishguard Transformed into Llareggyb by
   Dylan Thomas Film Makers." Times (London), 1 February, p. 3.
       Gives a report on the progress of the film production of
   Under Milk Wood and explains why Fishguard was chosen as the
   appropriate setting.

8 GILBERTSON, PHILIP NATHAN. "Time and the Timeless in the
   Poetry of T.S. Eliot, Dylan Thomas, and Edwin Muir." Ph.D.
   dissertation, University of Kentucky, 215 pp.
       Discusses the similar responses to the problem of time
   found in the poetry of Thomas, Eliot, and Edwin Muir. The poets,
   in general, start on a poetic journey arising from darkness and
   leading to an affirmative lighted place existing forever in the

temporal context. At first desperate about the weight of
endless process, Thomas grew to understand that the problem of
time could be best dealt with by means of mythical ritual and
fable. See Dissertation Abstracts International 33 (1972):752A.

9   GILMORE, HAYDN. "Dylan Thomas as Journalist." Journalism
     Quarterly 48 (Autumn):554-58.
         Looks at Thomas's experience in journalism, suggesting that
     his brief career in this line "perhaps saved him from complete
     verbal obscurity." Thomas's writing seems to prove the fact that
     "there is a tension between bad journalism and good poetry."

10   GINGERICH, MARTIN E. "Dylan Thomas and the Ark of the
     Covenant." Anglo-Welsh Review 19 (Spring):183-85.
         Investigates the correspondences between Thomas and Noah of
     the Ark, with whom the poet compares himself in the "Author's
     Prologue." They were essentially alike in their faiths, doubts,
     and hopeful work.

11   _____. "Rhetoric and Meaning in 'A Refusal to Mourn.'" Notes
     on Contemporary Literature 1 (January):5-6.
         Paraphrases "A Refusal to Mourn" by way of showing the sig-
     nificance of rhetorical usage. The rhetorical style reveals the
     writer's feelings about death. The purposeful simplicity of
     style adds to the depth of emotion.

*12 GOODMAN, R. "Three Poems by Dylan Thomas." UNISA English
     Studies 9 (March):27-29.
         See Annual Bibliography of English Language and Literature
     46 (1971):703.

13   "Home of Dylan Thomas is Sought as Memorial." New York Times,
     18 March, p. 20.
         Reports on the efforts of the Dylan Thomas Society of the
     Netherlands to raise funds for the purchase of the poet's home
     in Laugharne.

14   JONES, RICHARD. "Verses and Conundrums." Times (London),
     14 June, p. 8.
         Reviews Daniel Jones's Dylan Thomas: The Poems and Clark
     Emery's The World of Dylan Thomas. Jones offers little new
     knowledge and, by including many previously unpublished poems,
     does more harm than good to Thomas's reputation. Emery's expli-
     cations are praised for their clear reasoning and great learning.

15   JONES, T. JAMES. "A Bilingual Llareggyb." Planet 8
     (October-November):29-32.
         Points out some of the problems of translating Under Milk
     Wood into Welsh, particularly with reference to various images,
     phrases, and rhymes.

16   KARRER, WOLFGANG. Die Metaphorik in den Collected Poems von
      Dylan Thomas: Eine syntaktische Untersuch. Bonn: Bouvier
      Verlag Herbert Grundmann, 175 pp.
          Attempts to arrive at a new understanding and appreciation
      of the Collected Poems by means of a systematic analysis of the
      syntactic structures of Thomas's poetry.

17   KORG, JACOB. Review of Dylan Thomas' Early Prose. Western
      Humanities Review 25 (Winter):90-91.
          Believes Annis Pratt's study to be a useful examination of
      the relationship between the short stories and "their mythic
      analogues," especially since the critic "defines the distinguish-
      ing quality that differentiates Thomas from other revivers of
      legend and mythology; the others regard them as primitive ver-
      sions of modern insights, but to Thomas the myths are still
      myths."

18   MAYOUX, JEAN-JACQUES. "Dylan Thomas au Bois lacté." Critique
      27 (September):675-87.
          Praises Under Milk Wood as a work in which Thomas accom-
      plished what he truly intended. It works particularly well as
      an expression of the writer's sympathy for the universal condi-
      tion of man.

19   MELLER, HORST. "Dylan Thomas." In Englische Dichter der
      Moderne: Ihr Leben und Werk. Edited by Rudolph Sühnel and
      Dieter Riesner. Berlin: Schmidt, pp. 489-509.
          Surveys the life and work of Thomas.

20   MELLOWN, ELGIN W. Review of Dylan Thomas in Print. South
      Atlantic Quarterly 70 (Summer):432-33.
          Reviews Ralph Maud's work, finding the bibliography to be
      an "excellent" study aid despite its "idiosyncratic form."

21   MEYER, ROBERT H. "Dylan Thomas: The Experience, the Picture,
      and the Message." English Journal 60 (February):199-204.
          Shows Thomas's poems moving consciously from experience to
      picture to theme. The poetic technique "imitates and reflects
      the paradoxes and seeming disparities of existence," arriving
      like life at a "unified whole."

22   PARSHALL, PETER F. "Thomas' 'The force that through the green
      fuse drives the flower.'" Explicator 29 (April): item 65.
          Interprets the last stanza of the poem as being dominated
      by the creative mood with the "destructive motif" serving as the
      paradoxical negative "echo."

23   PEARSON, GABRIEL. "Gabriel Pearson on Dylan Thomas."
      Spectator 227 (20 November):731-32.
          Complains about the "marked indifference" that met the
      publication of Dylan Thomas: The Poems and Dylan Thomas: The
      Early Prose Writings. Speculates that the Thomas "legend" is
      the enemy of a true appreciation of his great achievements.
      Finds many points of comparison between Thomas and W.H. Auden,

concluding that the two together represented the "sundered halves
of the great modernist poet that English poetry, after Eliot,
failed to throw up."

24   RAY, PAUL C. The Surrealist Movement in England. Ithaca,
      N.Y.: Cornell University Press, pp. 277–86 passim.
      Claims that Thomas was influenced by surrealism more than
any other major poet of our time. He was not a pure surrealist,
however, because it's clear that he "deliberately uses the sur-
face effects of surrealism," never giving in to "automatism" in
his creative process. Thomas managed to create the surrealistic-
like merging of dream and reality by employing "rigidly controlled artistry."

25   REDMOND, JOHN. "Dylan Thomas." Library Review 23 (Fall):
      117–18.
      Reviews Emery Clark's The World of Dylan Thomas and Daniel
Jones's edition of The Poems. Faults Clark for a rather forced
expositional approach but commends Jones's work, especially the
background information that accompanies what "will have to be"
the "standard edition" of Thomas's poems.

26   _____. "Early Thomas." Library Review 23 (Winter):163.
      Reviews Walford Davies's edition of Early Prose Writings.
The main value of the book lies in its strengthening the common
knowledge about Thomas's "interest in eccentrics, his preference
for 'dark, passionate beauty,'" and the fact that "from the first
his gift was 'imaginative and verbal.'"

27   Review of Dylan Thomas' Early Prose: A Study in Creative
      Mythology. Choice 8 (October):1020.
      Recommends Annis Pratt's study mainly for its insights into
the mythic aspects of the early work of Thomas.

28   Review of Dylan Thomas in Print: A Bibliographical History.
      Choice 8 (December):1319.
      Finds Ralph Maud's bibliographical work to be cumbersome
and difficult to use.

29   SISSON, C.H. "The Forties: George Barker; Dylan Thomas;
      Patrick Kavanagh; David Gascoyne." In English Poetry, 1900–
      1950: An Assessment. New York: St. Martin's Press,
      pp. 249–51, 254.
      Agrees that, as Thomas once said, he was a "freak user of
words," finds that he lacked emotional and intellectual development, and concludes that he is thus only historically significant as the "prototype of much of the literary pretensions of
the forties."

30   TANE, MIRIAM. "In Dylan Thomas's Footsteps." New York Times,
      17 January, sec. 10, pp. 2–3.
      Takes a tour of the most memorable places in Thomas's
life, using biographical information and key lines as reference
markers.

31   "Then Nothing New." Times Literary Supplement, 30 July,
     p. 893.
        Reviews Clark Emery's The World of Dylan Thomas and Daniel
     Jones's edition of Dylan Thomas: The Poems. Dismisses Emery's
     work as a collection of "suspect" paraphrases. The publication
     of The Poems is not enthusiastically applauded because the addi-
     tion of many poems that Thomas chose not to include in Collected
     Poems shows clearly that he was "better than most poets at decid-
     ing what was his best work."

32   THWAITE, ANTHONY. "Early Spring in Cwmdonkin Drive." New
     Statesman 81 (28 May):738–39.
        Reviews Clark Emery's The World of Dylan Thomas and Daniel
     Jones's edition of Dylan Thomas: The Poems. Emery's work is
     dismissed as another volume of "bad" Thomas criticism. It draws
     a "thick web of unhelpful verbiage over the poems it discusses."
     Jones's work is especially valuable in revealing "more clearly
     than ever before the rise and fall of a poet."

33   TODD, RUTHVEN. "Dylan Thomas, a Personal Memoir."
     Mediterranean Review 1 (Spring):15–23.
        Gives a sampling of the projected book by Todd promising
     to tell Thomas's story, with particular stress on the London
     days in the thirties when the author knew the poet as a young
     friend.

34   TRITSCHLER, DONALD. "The Stories in Dylan Thomas' Red Note-
     book." Journal of Modern Literature 2 (September):33–56.
        Looks at the short stories appearing in Thomas's "Red
     Notebook." The ten stories reveal Thomas exploring most of his
     major themes before he reached twenty. As in his early poems,
     in these stories Thomas concentrates on such issues as the para-
     doxes of creation, man's loss of innocence, the omnipresence of
     death and evil, and the struggle between flesh and spirit.

35   WHITE, WILLIAM. "Everything by and about Dylan Thomas."
     American Book Collector 21 (March–April):2.
        Recommends Ralph Maud's Dylan Thomas in Print to anyone
     who is an admirer of Thomas's "wonderful but disturbing poetic
     personality."

36   WHITTINGTON-EGAN, RICHARD. "More of Dylan Thomas."
     Contemporary Review 219 (July):52–53.
        Reviews Daniel Jones's edition of Dylan Thomas: The Poems
     and Clark Emery's The World of Dylan Thomas. Jones's work is
     especially important for the chronological arrangement of the
     poems, thus allowing one to discover the technical growth and
     the development of innovative imagery in the work as a whole.
     While Emery's explications are not indispensable, they provide
     useful "calibrations" to set against the interpretations of Elder
     Olson and William York Tindall.

37   WILLINGHAM, JOHN R. Review of <u>The Poems of Dylan Thomas</u>.
      <u>Library Journal</u> 96 (July):2325.
      Recommends Daniel Jones's edition of the poems. By adding
many poems not contained in <u>Collected Poems</u> and providing important bibliographical and technical notes, Jones has "strongly
enhanced" Thomas's reputation as a major poet.

38   WOODCOCK, GEORGE. "A Dubious Thomas." <u>New Leader</u> 54
      (1 November):18-19.
      Reviews Daniel Jones's edition of <u>The Poems of Dylan
Thomas</u>. This new collection, which adds more than one hundred to
the ninety included in <u>Collected Poems</u>, is an "ambivalent gift"
because it fails to give the reader anything new that represents
the poet "at his best." Also comments on how much attitudes on
Thomas had changed since his death.

                                   1972

1   BARNES, CLIVE. "Stage: Thomas, Poet Too." <u>New York Times</u>,
      8 February, p. 25.
      Reviews a revival of Sidney Michael's <u>Dylan</u>, a play that
offers a "fascinating documentary picture" of Thomas's painful
last years. This is a "good slick" dramatization that provides a
"portrait of the artist as old dog" howling at the "failure of
his moon."

2   BERNARD, JACQUELINE. "La topographie poétique de Dylan
      Thomas: 'Le Bois lacté' entre 'La carte du tendre' et 'le
      pays du ciel.'" <u>Études anglaises</u> 25 (April-June):261-71.
      Argues that <u>Under Milk Wood</u> represents not a divergence on
the part of Thomas from his "difficult" poetry but a work that
illustrates a consistent, progressive "evolution" in his art.

3   BRINK, A.W. "Psychoanalysis and Literature." <u>Queen's
      Quarterly</u> 79 (Winter):572-74.
      Praises David Holbrook's <u>Dylan Thomas: The Code of Night</u>
as an excellent Freudian study of the artist's "unconscious"
creative process. Merging "compellingly" humanism and psychoanalysis, the critic succeeds in placing Thomas's poetry in the
"context of a struggling ego," thus clarifying much of the poet's
"obscurity."

4   BURDETTE, ROBERT KENLEY. <u>The Saga of Prayer: The Poetry of
      Dylan Thomas</u>. Studies in English Literature 67. The Hague:
      Mouton, 160 pp.
      Recognizes the difficulties of interpreting Thomas's
poetry at the start, then goes on to show that the poet's work
actually contains a consistent and unified vision and meaning.
The central vision is akin to gnosticism, and the grand vision
of Thomas can be discovered by linking the doctrine and imagery
of gnosticism with his thought and poetic language. Based on a
detailed examination of some of Thomas's long poems, the conclusion is drawn that the writing expresses an "ecstatic awareness

of the beauty that is sacred in this world" and that this mystic
vision ultimately places the work in the mainstream of modern
poetry inspired by essential religious attitudes.

5   BURKE, THOMAS EDMUND. "A Descriptive Catalogue of the Dylan
     Thomas Collection at the University of Texas at Austin."
     Ph.D. dissertation, University of Texas, 343 pp.
          Describes the holdings of the Dylan Thomas Collection at
     the University of Texas and surveys the materials with an eye
     toward their usefulness. The descriptive catalog is categorized
     to help the researcher specifically interested in bibliographi-
     cal, textual, analytical, and biographical work. See Disserta-
     tion Abstracts International 32 (1972):6414A.

6   CREWE, J.V. "The Poetry of Dylan Thomas." Theoria 38:65-83.
          Gives an overview of the achievement of Thomas.

7   DAVIES, WALFORD D. Dylan Thomas. Cardiff: University of
     Wales Press on behalf of the Welsh Arts Council, 94 pp.
          Looks at Thomas's life and work as a whole. His last poems
     "attempt to merge and submerge personal elegy in an awareness of
     a more general mortality whose pattern is not annihilation but
     change." If these poems exhibit any technical "danger," it's the
     tendency for "too much verbal glamour."

8   _____. Review of "Under Milk Wood": Account of an Action to
     Recover the Original Manuscript. Notes and Queries 19
     (February):71-72.
          Suggests that, based on the evidence in J.S. Cox's account,
     Thomas would have "enjoyed" being present at the legal proceed-
     ings held to decide who was the rightful owner of the manuscript
     of the play-for-voices.

9   _____, ed. Dylan Thomas: New Critical Essays. London: J.M.
     Dent, 291 pp.
          Collects eleven critical essays that reflect how Thomas's
     reputation stands some twenty years after the publication of
     Collected Poems. Various writers see Thomas as a supreme artist,
     psychological oddity, wounded genius, profound metaphysical or
     religious voice. Five of the essays take a phenomenological look
     at his work. While most of the pieces deal with the nature of
     the poet and the poetry, the last one focuses on Under Milk Wood.
     In the introduction, the editor suggests that it is now time to
     look critically at the poetry of Thomas independent of what kind
     of man he was supposed to have been.

10   EVANS, D.R., and HARDY, J.P. "Dylan Thomas." Times Literary
     Supplement, 23 June, p. 719.
          Shows that Thomas was influenced by Milton, that his in-
     terest in the great poet was "early and lasting."

11   "For Cash, Rather Than Posterity." Times Literary Supplement,
      3 March, p. 254.
           Reviews Early Prose Writing and Ralph Maud's Dylan Thomas
      in Print. Having the knack of "creative rejection," Thomas would
      have been the first to admit that little of his prose need be
      saved for posterity. His primary prose talent seemed to lie in
      "comic-fantastic dialogue." Maud's work is very helpful in
      charting the crooked path of Thomas's reputation.

12   GRUEN, JOHN. The Party's Over Now: Reminiscences of the
      Fifties. New York: Viking Press, pp. 25, 27–30.
           Recalls a party given by Oscar Williams for Thomas. The
      poet drank heavily, but when he spoke of his home or read poetry,
      the experience was "literally breathtaking."

13   HAVARD, ROBERT G. "The Symbolic Ambivalence of 'Green' in
      García Lorca and Dylan Thomas." Modern Language Review 67
      (October):810–19.
           Shows that, like Lorca, Thomas used the color green as a
      symbolic expression of conflict. There is evidence (specifically
      in Lorca's "Roman Sonámbulo" and Thomas's "Fern Hill") that both
      poets were consciously attempting to express "archetypal rather
      than idiosyncratic or esoteric values" through the symbol.

14   HOGLER, RAYMOND LOUIS. "Diction and Metaphor in the Poetry of
      Dylan Thomas." Ph.D. dissertation, University of Colorado,
      218 pp.
           Argues that the many frustrated attempts to interpret some
      of Thomas's difficult poetry stems from a conceptual failure to
      understand the unique language of the poems. The study system-
      atically examines a number of critical evaluations of the poet,
      goes on to discuss the development of his distinct idiom, and
      ends by focusing on his use of diction and metaphor and his
      relation to literature as a tradition. See Dissertation
      Abstracts International 33 (1973):4417A.

15   _____. "Dylan Thomas: The Development of an Idiom." Anglo-
      Welsh Review 21 (Summer):113–23; (Winter):102–13.
           Analyzes Thomas's unique poetic style. Although difficult,
      it's "by no means incomprehensible or nonsensical." He developed
      this style after an "arduous period of experimentation and
      apprenticeship." Once he developed his personal style, he never
      abandoned it.

16   HOLBROOK, DAVID. Dylan Thomas: The Code of Night. London:
      Athlone Press, University of London, 271 pp.
           Employs new psychological discoveries in trying to show
      that Thomas was essentially a schizoid person whose writing was
      an "anguished attempt" at self-identification. The schizoid
      diagnosis reveals a "strategy of survival" in face of the "ter-
      rible truth" that Thomas's vitality "asserts life" even while it
      "conceals death and destruction."

17　LEITCH, VINCENT B.　"Herbert's Influence in Dylan Thomas's 'I see the boys of summer.'" Notes and Queries 19 (September): 341.
　　Points out the close resemblance between George Herbert's dialectical Christian image used in "The Search" and Thomas's "kissing poles" image used in "I see the boys of summer."

18　LOESCH, KATHARINE TAYLOR.　"The Shape of Sound: Configurational Rime in the Poetry of Dylan Thomas." In Studies in Interpretation. Edited by Esther M. Doyle and Virginia H. Floyd. Amsterdam: Rodopi N.V., pp. 33-66.
　　Reprint of 1968.13.

19　NORMAN, BARRY.　"Aquarius." Times (London), 6 March, p. 10.
　　Describes what was contained in ITV's "quiet memoir" of the poet.

20　NYE, ROBERT.　"The Death of Dylan Thomas." Books and Bookmen 18 (October):i-vii.
　　Looks at Thomas's failures as a poet and human being.　The totally self-centered view of life in his early poetry never did develop into anything more.　The real subject of his early work is masturbation.

21　PRITCHARD, WILLIAM H.　"Youngsters, Middlesters, and Some Old Boys." Hudson Review 25 (Spring):129-30.
　　Reviews The Poems of Dylan Thomas and discovers that during the course of the years he has regretfully come to agree with Geoffrey Grigson's assessment that there was too much verbal acrobatics and too little fun in Thomas's poetry.

22　Review of Dylan Thomas: Early Prose Writings. Choice 9 (November):1134.
　　Finds Walford Davies's edition to be a collection of mostly superficial items, valuable perhaps for the Thomas scholar but dull for the general reader.　It "adds nothing important to the Thomas canon."

23　Review of The Poems of Dylan Thomas. Choice 9 (July):648.
　　Recommends Daniel Jones's edition of Thomas's poems.　This collection gives a fuller picture of the poet's development than the Collected Poems volume by including about one hundred additional numbers.

24　SCHERTING, JACK.　"Echoes of Look Homeward Angel in Dylan Thomas's A Child's Christmas in Wales." Studies in Short Fiction 9 (Fall):404-6.
　　Argues that Thomas's A Child's Christmas in Wales is based not only on childhood memories but also on recollections from reading Thomas Wolfe's Look Homeward Angel.　There are too many "striking parallels" between the story and the novel to be mere coincidences.

25 THOMAS, AERONWY. "Dylan Thomas's Daughter, Aeronwy, Talks to
    Mervyn Levy About Her Childhood at Laugharne in Wales."
    Listener 88 (5 October):433-5.
        Describes Thomas's writing and drinking habits as recalled
    by his daughter.

26 TURPIN, ELIZABETH RICE. "Rhetoric and Rhythm in Twentieth-
    Century Sonnets by Hopkins, Auden, Frost, Cummings, Thomas,
    and Merrill Moore." Ph.D. dissertation, Texas A&M University,
    385 pp.
        Discusses the sonnet's tradition, emphasizing the need to
    consider it as a genre instead of a form. Looks at selections
    from several important poets who have helped to continue the life
    of the sonnet in the present century. All the poets under dis-
    cussion are found to have written sonnets that relate back to the
    early Italian sonnets, especially with reference to the charac-
    teristic employment of rhetoric, rhythm, persona, theme, and
    structure. See Dissertation Abstracts International 33 (1973):
    4368A.

27 WILLIAMS, HARRY. "Dylan Thomas's Poetry of Redemption: Its
    Blakean Beginnings." Bucknell Review 20 (Winter):107-20.
        Shows that the Blakean theme of "generation and creation"
    was an obsessive one in Thomas's early poetry. Thomas's Note-
    books provide a great deal of evidence of just how powerful
    Blake's influence was on him. Ultimately, the role language
    played for the two poets is different, with Blake's ideal "sung"
    by Thomas to fulfill the "vanity of realization."

                               1973

1   BRUNS, GERALD L. "Daedalus, Orpheus, and Dylan Thomas's
    Portrait of the Artist." Renascence 25 (Spring):147-56.
        Compares Thomas's Portrait of the Artist with Joyce's.
    Joyce's protagonist dreams of poetic flight into "transcendence";
    Thomas's is "dominated by the earth and its people." The effect
    of Thomas's stories is to discover "an artist distinguished by
    his humanity . . . not by any god-like or transcendent powers that
    he may be supposed to possess." The task of Thomas's poet is
    "to discover words present in the world, and by this discovery
    to become . . . the medium by which the Logos expresses itself."

2   CANBY, VINCENT. "Under Milk Wood Arrives on Screen." New
    York Times, 22 January, p. 20.
        Reviews Andrew Sinclair's film version of Under Milk Wood.
    Finds the attempt to discover visual counterparts to the words
    at best "redundant" and at worst "banal, misleading or wrong."
    There isn't a great deal for the camera eye to do except "to try
    desperately to keep up with the language--but the language wins."

3   CLEVERDON, DOUGLAS. "Dylan Thomas and Broadcasting." Poetry
    Wales 9 (Autumn):85-92.
        Describes Thomas's broadcasting experience as a reader,
    writer, and actor. He was a supreme master of the medium.

4   CREWE, J.V. "Dylan Thomas." Theoria 40:69-71.
        Follows up on a general article about Thomas appearing the
    previous year in Theoria. See 1972.6.

5   DAVIS, W. EUGENE. "The Making of A Child's Christmas in
    Wales." Arizona Quarterly 29 (Winter):342-51.
        Gives an account of the reshaping that Thomas's "lyrical"
    Christmas essay underwent. Using material from two earlier
    essays, Thomas dealt with a "special set of problems," and this
    gives us insights into the creative process employed and the
    various strategies he consciously used to affect the reader.

6   DONALD, J. WALLACE, and JOHNSTON, KENNETH G. "'Do not go
    gentle . . .': In the Classroom: Dylan Thomas's Good Night."
    English Quarterly 6 (Winter):321-5.
        Describes "Do not go gentle" as an elegy that goes against
    the grain of simple resignation. Suggests teaching the poem in
    conjunction with Shakespeare's Romeo and Juliet for the purpose
    of highlighting the tragic theme.

7   GARLICK, RAYMOND. "The Shapes of Thoughts." Poetry Wales 9
    (Autumn):40-48.
        Considers the influence of Herbert and Donne on the poetry
    of Thomas. Both Herbert and Donne used visual shapes and images
    that occur in some manner in certain of Thomas's poems. Donne's
    distinctive diction also appears to have influenced Thomas's
    language.

8   GINGERICH, MARTIN E. "Dylan Thomas: Curse-Bless." Anglo-
    Welsh Review 22 (Spring):178-82.
        Discusses the recurrent "curse, bless" paradox at work in
    Thomas's poetry, particularly as the dichotomy appears in some
    later poems and in Under Milk Wood.

9   GREGORY, HORACE. "The Black-Stockinged Bait and Dylan
    Thomas." In Spirit of Time and Place. New York: W.W. Norton
    & Co., pp. 191-200.
        Stresses Thomas's regional identity, original imagination,
    and affinity with neoromantic literature in attempting to gauge
    the special quality of his poetry. Considers some of the criti-
    cal labels sometimes attached to Thomas--such as Freudian,
    pantheist, symbolist, and surrealist. Concludes that in Thomas's
    finest poems "there is 'a perfect fusion' of the opposites, a
    precarious welding together of the two extremes--a 'dead body'
    and 'the soul.'"

10 HARDY, BARBARA. "The Personal and the Impersonal in Some of
    Dylan Thomas's Lyrics." Poetry Wales 9 (Autumn):75-83.
        Points out that Thomas's lyrics are unusual in that they
    rarely center around a personal point of view. Usually, they
    grow out of abstract occasions and are expressed in sensuously
    abstract imagistic and dramatic ways.

11 HEINEMANN, ALISON. Review of Dylan Thomas: The Country of
    the Spirit. Library Journal 98 (1 October):2862.
        Recognizes Rushworth Kidder's study as an illuminating,
    systematic analysis of Thomas as a religious poet.

12 JONES, GLYN. "18 Poems Again." Poetry Wales 9 (Autumn):
    22-26.
        Rereads 18 Poems after four decades and comes away with a
    loss of some of the excitement of the past. Still calls atten-
    tion, however, to Thomas's original diction and surrealistic
    tendencies that are impressive. Also, the poems now seem less
    obscure.

13 KIDDER, RUSHWORTH MOULTON. Dylan Thomas: The Country of the
    Spirit. Princeton, N.J.: Princeton University Press, 237 pp.
        Illustrates Thomas's use of three types of religious
    imagery--categorized as referential, allusive, and thematic
    imagery. Ultimately, this critical approach reveals that while
    Thomas used religious language in his earlier poetry to apprehend
    the world, eventually he rose above the limits of fixed cate-
    gories. His mature work "culminates in ritual and sacramental
    expression of religious matters."

14 LEWIS, PETER ELFED. "Return Journey to Milk Wood." Poetry
    Wales 9 (Autumn):27-38.
        Defends Under Milk Wood against critical attacks that fail
    to see the creation for what it tries to be. It should be under-
    stood that Thomas wrote a play for voices, in which he set out
    (successfully) to "produce aurally-exciting verbal textures"
    joined creatively with "an atmosphere, a mood, a place."

15 MATHIAS, ROLAND. "A Niche for Dylan Thomas." Poetry Wales 9
    (Autumn):51-74.
        Considers the influence of Thomas's Welsh heritage and
    environment on his works. In his poetry the Welsh influence is
    especially obvious when a biblical tone appears. His complex
    versification is another sign of this influence. Deficient as
    an intellectual, he substituted subjective intensity for deep
    thought.

16 O'CONNOR, JOHN. "Dylan Thomas Study Repeated Tonight." New
    York Times, 7 November, p. 95.
        Previews the television rerun of Perry Miller Adato's Emmy
    Award winning N.E.T. production "Dylan Thomas: The World I
    Breathe." A combination of interviews, readings, photographs,
    and a previous film documentary, the program effectively pays
    tribute to the man and debunks the legend.

17   PIXLEY, DOROTHY, ed. "'Author's Prologue' to Collected Poems
      by Dylan Thomas." Connecticut Critic 7 (March):35-38.
         Examines the extended meaning of "Author's Prologue," giv-
      ing special praise to Thomas's expressive and energetic imagery.

18   REES, ALAN. "Dylan Thomas and the B.B.C." Listener 90
      (18 October):516-17, 520-21.
         Combines extracts from the B.B.C.'s written archives in the
      course of surveying Thomas's experience with the network.

19   Review of Dylan Thomas: The Code of Night. Choice 10 (July-
      August):776.
         Criticizes David Holbrook's study as a "depth psychology"
      analysis whose main value lies in emphasizing the behavior of the
      man without adding much understanding of the artist and his
      creations.

20   Review of Dylan Thomas (Writers of Wales). Choice 10 (June):
      616.
         Recommends Walford Davies's study as an "excellent intro-
      duction" to Thomas, especially to his "Welshness."

21   Review of The Saga of Prayer: The Poetry of Dylan Thomas.
      Choice 10 (June):615.
         Criticizes Robert K. Burdette's work for being "overly
      concerned" with developing the thesis that Thomas may be read as
      a gnostic.

*22   SANDERS, WILLIAM. "Dylan Thomas: 'A Law Unto Himself.'"
      Junction 1972, pp. 50-56.
         Focuses on the anarchic side of Thomas. See MLA Inter-
      national Bibliography, 1973, p. 124.

23   SINGLETON, ROBERT R. "Thomas' 'In the white giant's thigh.'"
      Explicator 31 (January): item 34.
         Speculates that the actual setting Thomas was imagining
      when writing the poem was the Cerne Abbas Giant's fertility
      site.

24   STARK, BRUCE RODERICK. "An Essay in the Linguistic Analysis
      of Literature: Bloomfieldian Linguistics and Dylan Thomas'
      'After the funeral.'" Ph.D. dissertation, Columbia Univer-
      sity, 395 pp.
         Analyzes Bloomfieldian linguistic theory on structure and
      meaning, and applies the findings to an examination of "After
      the Funeral." The primary focus of the study is the paradigm
      itself; the interpretation of the poem is "merely one of its
      by-products." See Dissertation Abstracts International 34
      (1973):2600A.

25   "Thomas by Thomas." Sunday Times (London), 28 January, p. 32.
         Reports on the latest effort to sell the Boathouse and on
      Aeron's thoughts about the place and the poetry of her father.

26   THOMAS, R. GEORGE. "Dylan Thomas and Some Early Readers."
     Poetry Wales 9 (Autumn):3-19.
         Compares the kind of reception Thomas's writing tended to
     get before and after the Second World War. The early readers
     tended to respond sympathetically to Thomas's fantasy-filled,
     nightmarish work of the thirties and forties. After the war,
     readers were less responsive to these literary qualities.

                                1974

1   BARONE, JOSEPH M. "Semantic Sets and Dylan Thomas' 'Light
     breaks.'" Poetics 10:97-129.
         Goes through a rigorous analysis of "Light breaks" in order
     to discover what a semantic reading can reveal about the notions
     of "metaphor," "semantic deviance," and poetic language in gen-
     eral. The poet's language "is no more obscure to him than the
     theory of relativity was to Einstein. He simply 'thinks that
     way.'" To the poet language "is the exercise of his quantita-
     tively different linguistic faculty."

2   BIVENS, WILLIAM P., III. "Noun Phrase Case Schemes in the
     Deep Structure of Poems." Style 8:305-21.
         Applies Charles Fillmore's case grammar theory to some of
     the poetry of Thomas and Yeats to see how the case role model
     can help in the understanding of poetry.

3   BLACKBURN, THOMAS. "Dylan Thomas." In The Price of an Eye.
     Westport, Conn.: Greenwood Press, pp. 111-23.
         Reprint of 1961.4.

4   DONER, DEAN. Review of Dylan Thomas' Early Prose: A Study in
     Creative Mythology. Modern Fiction Studies 20 (Summer):
     248-49.
         Considers Annis Pratt's book to be a valuable study of the
     mythological influences on Thomas even though the work does suf-
     fer from too much speculation and has a "dissertation-like
     character."

5   FAERBER, ROBERT. "Analyse sémantique d'un poème de Dylan
     Thomas." Recherches anglaises et américaines 7 (Summer):
     116-31.
         Gives a close semantic reading of "Poem in October." The
     pleasure (or displeasure) of the experience of reading the poem
     depends on the creation's own semantic world.

6   GATES, BARBARA T. "Thomas' 'In my Craft or Sullen Art.'"
     Explicator 32 (May): item 68.
         Draws a parallel between this poem and Theseus's famous
     speech in A Midsummer Night's Dream. Such a reading suggests
     that the poem's narrator, like Theseus, expresses the element of
     necessary "lunacy" that poets and lovers contain.

7   GENG, VERONICA. "Ode to a 'Y.'" New York Times, 31 March,
pp. 69-71.
Discusses the development of New York's Poetry Center.
John Malcolm Brinnin recalls that Thomas's appearance provided
the Center with a much-needed infusion of excitement.

8   HARDESTY, MARGARET ANNE. "An Examination of the Sacramental
Vision of Dylan Thomas: Its Sources, Analogues, and Its
Expression in His Poetry." Ph.D. dissertation, State University of New York at Binghamton, 213 pp.
Looks at Thomas as the foremost romantic poet of the century, one who believed that poetry was the main means of reconciling the sensual and the spiritual. His poetry as a whole,
reflecting the way of Christian redemption, moved from darkness
to reconciling, spiritual light. See Dissertation Abstracts
International 34 (1974):6641A.

9   JOHNSON, PAMELA HANSFORD. "Dylan." In Important to Me:
Personalia. London: Macmillan, pp. 140-49.
Recounts her relationship with young Thomas. She remembers
him as "essentially a life-giver, partly because it was in his
nature, and partly because life was what he loved to give."

10   KILLINGSLEY, SIEW-YUE. "Lexical, Semantic and Grammatical
Patterning in Dylan Thomas: Collected Poems 1934-1952."
Orbis 23:285-99.
Attempts to apply stylistics to Thomas's Collected Poems in
such a way as to make the findings "acceptable to both the
linguist and the literary critic." Comments on linguistics and
content are consciously linked.

11   LOWREY, NORMAN EUGENE. "A Child's Christmas in Wales: A
Setting of Dylan Thomas' Poem for Narrator and Orchestra."
Ph.D. dissertation, University of Rochester, Eastman School
of Music, 53 pp.
Sets A Child's Christmas in Wales to a seven-part composition with the intent of giving additional life and accessibility
to the text. See Dissertation Abstracts International 36 (1976):
4841A.

12   McKAY, D.F. "Aspects of Energy in the Poetry of Dylan Thomas
and Sylvia Plath." Critical Quarterly 16 (Spring):53-67.
Shows how the poetry of Thomas and Sylvia Plath are related
in their concentration on linguistic energy, the essential energy
conducted by meaning. Both poets "demonstrate a desire to regain
the simultaneity of experience by the strategic manipulation of
language: to bring together dancer, the art of dancing and the
dance." The thematic meaning is expressed dramatically by the
(often kinesthetic) action of the poetry.

13   MIDDLETON, DAVID. "Twenty Years A-Growing: New Criticism of
        Dylan Thomas." Southern Review 10 (Spring):529-33.
           Looks at three new critical studies that confront the issue
        of Thomas's true achievement. Rushworth Kidder's Dylan Thomas:
        The Country of the Spirit has little new to say in its depiction
        of Thomas as a religious poet. David Holbrook's Dylan Thomas:
        The Code of Night is more impressive in its attempt to prove that
        Thomas suffered from "ontological insecurity," but as an example
        of psychological criticism it falls into the "fallacy of
        methodological transference." Walford Davies's Dylan Thomas:
        New Critical Essays provides the "centrist view" of Thomas as the
        author of a "few" of the "best short poems in the Romantic
        tradition."

14   PAGE, CHRISTOPHER. "Dylan and the Scissormen." Anglo-Welsh
        Review 24 (Summer):76-81.
           Examines Thomas's use of recurrent imagery taken from the
        nursery rhyme Struwwelpeter.

15   PEEL, MARIE. "Welsh Dylan." Books and Bookmen 19 (January):
        37-38.
           Focuses on the achievement of Under Milk Wood. It succeeds
        in portraying the surface complexity of Wales by means of origi-
        nal lyrical language; however, it fails to portray the soul of
        the land and people with the same power.

16   Review of Dylan Thomas: The Country of the Spirit. Choice 11
        (March):90.
           Criticizes Rushworth Kidder's study for occasionally labor-
        ing over points that are meant to prove that "taking over the
        language of Christian thought" led Thomas to eventually "think as
        a Christian."

17   Review of Dylan Thomas: The Country of the Spirit. Virginia
        Quarterly Review 50 (Winter):xvi-xvii.
           Praises Rushworth Kidder's study of Thomas as a religious
        poet. By focusing on referential, allusive, and thematic
        imagery, the analysis shows convincingly the development of
        religious thought in the poetry.

18   SAUTTER, DIANA. "Dylan Thomas and Archetypal Domination."
        American Imago 31 (Winter):335-58.
           Gives Thomas's poetry an archetypal analysis, using the
        approach as "an opening to resonance rather than definition,"
        attempting in the end to mediate between the critical poles
        represented by Jacob Korg ("mystical infatuation") and David
        Holbrook ("Freudian rationalization"). Thomas was a person
        "under the dominance of an archetype, who suffered the particular
        antinomies between the Eros of the archetype and the Death of
        Separation in the imagery of one crucified."

19   SMOOT, GEORGE ALBERT. "The Poetry of Dylan Thomas: Processes
      in the Weather of the Heart." Ph.D. dissertation, Syracuse
      University, 208 pp.
         Explicates "Ballad of the Long-legged Bait," "Vision and
      Prayer," and "A Winter's Tale," focusing on their emotional con-
      cerns. The study ultimately shows the culminating, transcending
      reconciliation of physical and spiritual love. See <u>Dissertation</u>
      <u>Abstracts International</u> 36 (1975):330A.

20   SUNDERMAN, PAULA. "Dylan Thomas' 'A Refusal to Mourn': A
      Syntactic and Semantic Interpretation." <u>Language and Style</u> 7
      (Winter):20-35.
         Interprets "A Refusal to Mourn the Death, by Fire, of a
      Child" by means of a close analysis of the syntactical and seman-
      tic interrelationship. Uses two complementary critical approaches
      (Samuel Levin's theory of coupling and Archibald Hill's meta-
      literary methodology) and draws upon "extralinguistic material"
      in order to provide a convincing "literary" interpretation based
      on the poem's own language.

*21   YOUNG, A. "Aspects of the Reaction to Dadaism and Surrealism
      in English Literature, 1916-1946, with Particular Reference to
      the Writings of Dylan Thomas." Ph.D. dissertation, University
      of Manchester.
         See <u>Annual Bibliography of English Language and Literature</u>
      49 (1974):609.

                              1975

1   ANDREWS, PETER. "A Coffee-Table Miscellany." <u>Saturday Review</u>
      3 (29 November):27.
         Admires the "crisp narrative" of Andrew Sinclair's <u>Dylan</u>
      <u>Thomas: No Man More Magical</u>. Concludes that Thomas is "our
      Shelley" in the sense that his "extravagant life overshadows his
      poetry."

2   BLUNDEN, ALLAN. "Beside the Seaside with Georg Heym and Dylan
      Thomas." <u>German Life and Letters</u> 29 (October):4-14.
         Compares Thomas with Georg Heym, the German expressionist.
      There are some striking but essentially superficial similarities
      between them. The most significant similarity exists in their
      concern with the theme of man's suffering; but here the differ-
      ence in how they treat this theme becomes particularly instruc-
      tive.

3   DAVIE, DONALD. "Dylan Thomas." <u>New York Times</u>, 9 November,
      sec. 7, p. 7.
         Reviews Andrew Sinclair's <u>Dylan Thomas: No Man More</u>
      <u>Magical</u>, finding it a "responsible" book, although it does fail
      to deal effectively with the question of just how dangerous fame
      was in the case of this poet. His "gifts were very great; but
      he used them to achieve effects which are, though powerful,
      artistically coarse."

4   DAVIN, DAN. "A Spinning Man." In Closing Time. London:
    Oxford University Press, pp. 121-50.
        Records his recollections of the Thomas he knew during the
    final year of the war. His purpose is not to get involved in a
    critical discussion of the poetry; instead, it's to depict what
    this "difficult" man was like. Thomas "needed an intense life,
    a life of drama, and he could not get it entirely from within
    himself." However much he was an "egoist," he wasn't a solipsist
    but affectionate, gregarious."

5   DAVIS, CYNTHIA. "The Voices of Under Milk Wood." Criticism
    17 (Winter):74-89.
        Arguing against the common view that Under Milk Wood is the
    expression of a single persona, shows how Thomas actually used
    careful, complex patterns in allotment of roles, verbal varia-
    tions, and levels of thematic significance. The dramatic pro-
    gress toward thematic understanding "works through many indi-
    vidual situations." The Second Voice expresses in "mythic lan-
    guage" the visionary link between all the characters; the First
    Voice acts as the "shaping artist" presenting a "unified vision
    of the human struggle to see, to understand, and to love" by
    means of description, declaration, figurative language, and word
    play.

6   "Dylan Thomas Museum Opens." Sunday Times (London), 1 June,
    p. 3.
        Notes the opening of the Boathouse as a permanent museum.

7   FERGUSON, SUZANNE. "Fishing the Deep Sea; Archetypal Patterns
    in Thomas' 'Ballad of the Long-legged Bait.'" Modern Poetry
    Studies 6 (Spring):102-14.
        Gives "Ballad of the Long-legged Bait" a Jungian reading.
    In the climactic part of the poem "we may perceive the crisis of
    the actual process of self-discovery, called by Jung the 'arche-
    type of transformation.'"

8   FITZGIBBON, CONSTANTINE. "Dylan Thomas Letters." Times
    (London), 22 November, p. 13.
        Elaborates on Geraldine Norman's story concerning Sotheby's
    planned sale of some of Thomas's letters.

9   FOSBERG, MARY DEE HARRIS. "Computer Collation of Manuscript
    Poetry: Dylan Thomas' 'Poem on his birthday.'" Ph.D. dis-
    sertation, University of Texas at Austin, 196 pp.
        Collates close to two hundred pages of "Poem on his birth-
    day" manuscripts, thereby producing a history of the evolution of
    the poem that reveals previously unrecognized aspects of Thomas's
    art. The results of the collation essentially help one under-
    stand how the poet worked and what some of his most difficult
    poems mean. See Dissertation Abstracts International 36 (1976):
    6700A.

10   FREEMAN, DONALD C. "The Strategy of Fusion: Dylan Thomas's
     Syntax." In Style and Structure in Literature: Essays in the
     Stylistics. Edited by Roger Fowler. Ithaca, N.Y.: Cornell
     University Press, pp. 19-39.
          Illustrates the essential connection between linguistic and
     poetic design in Thomas's art by means of a transformational-
     generative critical approach. Shows how certain syntactic
     strategies ("yoking of immediate syntactic constituents which
     are contradictory; . . . intensive use of the relative clause
     formation and related transformations; . . . various kinds of
     preposing transformations") are used to express Thomas's unifying
     vision of natural process. He is "above all a poet of fusion,"
     always attempting "to fuse natural process and human physiology,
     the forces of nature and human mortality and . . . man's indi-
     vidual life and death with collective human and cosmic history."

11   GRIGSON, GEOFFREY. "Shinies." Spectator 235 (29 November):
     702.
          Criticizes Andrew Sinclair's Dylan Thomas: Poet of His
     People (published in the United States as No Man More Magical)
     for its "unctuosity, its enormous grovel and ecstasy; and
     ignorance about poetry."

12   HIGHAM, DAVID. "Dylan Thomas Letters." Times (London),
     8 December, p. 13.
          Comments on Sotheby's failed attempt to sell some of
     Thomas's letters, perhaps due to copyright questions.

13   HOLROYD, MICHAEL. Augustus John. New York: Holt, Rinehart &
     Winston, pp. 445 passim.
          Describes the sometimes "turbulent" relationship between
     Thomas and the artist who introduced Caitlin to the poet.

14   JACOBS, NICOLAS. "Reviews." Notes and Queries 22 (October):
     475-80.
          Reviews three recent books concerning Thomas and finds them
     all less than successful or very significant. Walford Davies's
     edition of Dylan Thomas: Early Prose Writings contains material
     previously uncollected probably because so much of it degenerates
     into "wearisome," sprawling "self-parody." Davies's Dylan
     Thomas: New Critical Essays anthologizes essays that represent
     a "fair cross-section of all those critics whose attitude to
     Thomas is not one of outright rejection." David Holbrook's
     Dylan Thomas: The Code of Night is "frequently turgid and at
     times plain silly" in its earnest effort to psychoanalyze the
     poet.

*15 LAMONT, C.C. "A Survey of Criticism of Dylan Thomas's Poetry
     from 1934 to 1954 and a Bibliography from 1934 to 1966."
     Ph.D. dissertation, University of Edinburgh.
          See Annual Bibliography of English Language and Literature
     50 (1975):15.

16   MIDDLETON, DAVID. "Thomas' 'Author's Prologue.'" Explicator
     34 (October): item 12.
        Shows that the probable source of the ambiguous phrase
     "cities of nine / Days' night" in "Author's Prologue" was Blake's
     "The Four Zoas."

17   MONTAGUE, GENE. "Thomas' 'Because the pleasure-bird
     whistles.'" Explicator (December): item 30.
        Disagrees with William York Tindall's assertion that the
     poem is "about the experience of making a poem about an expe-
     rience in the bum city." Actually, the "narrative heart" depicts
     sodomy, and the poem "explains, justifies, and apologizes for the
     act."

18   MONTGOMERY, Brother BENILDE. "The Function of Ambiguity in
     'A Refusal to Mourn the Death, by Fire, of a Child in London.'"
     Concerning Poetry 8 (Fall):77-81.
        Interprets "A Refusal to Mourn" as a poem expressing "nega-
     tive affirmation." Thomas's vision comes from his awareness of
     the "creative process" described in Genesis and of his work's
     nature. The essential tension in Thomas is "between his own
     self-conscious humanity . . . and his all-humbling awareness that
     certitude leads only to death." His use of "deliberate ambi-
     guity" comes from his attempt to balance the two extremes.

19   NEMER, MONIQUO. "Dylan Thomas, poète français." Revue des
     sciences humaines 158 (Summer):213-22.
        Based especially on the evidence of "And death shall have
     no dominion," the conclusion is drawn that Thomas's poetry
     served to rehabilitate the particularly "French" idea of the
     poet as bard.

20   NORMAN, GERALDINE. "Letters from the Heart of an Incomparable
     Wordsmith." Times (London), 20 November, p. 16.
        Gives a sampling of some of Thomas's letters about to be
     sold by Sotheby's.

21   NYE, ROBERT. "Magic Eludes This Thomas Biographer."
     Christian Science Monitor, 24 December, p. 23.
        Reviews Andrew Sinclair's Dylan Thomas: No Man More
     Magical, dismissing it as a disappointing account because it's
     basically a "rehash" of familiar material.

22   PAGE, MICHAEL. Review of Dylan Thomas: No Man More Magical.
     Library Journal 100 (1 December):2243.   ·
        Believes that the primary value of Andrew Sinclair's work
     lies in its being an "appreciation" that shows the "polarities"
     between Thomas's life and work.

23   PERKINS, D.C. The World of Dylan Thomas. Swansea: Celtic
     Educational, 79 pp.
        Looks at the (mainly Welsh) environment that Thomas came
     from and the world that concerned him in his work.

24   PIKOULIS, JOHN. Review of <u>Dylan Thomas: Selected Poems</u>.
     <u>Anglo-Welsh Review</u> 24 (Spring):208–11.
        Questions the value and objectivity of Walford Davies's
     selection, arrangement, annotation, and introductory commentary.

25   "Poet's Home to Stay in Welsh Hands." <u>Times</u> (London),
     4 January, p. 2.
        Reports on the purchase of the Boathouse by the Wales
     Tourist Board and an educational trust.

26   POOLE, RICHARD. "Dylan Thomas, Ted Hughes and Byron: Two
     Instances of Indebtedness." <u>Anglo-Welsh Review</u> 25 (September):
     119–24.
        Points out that a line in the middle stanza of "Do not go
     gentle" is indebted to a stanza in Byron's "Child Harolde's
     Pilgrimage."

27   Review of <u>Dylan Thomas: No Man More Magical</u>. <u>Booklist</u> 72
     (15 December):541.
        Praises Andrew Sinclair's work as an appreciation that is
     "admiring yet critical."

28   Review of <u>Dylan Thomas: No Man More Magical</u>. <u>Publishers
     Weekly</u> 208 (22 September):125.
        Criticizes Andrew Sinclair's work for not actually proving
     that Thomas was "the finest lyric poet of his age," but praises
     the honest account of the man's "deeply divided" nature.

29   SCHVEY, HENRY I. "Dylan Thomas and Surrealism." <u>Dutch
     Quarterly Review of Anglo-American Letters</u> 5:83–97.
        Documents Thomas's relation to surrealism and shows impor-
     tant similarities and discrepancies between his poetry and the
     movement. Like the surrealists, Thomas applied Freudian psychol-
     ogy to his art, used paradoxical images "dredged up from the
     subconscious," and tried to "liberate" his creations from stale
     methods. Unlike the surrealists "bent upon the revolutionary
     destruction" of accepted reality, including art, Thomas believed
     in the essential life of art.

30   SINCLAIR, ANDREW. <u>Dylan Thomas: No Man More Magical</u>. New
     York: Holt, Rinehart & Winston, 240 pp.
        Describes the life and development of the "contradictory
     poet" and his "impossible" search for "unity in divergence, a
     sweet final resolution of the soul." Beginning with an outline
     of Thomas's Welsh heritage, the study arrives at the conclusion
     that "the finest lyric poet of his age" was essentially (though
     "willy-nilly") a Welsh bard and minstrel. Published in England
     as <u>Dylan Thomas: Poet of His People</u> by London's Joseph.

31   WALLACE, RONALD. "Thomas' 'Especially when the October wind.'"
     <u>Explicator</u> 34 (September): item 3.
        Focuses on the ambiguous meaning of the phrase "some let
     me make you" in the poem. Suggests that the poet is thinking of
     the magical ability of words to "make" or transform things or
     people.

32 YOUNG, ALAN. "Image as Structure: Dylan Thomas and Poetic Meaning." Critical Quarterly 17 (Winter):333-45.
Takes up the "odd" case that Thomas's consistent denial of being influenced by the surrealist movement has frequently been ignored or challenged by certain critics. Proposes that Thomas's images "make sense mainly within a coherence theory of poetic meaning and truth rather than within a correspondence theory." One of his poems acquires an artistic completeness "only if the actual 'correspondences' are assimilated into the heart of the poem, taking a new life in the poem."

1976

1 "Appeal." Washington Post, 8 February, p. D17.
Reports on Caitlin Thomas's attempt to sell some of her husband's letters. While letters by Browning and some other figures were fetching impressive bids, only two unacceptably low offers were made for the mementos handled by Sotheby's.

2 BARNES, CLIVE. "1-Man Show of Shows." New York Times, 13 October, p. 34.
Reviews Emlyn Williams's "Dylan Thomas Growing Up," the monologue he has been performing since 1955. Williams presents the stories with "bardic relish" and captures the essence of the poet.

3 BRIDGES, LINDA. "His Own Best Enemy." National Review 28 (23 July):797.
Reviews Andrew Sinclair's Dylan Thomas: No Man More Magical, praising this "unblinking" appraisal for keeping the various sides of Thomas "skillfully in balance." Also notes the author's "polemical purpose" of defending the poet's reputation as a great lyric poet.

4 CLEVERDON, DOUGLAS. "Swansea Singer." Sunday Times (London), 4 January, p. 38.
Reviews Andrew Sinclair's Dylan Thomas: Poet of His People. Commends the author for expressing his "enthusiasm" while still retaining a "sense of proportion." The commentary on Thomas's Welshness is particularly useful.

5 COE, RICHARD L. "A Jubilant 'Thomas.'" Washington Post, 27 October, pp. C1, C6.
Praises Emlyn Williams for re-creating the vital, essential Thomas in his "Growing Up" performance. Williams's "winnowing" from the sources results in "a sensitive salute to his country-man."

6 DAVENPORT, DIANA. "The Malting House Summer." New Review 3: 66-70.
Describes the background story behind the collaboration between John Davenport and Thomas on The Death of the King's Canary.

7   DUNCAN, RONALD. "The Druid of DT's." Books and Bookmen 21
    (March):18-19.
        Reviews Andrew Sinclair's Dylan Thomas: Poet of His
    People. Takes exception with the exaggerated praise throughout
    the study.

8   "Dylan Thomas Novel to be Published." Times (London),
    27 July, p. 3.
        Reports on the impending publication of The Death of the
    King's Canary, attributing the delay of thirty-five years to the
    "libellous" nature of the work.

9   ELY, ROBERT. "'The Wordy Shapes of Women' in the Poetry of
    Dylan Thomas." English Studies in College 2:1-14.
        Concentrates on the appearance of women in Thomas's poetry.

10 FENTON, JAMES. "Jesuitical." New Statesman 91 (2 January):
    16.
        Reviews Andrew Sinclair's Dylan Thomas: Poet of His
    People, calling it a "conscientious, professional pot boiler"
    that gives an honest depiction of the poet's life but says little
    of significance about the poetry.

11 FITZGIBBON, CONSTANTINE. Introduction to The Death of the
    King's Canary. New York: Viking Press, pp. v-viii.
        Accounts for the long delay of the book's publication.

12 FULLER, ROY. "A Lludyldaed Mystery." Times Literary Supple-
    ment, 1 October, p. 1229.
        Reviews The Death of the King's Canary, finding it to be a
    disappointing "squib" that fails to "explode." The surrealistic
    marks are particularly tedious.

13 GILL, BRENDAN. Here at the New Yorker. New York: Random
    House, pp. 248, 257.
        Repeats popular stories of Thomas's sexual escapades. Also
    notes James Laughlin's sponsorship of him and other young, un-
    known writers.

14 GINGERICH, MARTIN E. "The Timeless Narrators of Dylan Thomas'
    'In Country Heaven.'" Modern Poetry Studies 7 (Autumn):
    109-21.
        Examines Thomas's use of narrators. In In Country Sleep
    they initially are poised to choose between "curse" and "bless."
    But they "come to learn that the alternatives are either to
    choose 'curse' and 'bless' or to exclude them, in which latter
    case they become like the animals who have no choice at all."
    Through the last three poems of this collection Thomas arrives at
    an understanding and acceptance of man's "temporality."

15 GRIGSON, GEOFFREY. "Sub-satirical." Listener 96
    (30 September):409.
        Dismisses The Death of the King's Canary as a tedious
    "pasquinade."

16   HAAS, RUDOLF. "Dylan Thomas: Under Milk Wood." In Das
     moderne englische Drama: Interpretationen. Edited by Horst
     Oppel. Berlin: Erich Schmidt, pp. 288-301.
         Interprets Under Milk Wood, focusing on questions of influ-
     ence, originality, dramatic form, and regional and universal
     appeal.

17   HILTON, IAN. "Deutsch-Walisische literarische Beziehungen im
     20. Jahrhundert." Jahrbuch für internationale Germanistik 2,
     no. 4:290-98.
         Discusses the importance of Thomas and Vernon Watkins from
     a European point of view, pointing out the distinct qualities of
     both, qualities that fell out of favor during the sixties, when
     a preference for a more "laconic" poetry began to grow.

18   JACKAMAN, ROB. "Man and Mandala: Symbol as Structure in a
     Poem by Dylan Thomas." Ariel 7 (October):22-33.
         Points out that, when reading Thomas, one is "confronted by
     a landscape in which everything is symbolic" on a "cosmic scale."
     The archetypal symbol of the mandala is chosen to illuminate the
     "functional complexity" of Thomas's symbols in general. At his
     best, Thomas employed a symbolic language that expressed a "posi-
     tively archetypal affirmation."

19   KERSHNER, R.B., Jr. Dylan Thomas: The Poet and His Critics.
     The Poet and His Critics Series, edited by Charles Sanders.
     Chicago: American Library Association, 285 pp.
         Explores Thomas's major aspects through the critical writ-
     ing that surrounds his work. After a general introduction, chap-
     ters focusing on the issues of Thomas's legend, personality,
     religious vision, situation in literary contexts, and poetic
     technique follow. Throughout, the consciously objective approach
     is meant to reflect on Thomas's poetry as a whole instead of
     individual selections. Each chapter ends with a listing of the
     references used within it; and, to further aid readers of this
     "most thoroughly and frequently explicated modern poet," the book
     ends with an outline of basic sources, a chronology, and an index
     of explications. "Undeniably the body of his work includes
     failures--usually interesting failures--but there is surprisingly
     little critical unanimity as to just which poems these are."
     Thomas's poems "demand reading in their own terms," and if it's
     necessary that we discover "new methods for unravelling them and
     a new vocabulary to hint at their working, then that is one
     measure of their success."

20   KING, FRANCIS. "Old Boys." Spectator 237 (2 October):24.
         Reviews The Death of the King's Canary, finding Thomas's
     collaboration with John Davenport on this parody of the contempo-
     rary poetic scene during the book's writing to be only "inter-
     mittently fascinating" and finally an "unsatisfactory read."

Writings about Dylan Thomas, 1934–1985

21 LANE, GARY. A Concordance to the Poems of Dylan Thomas.
    Metuchen, N.J.: Scarecrow Press, 702 pp.
       Bases the concordance on the 1971 publication of The Poems
    of Dylan Thomas. The three parts of the concordance consist of
    the listing of all words and numbers occurring in the poetry,
    the listing and cross-referencing of the components of the
    hyphenated compounds, and the listing of the words in descending
    order of the frequency with which they appear.

22 McKAY, DONALD F. "Image of Energy: The Vortex in Dylan
    Thomas." English Studies in Canada 2 (Fall):314-28.
       Looks at Thomas as a "vorticist." In this poetry, vortex
    "exemplifies the human apotheosis" that joins the "contrary
    extremeties, the centre and circumference of existence" and
    "reconciles the creative and destructive versions of energy."
    In his writing, the vortex represents an energy that is "gener-
    ated when the human will is exercised against . . . the bounds
    of universal necessity."

23 McLELLAN, JOSEPH. "'Trilogy': A Rich Musical Tribute on the
    Life of Dylan Thomas." Washington Post, 26 April, p. B7.
       Reviews "A Dylan Thomas Trilogy," John Corigliano's musical
    composition based on "Fern Hill," "Poem in October," and "Poem on
    his birthday." The final section of the tribute is especially
    praiseworthy for the "dark, ominous, brooding music" that cap-
    tures Thomas's death-anticipating mood.

24 NORMAN, GERALDINE. "File on Dylan Thomas Project Sold for
    £1,550." Times (London), 18 December, p. 14.
       Reports on Sotheby's sale of some of Thomas's letters and
    a file of an unfinished and unrecorded projected book.

25 NOVAK, ROBERT. "Dylan Thomas Hidden in a Novel." Windless
    Orchard 27 (Fall):14-20.
       Points out the fictional presence of Thomas in Pamela
    Hansford Johnson's novel The Survival of the Fittest.

26 PALMER, RICHARD ALLEN. "Dylan Thomas and the Metaphysical
    Mode: A Study of Shared Sensibilities." Ph.D. dissertation,
    University of Illinois, 292 pp.
       Argues that looking at Thomas as a poet clearly rooted in
    the metaphysical poetic tradition provides the most illuminating
    guide to his complex poetry. The similarities between Thomas and
    the metaphysical poets cover the aspects of technique, universal
    vision, and various major thematic issues and concerns. See
    Dissertation Abstracts International 37 (1977):6508A.

27 PARTRIDGE, A.C. "New Lines, Dylan Thomas, and Conclusions."
    In The Language of Modern Poetry: Yeats, Eliot, Auden.
    London: Andre Deutsch, pp. 319-24 passim.
       Regards Thomas as a symbolic poet who was essentially a
    Cymric Celt. Because his response to nature was earthy, the
    images are sensuous instead of profound. His obscurity can

largely be ascribed to his failure to differentiate between
literal and figurative description.

28   PESCHMANN, HERMANN. "Romp--or Damp Squib?" Times Educational
     Supplement, 31 December, p. 13.
     Believes that the real reason The Death of the King's
Canary was published posthumously is because Thomas knew that the
book was a failure. There are serious problems with confusing
characterizations, vague style, and surreal atmospherics.

29   Review of Dylan Thomas: No Man More Magical. Choice 12
     (February):1576.
     Finds that Andrew Sinclair's work adds no new biographical
facts and "counts for very little" as criticism of the poet's
writing.

30   RICKS, CHRISTOPHER. "The Famous and the Fatuous." Sunday
     Times (London), 3 October, p. 40.
     Doubts that anyone really cares any longer about the sur-
realistic satire found in The Death of the King's Canary.

31   SCHOBERT, TIMOTHY. Review of A Concordance to the Poems of
     Dylan Thomas. Library Journal 101 (1 November):2267.
     Declares that Gary Lane's A Concordance to the Poems of
Dylan Thomas supersedes Robert C. Williams's earlier concordance
since this one is keyed to an expanded collection of Thomas's
poems.

32   WAIN, JOHN. "Dylan Thomas." In English Poetry. Edited by
     Alan Sinfield. London: Sussex, pp. 216-28.
     Considers the achievement of Thomas. Stresses and traces
his "bardic" quality. The unevenness of the work is recognized,
but so is the splendid use of language and the genuine feeling
for common people found particularly in the short stories and
later poetry.

33   WILLIAMS, HUGO. "Home Front." New Statesman 92 (10 October):
     456.
     Dismisses The Death of the King's Canary as a boring
"whodunit" hardly worth mentioning.

                                 1977

1   BERGES, EMILY T. Review of Dylan Thomas: The Poet and His
    Critics. Library Journal 102 (August):1648-49.
     Finds R.B. Kershner's work to be flawed but still valuable
as an overview of the scholarship concerned with the poet.

2   BERTHOUD, ROGER. "Mr. Carter Speaks Up for Dylan Thomas."
    Times (London), 9 May, p. 4.
     Reports on President Jimmy Carter's effort to have Thomas
included in Westminster Abbey's Poets' Corner.

3   BROYARD, ANATOLE. "Ironic, Parodic, Hip." New York Times,
    15 May, sec. 7, p. 12.
    Reviews The Death of the King's Canary, dismissing the
parodic satire as a failure with the exception of the section
aimed at Empson.

4   CADDEL, RICHARD. Review of Dylan Thomas: The Poet and His
    Critics. Library Review 26 (Summer):162-65.
    Commends R.B. Kershner's work for managing with admirable
success to give a comprehensive view of the mass of Thomas criticism ranging from the "often idiosyncratic" early studies to the
more comprehensive studies that follow.

5   CAHILL, DANIEL J. Review of The Death of the King's Canary.
    World Literature Today 51 (Autumn):619.
    Thinks that in collaborating on this satirical novel, Thomas
and John Davenport have succeeded in writing only a "mildly
amusing" parody of their contemporary literary scene.

6   CHERRY, KELLY. "Two Trapped Poets and Their Struggle to Break
    Free." Chicago Tribune, 20 November, sec. 7, p. 1.
    Reviews Paul Ferris's Dylan Thomas along with a biography
of Delmore Schwartz. The biographers argue that their subjects
both were caught "in a kind of creative adolescence, in the
narcissistic rhetoric of the romantic mind, words in love with
words." The reviewer believes that the poets arrived at greatness precisely because they "could not forget themselves."

7   COHEN, GEORGE. "Biting Parodies--37 Years Later." Chicago
    Tribune, 8 May, sec. 7, p. 2.
    Reviews The Death of the King's Canary. Although contempo-
rary readers would have to be scholars to discover all the
sources for the parodies, it's still recommended for those who
enjoy "satiric, biting farce."

8   COONEY, SEAMUS. Review of Dylan Thomas: A Biography.
    Library Journal 102 (15 October):2162-63.
    Commends Paul Ferris's biography for such virtues as common
sense and liveliness but complains that the author never succeeds
in making us appreciate Thomas's "extraordinary talent" or even
why this poet "really mattered."

9   DAVIES, JAMES A. "Dylan Thomas' 'One Warm Saturday' and
    Tennyson's Maud." Studies in Short Fiction 14 (Summer):
    284-86.
    Argues that an "awareness" of Tennyson's Maud is "basic" to
a complete grasp of the meaning of "One Warm Saturday." Points
out several kinds of links between the poem and the story, with
the final one being the fact that in both "a harsh reality eventually dominates the romantic relationship and the imagination
provides no permanent escape."

10   DAVIES, RICHARD A. "Dylan Thomas's Image of the 'Young Dog'
     in the Portrait." Anglo-Welsh Review 26 (Spring):68-72.
     Shows the irony of the "young dog" pose struck in the
     Portrait of the Artist stories. There is actually a pattern of
     a "gradual loss of courage and boldness, a consequent increase
     in fears and terrors" until in the end the young protagonist
     becomes a "terrified prig of a love-mad young man."

11   DAVIS, L.J. Review of The Death of the King's Canary. New
     Republic 177 (17 September):42.
     Grants that the satirical novel, the collaborative work of
     Thomas and John Davenport, has such flaws as thin plot and
     sketches that mean perhaps nothing to contemporary "lay" readers.
     But says, nevertheless, that the satiric comedy works on the
     whole because of the "unholy glee" with which the writers
     "slander" certain cultural figures of their time.

12   ELLMANN, RICHARD. "Richard Ellmann on Biography." New
     Republic 177 (26 November):26.
     Criticizes Paul Ferris's Dylan Thomas as a biography that
     in effect "dwells on diminution" because it fails to make the
     essential connection between the facts of the man's life and the
     creation of his poetry.

13   FERLAZZO, PAUL J. "Dylan Thomas and Walt Whitman: Birth,
     Death, and Time." Walt Whitman Review 23 (September):136-41.
     Contrasts Thomas's and Whitman's view of time. Whitman is
     "at peace" with the flow of time; Thomas fights it desperately.
     Whitman's "supreme achievement" is the "reconciliation" with
     death and "organic" time; Thomas protested against time as a
     "destructive force."

14   FERRIS, PAUL. Dylan Thomas: A Biography. New York: Dial
     Press, 399 pp.
     Attempts to separate the facts from the legends surrounding
     the poet's life. To support the conclusions, Ferris has brought
     in a great deal of fresh material, particularly from American
     archives, numerous interviews, and the medical records surround-
     ing Thomas's death. Ultimately, the research suggests that the
     poet manufactured a "character for the world to be entertained
     by, part-poet and part-clown," that the "two went together," and
     that the "borderline between fact and fiction may have been
     blurred inside his head as well as outside it." The biography
     also contains two previously unpublished poems and a postscript
     on the literary industry built on the reputation of Thomas.

15   FRANCISCA, BEVERLY. "Chomsky's Linguistic Models as Indices
     of Poetic Creativity." Coranto 10:13-30.
     Uses "And death shall have no dominion" to illustrate the
     sense of Noam Chomsky's poetic theories, specifically his notion
     of the "interaction" of "deep and surface structures."

16   FRASER, GEORGE SUTHERLAND. "Dylan Thomas." In Essays on
     Twentieth-Century Poets. Tontowa, N.J.: Rowman & Littlefield,
     pp. 182-203.
          Reprint of 1957.17.

17   GALE, GEORGE. "The Poet As Boor." Spectator 238 (23 April):
     21-22.
          Reviews Paul Ferris's Dylan Thomas and Daniel Jones's My
     Friend Dylan Thomas. Accepts the portrait drawn by Ferris's
     biography: "Thomas was a thief, a braggart, a Welsh kind of
     lush, and a man who continually played the role of a poet."
     Ferris's "straight" account dwarfs Jones's memoir, whose major
     value lies in the detailing of the collaborative creations pro-
     duced by the two friends while still schoolboys.

18   HALL, DONALD. "Hastening to Death." New York Times,
     13 November, sec. 7, p. 13.
          Reviews Paul Ferris's Dylan Thomas, praising the biography
     for being "scrupulous, well-made, horrifying and judicious." The
     biographer neither advocates nor debunks, and he provides much
     new information, especially about how Thomas "hastened" toward
     death.

19   HARDY, BARBARA. "The Personal and the Impersonal in Some of
     Dylan Thomas's Lyrics." In The Advantage of Lyric: Essays on
     Feeling in Poetry. Bloomington: Indiana University Press,
     pp. 112-20.
          Shows that Thomas's lyric poetry, unlike most other lyric
     poetry, doesn't usually move from the particular to the general.
     "The high degree of impersonality . . . is a cause or an effect
     of Thomas's surrealism, his oddity, and his obscurity."

20   HART, DOMINICK. "The Experience of Dylan Thomas's Poetry."
     Anglo-Welsh Review 26 (Spring):73-78.
          Makes the case that, more than most poets, Thomas gives the
     "raw material of experience" in his lines and asks the reader to
     provide the "event." "Viewed this way, Thomas's poetry resolves
     itself into a series of powerful images." These are expressed by
     means of "the single line, phrase, or even word, whose relation
     to one another in any one poem may be of minimal importance to
     the hearer."

21   HOUGH, GRAHAM. "Not Going Gentle." Books and Bookmen 22
     (August):46-47.
          Reviews Paul Ferris's Dylan Thomas. Although the biography
     is an "ample, careful piece of work," it fails to solve the
     greatest mystery about Thomas--the real connection between his
     life and poetry.

22   HOWES, VICTOR. "Superb Biography of Thomas." Christian
     Science Monitor, 25 November, p. 27.
          Considers Paul Ferris's Dylan Thomas to be an outstanding
     "psychological" biography of a "brilliant, tormented genius."

23   _____. "Thomas Helped Cook Up This Puff-pastry Item."
        Christian Science Monitor, 1 June, p. 23.
        Reviews The Death of the King's Canary, calling it a
        "moribund tour de farce" that has "little or no literary or
        gossip value."

24   INGRAMS, RICHARD. Review of The Death of the King's Canary.
        Books and Bookmen 22 (January):58.
        Thinks that the novel is a "rich" satire that, unfortu-
        nately, is so dated by its publication delay that it's "unin-
        telligible."

25   JEFFERSON, MARGO. "Prodigal Poet." Newsweek 90 (7 November):
        93-94.
        Reviews Paul Ferris's Dylan Thomas, commending the biog-
        raphy for being a "sympathetic, psychologically astute" account
        that "eschews the myths for documented facts."

26   JONES, DANIEL. My Friend Dylan Thomas. London: J.M. Dent,
        117 pp.
        Presents a portrait of Thomas, depending mostly on memory.
        Lets the "work speak for itself." There appeared to be a psycho-
        logical and personal split in Thomas, "at first deliberately
        created, then widening perhaps beyond his control."

27   _____. "Overmilk'd Wood: The Myth of Dylan Thomas."
        Encounter 48 (May):23-28.
        Describes how, as his friend's literary trustee, he became
        victimized by the often dishonest or naive myth-making that
        followed Thomas's death. He "tried to defend Dylan against
        Dylanism"; Thomas, after all, "did not like himself very much,"
        and he "would have liked his myth even less. Least of all, he
        would have liked his influence."

28   JONES, GLYN. "Bringing Up the Prodigal." Guardian Weekly,
        1 May, p. 23.
        Reviews Paul Ferris's Dylan Thomas and Daniel Jones's My
        Friend Dylan Thomas. Finds that, surprisingly enough, both
        books provide some new information about the exhaustively
        written-about poet. Ferris's story of the poet's ancestry and
        early years are especially full of fresh revelations and Jones's
        account of his "devotion" to the man often provides surprising
        material.

29   KUCZKOWSKI, RICHARD. Review of The Death of the King's
        Canary. Library Journal 102 (15 April):950.
        Finds the farcical parody cowritten by Thomas and John
        Davenport to be only a "mildly amusing literary curiosity."

30   LAMBERT, J.W. "Dylan: The Reeling Road to Greatness."
        Sunday Times (London), 24 April, p. 41.
        Reviews Paul Ferris's Dylan Thomas and Daniel Jones's My
        Friend Dylan Thomas. Ferris is especially adept at bringing to
        life the social world into which Thomas was born, and he is also

successful in describing the "spontaneously disgraceful" side
that jarred with the poet's obsessive craftsmanship. Jones provides a striking picture of a man exulting in his "pantheistic
pessimism."

31 MacCAIG, NORMAN. "Some of the Angels." Listener 97 (12 May):
    632-33.
       Reviews Paul Ferris's Dylan Thomas and Daniel Jones's My
    Friend Dylan Thomas. Praises both accounts for being sympathetic
    and objective at the same time.

32 MASSIE, ALLAN. "Lives of the Lions." Punch 272 (4 May):
    814-15.
       Reviews Paul Ferris's Dylan Thomas, finding the biography
    to be "undeniably well documented" but seriously flawed by a
    "note of denigration" that runs throughout the account. The
    biographer "swallows and regurgitates all the least substantial
    and more melodramatic aspects of the myth, while at the same
    time constantly belittling the man."

33 MIDDLETON, DAVID. "Green Countries: Dylan Thomas Studies
    Today." Southern Review 13 (Autumn):845-52.
       Surveys five new books that confirm the fact that Thomas
    has an ongoing appeal for general readers and literary critics.
    The Death of the King's Canary is recognized as a wry parody of
    Thomas's poetic contemporaries in the form of a detective thril-
    ler. Walford Davies's edition Dylan Thomas: Selected Poems is
    especially praised for the elucidation of Thomas's "myth-making"
    art and the defense against the charge of "willful obscurantism."
    Gary Lane's A Concordance to the Poems of Dylan Thomas is found
    to be a less convenient research tool than Robert C. Williams's
    concordance. Andrew Sinclair's No Man More Magical is found to
    be little more than a "pleasant review" of what is generally
    known of Thomas. But R.B. Kershner's Dylan Thomas: The Poet
    and His Critics is praised as a "distinguished, comprehensive"
    accounting of all the important studies concerned with the
    various facets of the man and poet. Kershner "has mastered the
    critical stance" of all the major Thomas critics. His work
    signals "a new era" in Thomas criticism; the stages of "critical
    reaction" are over.

34 MORGAN, JOHN. "Swansea Song." New Statesman 93 (29 April):
    565-66.
       Reviews Paul Ferris's Dylan Thomas and Daniel Jones's My
    Friend Dylan Thomas. Ferris's "demythologizing" biography is
    commended especially for the account of Thomas's childhood.
    Jones's book is called "an affectionate memoir" that provides
    some "technical" information about the poet's writing. Under
    Milk Wood was "a work of perfect self-expression, the nearest
    thing" to Thomas's talk.

35   NEIKIRK, BILL. "Jimmy Campaigns for 'Sinner' Poet Dylan
     Thomas." Chicago Tribune, 9 May, sec. 1, p. 2.
     Reports on President Jimmy Carter's active interest in
     having Thomas commemorated in Westminster Abbey's Poets' Corner.

36   REES, GORONWY. "Back to the Boathouse." Times Literary
     Supplement, 29 April, p. 505.
     Reviews Paul Ferris's Dylan Thomas and Daniel Jones's My
     Friend Dylan Thomas. Complains that Ferris's biography fails to
     bring Thomas successfully to life. He does nothing to solve the
     paradox of the unpleasant details surrounding the man's life
     versus the fact he was a person "whom it was always a pleasure
     and a stimulation to meet and know." Jones's reminiscence is
     much more successful in providing a picture that helps us under-
     stand the man and the poetry. He fails, however, just like
     Ferris, to investigate carefully enough Thomas's Welsh back-
     ground, perhaps the most important key for unlocking his para-
     doxical art and personality.

37   Review of The Death of the King's Canary. Atlantic Monthly
     239 (June):94.
     Pans Thomas's and John Davenport's collaborative work as a
     dated series of lampoons with only occasional flashes of comic
     brilliance.

38   Review of The Death of the King's Canary. Booklist 73
     (15 April):1240-41.
     Gives the farce cowritten by Thomas and John Davenport only
     a mild endorsement mainly because the passage of time has made
     the story too "esoteric."

39   Review of The Death of the King's Canary. Choice 14
     (September):867.
     Imagines that Thomas and John Davenport had great fun
     writing the satire; but finds that the parody has become dated.

40   Review of The Death of the King's Canary. Kirkus Review 45
     (15 March):308.
     Complains that Thomas and his coauthor John Davenport have
     crammed too many "isolated" and by now dated jokes into the novel
     to make much comic sense to the contemporary reader.

41   Review of The Death of the King's Canary. Publishers Weekly
     211 (14 March):91.
     Gives the collaborative work of Thomas and John Davenport
     an unfavorable review since it's only funny on occasion, and
     mostly too bizarre and dated.

42   Review of Dylan Thomas: A Biography. Atlantic Monthly 240
     (December):111.
     Gives Paul Ferris's biography a favorable notice. It's a
     "fair-minded" account that is "skeptical of gaudy legend."

43   Review of <u>Dylan Thomas: A Biography</u>. <u>Booklist</u> 74
      (15 October):346.
           Gives a favorable review notice to Paul Ferris's biography.
      Its main accomplishment is a sensitive tracking of Thomas's
      "obsession" to become a poet.

44   Review of <u>Dylan Thomas: A Biography</u>. <u>Christian Century</u> 94
      (28 December):1231.
           Gives Paul Ferris's biography credit for vividly illus-
      trating the poet's path toward "self-destruction" but complains
      that the writer fails to "diagnose the daemon of this genius."

45   Review of <u>Dylan Thomas: A Biography</u>. <u>Kirkus Review</u> 45
      (1 September):965.
           Praises Paul Ferris's biography as an economically and
      gracefully written account that succeeds in debunking the Thomas
      myth "without deflating the man."

46   Review of <u>Dylan Thomas: A Biography</u>. <u>New Yorker</u> 53
      (21 November):230, 233.
           Gives Paul Ferris's biography a favorable notice, espe-
      cially because of its success in depicting Thomas's "intense
      desire" to become a poet.

47   SHAPIRO, HARVEY. "A Conversation with Jimmy Carter." <u>New
      York Times</u>, 19 June, sec. 7, pp. 1, 34.
           Reports how President Jimmy Carter became a devout reader
      of Thomas. During the interview Carter expresses his hope that
      Westminster Abbey would one day recognize Thomas's greatness by
      including him in the Poets' Corner.

48   SHEPPARD, R.Z. "An Inebriate of Words." <u>Time</u> 110
      (31 October):104.
           Reviews Paul Ferris's <u>Dylan Thomas</u>. Criticizes the biog-
      raphy as a "somewhat clinical and dry" account that seems pri-
      marily interested in showing the poet to be a case of "arrested
      adolescence." The book's main flaw is its "failure to render the
      only Dylan Thomas that really counts--the maker of pagan word
      music."

49   TERRELL, CARROLL F. "Thomas' 'Over Sir John's hill.'"
      <u>Explicator</u> 36 (Fall):24-26.
           Explicates the poem by emphasizing the death-in-life theme.
      "Time ordains the continuous overwhelming slaughter."

50   TINNISWOOD, PETER. "It Had to Happen." <u>Times</u> (London),
      21 April, p. 19.
           Reviews Paul Ferris's <u>Dylan Thomas</u> and Daniel Jones's <u>My
      Friend Dylan Thomas</u>, commending both accounts for avoiding
      stereotypical portrayals of a doomed poet. Both writers succeed
      in depicting the importance Wales played in the life and art of
      the man.

51   TOULSON, SHIRLEY. "Do Not Go Gentle." Times Educational
      Supplement, 5 August, p. 14.
          Reviews Paul Ferris's Dylan Thomas, Daniel Jones's My
      Friend Dylan Thomas, and Derek Stanford's Inside the Forties.
      Ferris is given credit for sympathetically depicting the enormous
      price paid by Thomas for a "determined dedication to his art."
      Jones shows that while Thomas was serious about his art he also
      retained a "boisterous" sense of fun with words. A "likeable"
      person emerges from Jones's account. Stanford reminisces about
      the Thomas he knew as part of London's literary scene of the
      forties.

52   VAN WERT, WILLIAM F. "Dylan: A Documentary." Antioch Review
      35 (Spring-Summer):274-82.
          Links Thomas's imagined progress toward decay with the
      fates of two other famous modern figures with like-sounding
      names--Marshall Dillon of Gunsmoke and Bob Dylan.

53   VAUGHAN-THOMAS, WYNFORD. "The Bomb in the Suitcase." Sunday
      Times (London), 17 April, p. 16.
          Tells about finding a forgotten Thomas poem while straight-
      ening old papers. The poem seems to provide the "first faint"
      hints of Under Milk Wood.

*54   WEICK, GEORGE P. "'I, in my intricate image': The Poetic
      Self-Portrait in the Poetry of Dylan Thomas." Ph.D. disser-
      tation, University of London, Queen Mary College.
          See Annual Bibliography of English Language and Literature
      53 (1978):679.

55   WINCH, TERENCE. "Dylan Thomas: Defiant Celtic Soul."
      Washington Post, 30 October, p. E5.
          Reviews Paul Ferris's Dylan Thomas, finding it to be one
      of the best literary biographies of the time. It's "unpreten-
      tious and fair," and it's also more candid than Constantine
      FitzGibbon's polite biography. Thomas was "torn apart" by his
      "identity as a poet." Ferris is very successful in revealing his
      "naked vulnerability."

56   _____. Review of The Death of the King's Canary. Washington
      Post, 12 June, p. E6.
          Gives the satiric novel a negative review. Thomas's col-
      laboration with John Davenport results in a "thin and obscure"
      parody.

57   YOUNG, ALAN. "Radical Tradition: Thomas Hardy and Dylan
      Thomas." Thomas Hardy Yearbook 7:39-47.
          Suggests that important similarities can be discovered
      between Thomas and Hardy, with the ultimate one being the fact
      that both poets could "take a look at the metaphysical Worst"
      and could discover "first hints" of "the Better" side that would
      allow man to remain human.

58 YOW, JOHN. "An Analysis of Dylan Thomas's' 'If I were tickled by the rub of love.'" Studies in Poetry 1:30–35.
Explicates "If I were tickled by the rub of love" for the graduate students' journal of Texas Tech University.

1978

1 BAKER, DENYS VAL. "'A Strange Country to Me': Dylan Thomas and Cornwall." Contemporary Review 233 (December):322–24.
Recounts Thomas's stay in Cornwall and points out the "curiously significant part" it played in his life, most importantly his marriage in Penzance to Caitlin.

2 BROWN, GEOFF. "Under Milk Wood." Plays and Players 25 (August):33.
Reviews the Welsh National Theatre's staging of Under Milk Wood. Although this production is "pleasantly unfussy," it still seems to be an unnecessary offering since the words so clearly "rule over everything."

3 CLARKE, GILLIAN. "In a Grafted Tongue?" Times Educational Supplement, 1 September, p. 14.
Gives Daniel Jones's edition of Dylan Thomas: The Poems a good notice even though many of the new poems previously rejected by the poet himself need not have been included in the volume. Thomas "as often excludes the reader as touches him." The critic is struck by the thought that the poetry gives the sense that "here is language being made without a history." Guesses that "this mysterious, exciting handling of a new stuff" possibly explains the "stir" Thomas's work caused.

4 COSGRAVE, MARY SILVA. "Outlook Tower." Horn Book Magazine 54 (Fall):76–77.
Reviews Paul Ferris's Dylan Thomas, applauding the biography as a "penetrating psychological study" that attempts to separate the facts from the myths surrounding the controversial poet.

5 COSTELLO, TOM. "Dylan Thomas and the October Wind." Anglo-Welsh Review 27 (Autumn):100–110.
Analyzes "Especially when the October Wind." The poem is ultimately about the "creative process itself."

6 DALE-JONES, DON. "Anglo-Welsh Literature in the Schools of Wales." Planet 45/46:26–34.
Discloses that of all the Welsh writers using the English language, Thomas is the most frequently taught in secondary schools in Wales.

7 DAVIE, DONALD. "Frost, Eliot, Thomas, Pound." New York Times, 19 February, sec. 7, pp. 15, 33.
Reviews Donald Hall's Remembering Poets, a reminiscence that is convincing (especially in the case of Thomas and Frost)

due to its being grounded on particular episodes. Agrees with
Hall that great poems are the results of "sanity maintained and
achieved."

8   FERRIS, PAUL. "Dylan: Verbaliser Incarnate." Listener 100
     (9 November):610–11.
         Anticipating the showing of the B.B.C. documentary film
     about Thomas for which he wrote the script, Ferris comments on
     the inspiration and preparation behind the work.

9   FLUDAS, JOHN. "Literary Gossip--The Memoir of a Distinguished
     Quartet." Chicago Tribune, 5 March, sec. 7, p. 3.
         Reviews Donald Hall's Remembering Poets. Thomas is remem-
     bered as "drunk when not hung over, edging closer to death with
     every shot of whisky."

10   FOSBERG, MARY DEE HARRIS. "Dylan Thomas's Use of Roget's
     Thesaurus During Composition of 'Poem on his birthday.'"
     Bibliographical Society of America Papers 72 (October-
     December):505–17.
         Shows how Thomas used Roget's Thesaurus in composing "Poem
     on his birthday." About eight percent (thirty-one words) of the
     words in the poem apparently were drawn from the source. Thomas
     seems to have depended mainly on his own "extensive collection
     of words," however.

11   FRANCO, JUNE W. "'The Living Skein': A Stylistic Study of
     Dylan Thomas." Ph.D. dissertation, North Texas State Univer-
     sity, 158 pp.
         Analyzes Thomas's use of rhythm, syntax, sound, and diction
     in selected early and late poems. The stylistic evidence shows
     that Thomas's later poetry is the "greater achievement," with
     his greatest "virtuosity" residing in the use of sound. See
     Dissertation Abstracts International 39 (1978):1586A.

12   FREEMAN, IRA HENRY. "A Dylan Thomas Pilgrimage to the
     'Strangest Town in Wales.'" New York Times, 9 July, sec. 10,
     pp. 9, 20.
         Takes the reader on a tour of Laugharne, the town Thomas
     once called "the strangest town in Wales." After stopping at all
     the highlights (the Boathouse, Brown's Hotel, the grave, etc.),
     he continues on to Swansea. The tour ends with the note that
     Swansea University College was sponsoring the fifth annual Dylan
     Thomas Summer School.

13   GRIMES, DOROTHY GATLIN. "Phonemes, Distinctive Acoustic Fea-
     tures, and Phonesthemes in Dylan Thomas's Collected Poems: A
     Chronological Study." Ph.D. dissertation, Auburn University,
     382 pp.
         Applying the Trager and Smith notation system, tries to
     discover Thomas's phonological style, specifically with reference
     to the appearance of segmental phonemes and the characteristic
     acoustic qualities. The main difference between the language
     found in Collected Poems and language norm is the greater

frequency of compact consonants and vowels. See <u>Dissertation</u>
<u>Abstracts International</u> 39 (1978):1518A.

14 HALL, DONALD. "Dylan Thomas and Public Suicide." <u>American</u>
    <u>Poetry Review</u> 7 (January-February):7-13.
        Prints a portion from Donald Hall's forthcoming <u>Remembering</u>
    <u>Poets</u> (see 1978.15). Declares that he knew Thomas "only the way
    everyone did--in pubs, late in his short life, drinking, laugh-
    ing, telling stories."

15 _____. "Dylan Thomas and Public Suicide." In <u>Remembering</u>
    <u>Poets: Reminiscences and Opinion: Dylan Thomas, Robert</u>
    <u>Frost, T.S. Eliot, Ezra Pound</u>. New York: Harper & Row,
    pp. 3-37.
        Recalls his acquaintanceship with this "most gregarious"
    of men. Thomas was the "maddest of word-mad young poets," and
    when he became one, he "joined the Devil's party."

16 HEYMANN, C. DAVID. "Poets Behind the Lines." <u>Washington</u>
    <u>Post</u>, 26 February, p. E3.
        Complains that Donald Hall's <u>Remembering Poets</u> has in
    general a superficial quality. The section on Thomas is praise-
    worthy, however, because it skillfully illustrates Thomas's
    "self-destructive drive."

17 HILTON, IAN. "'The Poetic Medicine': Dylan Thomas and
    Germany." <u>Anglo-Welsh Review</u> 27 (Autumn):93-99.
        Looks at Thomas's reading and reviewing experience in
    German literature and at the "surge" of interest in his poetry
    that took place in Germany in the fifties and early sixties.

18 HOLBROOK, DAVID. "Reviews." <u>Anglo-Welsh Review</u> 27 (Spring):
    105-13.
        Reviews Paul Ferris's <u>Dylan Thomas</u> and Daniel Jones's <u>My</u>
    <u>Friend Dylan Thomas</u>, dismissing both biographical works as of
    little value because they fail to provide the essential, critical
    explanation of how the poet "sank from meaning into non-meaning
    and chaos."

19 JONES, TIM. "Poems and Prints to Remember Dylan." <u>Times</u>
    (London), 9 November, p. 1.
        Reports that Thomas "fever" was taking hold in Wales.
    Notes the production of a B.B.C. Wales program focusing on
    Thomas's "genius."

20 _____. "Society Formed to Honour Dylan Thomas." <u>Times</u>
    (London), 7 March, p. 4.
        Reports on the formation of Swansea's Dylan Thomas society.
    At the inaugural meeting Aeronwy read from her father's works.

21 KORG, JACOB. Review of <u>Dylan Thomas: A Biography</u>. <u>Georgia Review</u> 32 (Summer):444.
    Commends Paul Ferris for the extensive research he exhibits in the biography, but finds the account ultimately not very valuable. It has little new to say, and it appears to be guided by a deep suspicion that Thomas's "chronic insecurity" is the central explanation for the man's erratic behavior and his kind of poetry.

22 LLWYD, ALAN. "Cynghanedd and English Poetry." <u>Poetry Wales</u> 14:23-58.
    Points to Thomas as one of the poets who intentionally used the Welsh technique of alliterative and internal rhyme patterns known as cynghanedd.

23 MIDDLETON, DAVID E. "The Ultimate Kingdom: Dylan Thomas's 'Author's Prologue' to <u>Collected Poems</u>." <u>Anglo-Welsh Review</u> 27 (Autumn):111-23.
    Considers the "Author's Prologue" poem as Thomas's final comment on his major themes and his vision of the human situation.

24 MILLER, KARL. "The Outlaw." <u>New York Review of Books</u> 25 (6 April):13-14.
    Reviews Paul Ferris's <u>Dylan Thomas</u>, giving the biography only luke-warm praise because it fails to shed any new light on the connection between the personality and the creations of the controversial poet. Thomas's talent "awoke at puberty with the discovery of his body, and with the discovery that his body was an outlaw."

25 MONTGOMERY, BENILDE. "The Function of Ambiguity in 'A Refusal to Mourn the Death, by Fire, of a Child in London.'" <u>Anglo-Welsh Review</u> 27 (Autumn):125-29.
    Looks at the theme of "negative affirmation" found in "A Refusal to Mourn the Death by Fire." The death of the child is perceived as "a change in the cycle of created matter." The essential conflict in the poem is between Thomas's "self-conscious humanity" and his "all-humbling awareness that certitude leads only to death."

26 NISBET, ROBERT. "Young Dog in Swansea: Dylan Thomas's Artistic Relationship to the People of His Native Town." <u>Planet</u> 45/46:37-41.
    Investigates Thomas's prose that deals with his home town. In these writings, he concentrates on the themes of artistic isolation and Bohemianism. The persona of the creative narrator is that of a loner going on excursions during which he meets up with a variety of grotesques.

27 PIAZZA, PAUL. "Poetic Genius and Extravagant Failings." <u>Chronicle of Higher Education</u> 15 (23 January):18.
    Reviews Paul Ferris's <u>Dylan Thomas</u>, accepting the biography as an authoritative account. Compares Thomas with Delmore

Schwartz, concluding that they both were "their worst enemies."
Speculates that Thomas's poems are so "convoluted" because he
had an "anxiety to conceal his intellectual inadequacy."

*28   RAYNAL, ROSEMARY A.   "Tradition and Imagination in 'Fern
      Hill.'"   Innisfree, pp. 18-25.
      See MLA International Bibliography, 1978, p. 157.

 29   Review of The Death of the King's Canary. Virginia Quarterly
      Review 54 (Winter):23.
         Gives the collaborative work of Thomas and John Davenport
      a favorable notice. It's an "extremely funny" look at the
      "darker side of art."

 30   Review of Dylan Thomas: A Bibliography. Choice 15 (April):
      228.
         Recommends Paul Ferris's biography as a highly successful
      work that, told in a matter-of-fact way, encourages readers to
      "see through . . . the obscuring legend" to the real man and
      artist.

 31   ROBERTSHAW, URSULA.   "Choice for Children."   Illustrated
      London News 266 (December):127.
         Recommends A Child's Christmas in Wales as one of the
      finest Christmas books for children. The book has "magic of a
      potent and particular kind, the humdrum transformed by the vision
      of a poet."

 32   RODMAN, SELDEN.   "Three Neurotics."   National Review 30
      (1 September):1094.
         Compares Thomas with Tennessee Williams and Allen Ginsberg
      during the course of reviewing Paul Ferris's Dylan Thomas. Is
      struck in particular by Thomas's professional "humility," a
      quality lacking in the other two figures. Criticizes the
      biography for relentlessly concentrating on the "undoing" of the
      poet while throwing no meaningful light on the key issue--"how
      the magician of words evolved out of spoiled childhood and pro-
      longed adolescence."

 33   S., P.H.   "The Day that a Welsh Genius Came to Town."   Times
      (London), 16 May, p. 14.
         Summarizes Mark Goulden's recollections about discovering
      Thomas and thinking that a genius had appeared.

 34   SEIB, KENNETH.   "Portrait of the Artist as a Young Dog:
      Dylan's Dubliners."   Modern Fiction Studies 24 (Summer):
      239-46.
         Shows the essential connections between Joyce's Dubliners
      and Thomas's Portrait of the Artist. A careful consideration of
      Thomas's autobiographical stories reveals that they are "artful
      contrivances" that are as complex as some of his best poems.

35   SEYMORE, TRYNTJE VAN NESS. Dylan Thomas' New York. Owings
      Mills, Md.: Stemmer House, 133 pp.
        Highlighting this coffee-table book are pictures and quotes
      that refer to Thomas's experiences in New York.

36   SIMPSON, LOUIS. "The Color of Saying." In A Revolution in
      Taste: Studies of Dylan Thomas, Allen Ginsberg, Sylvia Plath
      and Robert Lowell. New York: Macmillan, pp. 3-42 passim.
        Combines biographical information with critical views of
      Thomas's career and works. While he lived, he "put on a terrific
      show" and he "reminded" people that they shouldn't forget that
      "poetry can be passionate speech, and that this proceeds from the
      life of an individual."

37   THWAITE, ANTHONY. "Dylan Thomas." In Twentieth-Century
      English Poetry: An Introduction. London: Heinemann,
      pp. 72-80.
        Traces Thomas's career, focusing on his stylistic methods,
      especially as they appear in "After the funeral." Not an intel-
      lectual, Thomas had "a narrow, instinctive, original talent" at
      which he worked very hard.

38   VARNEY, RONALD. "Legends to Live By." Sewanee Review 86
      (Spring):xlix, 1, lii.
        Praises Paul Ferris's biography as a "finely-tuned" work.
      Thomas emerges as a man "genuinely obsessed with his vocation."
      Written "with an almost bloodless passion," the study provides a
      great deal of fresh material.

39   WEICK, GEORGE P. "An Error of Transcription in Selected
      Letters of Dylan Thomas." Notes and Queries 25:336.
        Notes an error in the transcription of an important letter
      appearing in Constantine FitzGibbon's edition. Refers the reader
      to Henry Treece's Dylan Thomas: "Dog Among the Fairies" for the
      correct transcription.

40   _____. "Thomas' 'The spire cranes.'" Explicator 37 (Fall):
      21-22.
        Explicates the poem as one primarily concerned with the
      contrast between two types of poetry--that which is guided by
      "classical unity" and that which "exults in a sort of prodigal
      exuberance." In the poem, Thomas illustrates the latter type.

41   _____. "Thomas' 'Was there a time.'" Explicator 37 (Winter):
      26-27.
        Explicates the poem as one concerned with Thomas's per-
      sistent theme of the painful, necessary awareness of mortality.

42   "When We Were Young." Economist 269 (23 December):99.
        Reviews A Child's Christmas in Wales, praising it as a fine
      "celebration of childhood" that gains "incomparably" from Edward
      Ardizzone's illustrations.

1979

1   ACKERMAN, JOHN. Welsh Dylan: Dylan Thomas's Life, Writings, and His Wales. Cardiff: John Jones, 129 pp.
Admits that this book uses largely the material found in his 1964 study, Dylan Thomas: His Life and Work. He stresses, however, that some important new material that helps to illuminate Thomas's life and writing is incorporated. This added information comes from newly available letters and manuscript materials.

2   BENTLEY, GREGORY. "Dylan Thomas in Arcadia: The Pan Motif in the Collected Poems." Anglo-Welsh Review 64:91-104.
Shows that Thomas drew on the Pan tradition for some of his imagery, especially in his last six poems. He developed three aspects of Pan in particular: "Pan as the Universal All, the death of Pan, and Pan as an interior, psychological characteristic of Man."

3   CASTAY, MARIE-THERESE. "Nature and Some Anglo-Welsh Poets." Poetry Wales 15:100-110.
Discusses the important part nature plays in Anglo-Welsh poetry. In Thomas, nature usually appears not for its own celebration but as a means for expressing the themes of childhood and death. Points out the prevalence of earth and tree metaphors in his poetry.

4   FOSBERG, MARY DEE HARRIS. "Dylan Thomas, the Craftsman: Computer Analysis of the Composition of a Poem." Association for Literary and Linguistic Computing Bulletin 7, no. 2: 295-300.
Uses computer programming methodology to analyze Thomas's schematic writing in "Poem on his birthday." The collated data provides a history of the poem's composition and shows how Thomas used Roget's Thesaurus in the process.

5   GINGERICH, MARTIN. "'Especially when the October wind' and the 'Welsh Autumn.'" Anglo-Welsh Review 64:67-73.
Dwells on the important role weather and landscape play in "Especially when the October wind," which is then linked with the other birthday poems.

6   KERTZER, J.M. "'Argument of the Hewn Voice': The Early Poetry of Dylan Thomas." Contemporary Literature 20 (Summer): 293-315.
Considers how, in his early poetry, Thomas attempted to use, display, and dramatize ideas in a persuasive way. Shows that he consciously thought of poetry as a "vehicle of thought, debate, and persuasion"; that he "set himself within his poetic disputes"; and that he at least wished to be logical and systematic in presenting his poetic "arguments." He believed that poetry "must not state, but demonstrate." In his best early poetry, he managed to "reconcile" the faculties of head and heart, and he succeeds in exploiting a "finely crafted confusion"

to dramatize his wish "to understand and free himself or . . . to affirm a self he has failed to understand."

7 KIDDER, RUSHWORTH MOULTON. "Tracing the Pop and Jangle of Four Modern Poets." Christian Science Monitor, 22 January, p. 17.
   Reviews Louis Simpson's A Revolution in Taste, noting the author's view that Thomas was the "icebreaker" of modern poetry, the poet who "ended the Age of Auden."

8 LEVI, PETER. "Honey in the Rocks." New Statesman 98 (20 July):99–100.
   Reviews John Ackerman's Welsh Dylan, finding it a "pleasant memoir" that has nothing new to say about the most complicated issues surrounding Thomas.

9 LEWIS, PETER ELFED. "Under Milk Wood as Radio Poem." Anglo-Welsh Review 64:74–90.
   Argues that Under Milk Wood is as much a radio poem as a radio play. "The lyrical impulse behind his poetry and the comic impulse behind much of his prose . . . came together in the prose-poem-play."

10 McGANN, MARY EVELYN. "Voices from the Dark: A Study of the Radio Achievement of Norman Cornwin, Archibald MacLeish, Louis MacNeice, Dylan Thomas, and Samuel Beckett." Ph.D. dissertation, Indiana University, 316 pp.
    Discusses the radio drama as a uniquely modern form, focusing on the major contributions to the form of five writers. The critical discussion depends essentially on the realization of the radio medium's dramatic nature and psychological force. Thomas's Under Milk Wood is shown to purposely place subjective issues against the public and social activities of the characters. See Dissertation Abstracts International 40 (1979):844A.

11 MIDDLETON, DAVID EDWARD. "Subject-Object Relations: The Romantic Version of an Epistemological Problem and Its Transformation in the Poetry of Dylan Thomas (Volumes I and II)." Ph.D. dissertation, Louisiana State University, 787 pp.
    Examines the reasons behind Thomas's being classified by critics as a romantic poet and undertakes to discover the relation between such romanticism and modernism. Traces the development of Thomas's work through his three recognizable phases, concluding with the discovery that at the very end Thomas did find a satisfactory way in his poetry to assert his vision of imaginative love joined to sacramental landscape, thus resolving the primary romantic issue of the link between the individual and the great world. See Dissertation Abstracts International 40 (1980): 6273A.

12   NISBET, ROBERT. "Dream and Innocence: On Dylan Thomas's
      Prose." Planet 48:37-43.
         Discusses the qualities of Thomas's prose. Influenced by
      his work for radio, much of his prose has a distinctly free-
      flowing, apparently illogical, yet vividly direct essence. In
      much of his prose writing he attempts to merge childhood inno-
      cence and dream. The main problem with Under Milk Wood is the
      failure to merge these two visions satisfactorily. The play
      winds up being too polemical and contains characters who can't
      really be taken seriously.

13   PHILLIPS, ARTHUR. "Dylan under Milkwood." South Atlantic
      Quarterly 78 (Autumn):428-35.
         Shows how much Under Milk Wood was inspired by the actual
      setting of Laugharne and some of its inhabitants. The play
      eventually reveals that the "ever-renewing beauty" of the town
      "was sinking slowly into him."

14   RAWSON, C.J. Review of A Concordance to the Poems of Dylan
      Thomas. Modern Language Review 74 (July):689-90.
         Describes the arrangement of Gary Lane's concordance,
      noting that it is keyed to the 1971 edition of The Poems of
      Dylan Thomas.

15   REID, B.L. "Four Winds." Sewanee Review 87 (Spring):273-88.
         Recalls encounters with Thomas, Frost, Eliot, and Pound.
      Thomas arrived for a reading in a deplorable state, but when he
      started to read "the miracle was immediate and complete." From
      the "ugly disordered body proceeded what seemed the world's most
      beautiful speaking voice, perfectly controlled, in flawless
      performance."

16   SCHMIDT, MICHAEL. "Dylan Thomas." In A Reader's Guide to
      Fifty Modern British Poets. London: Heinemann, pp. 278-84.
         Gives a biographical summary, a survey of the work's char-
      acter and aim, and critical commentary on the distinctive nature
      of Thomas's art. His best poems are marked by the "immediacy of
      their highly wrought language." The feeling that his poems
      "arise from sentiment . . . and resolve themselves in sentiment"
      explains their weaknesses as well as their popularity.

17   SCHWARZ, DANIEL R. "'And the Wild Wings Were Raised':
      Sources and Meaning in Dylan Thomas' 'A Winter's Tale.'"
      Twentieth Century Literature 25 (Spring):85-98.
         Argues that "A Winter's Tale" is perhaps Thomas's "central"
      poem because it "dramatizes how the poet achieves a vision of
      personal salvation through the imaginative process." Writing
      self-consciously against the backdrop of poetic tradition, Thomas
      expresses his belief in the possibility of creative "alterna-
      tives" to "personal despair, political turmoil, and technological
      dehumanization." The poem finally reveals Thomas's "rededication
      to creativity and his own discovery of religious faith."

18 STEPHENS, RAYMOND. "Dylan Thomas and the Biographers."
Planet 48:34-37.
Criticizes the biographies of Constantine FitzGibbon and
Paul Ferris for failing in a major way to bring Thomas to life.
Both fail to explore deeply enough the connection between life
and literature, between the outer and the inner character of a
creative writer. Ultimately, not biographical facts but the
poems themselves best reveal the poet's essential life and
character.

19 SUNDQUIST, ERIC J. "'In Country Heaven': Dylan Thomas and
Rilke." Comparative Literature 31 (Winter):63-78.
Draws comparisons between Thomas's "In Country Heaven"
poems and Rilke's Duino Elegies. Thomas, who once read the
Elegies with excitement, shares a similar final vision and
poetic "terrain." "Both explore a borderline realm inhabited by
the living and the dead, and for both . . . this territory is an
interior psychological construct as well as a projected . . .
world." Thomas's ultimate note of affirmation, however, is
"happier" and more complete than Rilke's.

20 WEICK, GEORGE P. "Thomas' 'It is the sinners' dust-tongued
bell.'" Explicator 38 (Fall):8-10.
Explicates the poem as one dwelling on the images the
living possess of the dead.

21 _____. "Thomas' 'Was there a time.'" Explicator 37 (Winter):
26-27.
Explicates the poem by concentrating on the paradox that
while one is perhaps happier in a state of "blissful ignorance"
one is also "incomplete."

1980

1 ANDERSON, ROBERT M. "Thomas' 'A Refusal to Mourn.'"
Explicator 38 (Summer):36-37.
Notes that the poem contains implanted stylistic effects
indicating the way in which it should be read.

2 FARRINGDON, JILLIAN M., and FARRINGDON, MICHAEL G., eds. A
Concordance and Word-Lists to the Poems of Dylan Thomas.
Oxford: Oxford Microform Publications, 30 pp. and microfiche
slides.
Provides a microfiche concordance keyed to Daniel Jones's
1978 edition of Dylan Thomas: The Poems. Also word lists together with their frequencies are provided.

3 GRAHAM, ROBIN. Wole Soyinka: Obscurity, Romanticism and
Dylan Thomas." In Critical Perspectives on Wole Soyinka.
Edited by James Gibbs. Washington, D.C.: Three Continents,
pp. 213-18.
Uses Thomas as an example of an "Arch-Romantic" whose
writing can lead into a true appreciation of Wole Soyinka's
obscure and "mythic" imagination.

4   GRIMES, DOROTHY G. "Sound and Meaning in Dylan Thomas's 'Author's Prologue.'" University of South Florida Language Quarterly 19:15-18.
        Shows that the texture of sound of "Author's Prologue" is an integral part of the poem's overall theme. Thomas's complex vision is supported by his combined use of density, diffuseness, harshness, and gravity.

5   HEINS, PAUL. Review of A Child's Christmas in Wales. Horn Book Magazine 56 (December):627-28.
        Praises the combination of the vigorous impressionistic quality of the text and Edward Ardizzone's appropriately good-humored illustration of Thomas's tale.

6   LAMB, BRUCE. "Thomas' 'All all and all the dry worlds.'" Explicator 38 (Summer):2-4.
        Explicates the poem as one opposing cyclic to progressive history. The contrast is revealed through reflective imagery and analogous structure.

7   McNULTY, FAITH. "Children's Books for Christmas." New Yorker 56 (1 December):223.
        Finds that A Child's Christmas in Wales is a difficult book for children precisely and ironically because it appears "not so much for a child as by a child."

8   STROUSE, JEAN. "Storybooks for Christmas." Newsweek 96 (1 December):104.
        Recommends A Child's Christmas in Wales as the "perfect coda" to a list of Christmas books.

9   WILLIAMS, ANNE. "Thomas' 'Over Sir John's hill.'" Explicator 38 (Summer):11-13.
        Explicates the poem as a pastoral elegy wherein "natural justice reveals irreconcilable differences between the worlds of mind and of matter."

10   ZARKIN, ROBERT. "Dylan Thomas Growing Up." Plays and Players 27 (March):29.
        Praises Emlyn Williams's one-man show in which he takes Thomas's words and adds the "colour of Theatre" to provide a "memorable evening."

1981

1   "Abbey Place for Dylan Thomas." Times (London), 6 October, p. 26.
        Reports the fact that the Poet's Corner memorial plaque would apparently be placed close to Byron and Hopkins.

2   BURNS, RICHARD. Ceri Richards and Dylan Thomas: Keys to
     Transformation. London: Entiharmon Press, 137 pp.
         Looks at the work of Thomas and Ceri Richards together,
     discovering that the "principle creative impulse which they
     shared was celebration of the recessive feminine principle."
     Points to a number of correspondences between the two artists
     that support the case for discussing them comparatively.

3   "Corner Place for Dylan." Times (London), 19 May, p. 14.
         Announces the success of the effort for Thomas's inclusion
     in the Poets' Corner of Westminster Abbey.

4   LEWIS, PETER. "The Radio Road to Llareggub." In British
     Radio Drama. Edited by John Drakakis. Cambridge: Cambridge
     University Press, pp. 72-110.
         Looks at the growth, history, and critical reputation of
     Under Milk Wood. Points to various misconceptions surrounding
     the radio play, one being that the work represented a radical
     change for the poet. Most of the play's critical misinterpreta-
     tions stem from the failure to relate its essential quality to
     the sound medium for which it was written. Although it's not
     "great literature," it is "great radio."

5   LINEBARGER, J.M. "Thomas' 'The hand that signed the paper.'"
     Explicator 39 (Spring):28-29.
         Suggests that in the poem Thomas is specifically inspired
     by thoughts about the Falange Española, Spain's Fascist party.

6   MILLER, MICHAEL G. "Whitman's Influence on Dylan Thomas's
     'Poem in October.'" Walt Whitman Review 27 (December):
     155-58.
         Presents the case that, based on the similarities found
     between "Poem in October" and "When Lilacs Last in the Dooryard
     Bloom'd" (section 14), Whitman's was a kind of "precursor" of
     Thomas's poem and the American writer may have been "the single
     most important influence" on him. Striking similarities are
     found in setting, action, imagery, phrasing, rhythm, and theme.

7   NOWOTTNY, WINIFRED. "'There was a Savior.'" In The Language
     Poets Use. London: Athlone Press of the University of London,
     pp. 187-219; New York: Oxford University Press, pp. 174-222.
         By carefully explicating "There was a Savior," Nowottny
     discovers that Thomas's style was exceedingly sophisticated and
     suggestive while at the same time having an almost childlike
     directness. Reprint of essay in 1966.8.

8   SONDRUP, STEVEN P. "The Psalm of Nephi: A Lyric Reading."
     Brigham Young Studies 21 (Summer):360-62.
         Refers to Thomas's use of parallelism as an organizing
     principle in the process of discussing the poetic strategies
     employed in "Psalm of Nephi."

9   TINKLER, VALERIA. "Dylan Thomas as Poet and Story-Teller."
    <u>Dutch Quarterly Review of Anglo-American Letters</u> 11, no. 3:
    222-37.
    Assesses the difference between what Thomas achieved in his
    prose as opposed to his poetry. In the end, Thomas's prose is
    especially marked by his "continuous, controlled exploration" of
    human existence.

10 WATSON, PETER. "Disarming Words." <u>Times</u> (London),
    4 November, p. 10.
    Reports on an episode in 1945 when Thomas was in danger of
    being killed by an enraged Greek army captain who exploded into
    a random shooting spree.

                              1982

1   ADUBATO, ROBERT A. Reviews <u>The Doctor and the Devils</u>.
    <u>Theatre Journal</u> 34 (1 March):120-21.
    Reviews Carol Corwen's stage adaptation of <u>The Doctor and
    the Devils</u>. Corwen managed to condense the more than fifty
    original scenes into two acts. Thomas's characteristic "wit and
    cynicism on the vicissitudes of alcohol and other matters are
    apparent" throughout.

2   "Appeal to U.S. Over Sale of Poet's Home." <u>Times</u> (London),
    11 October, p. 2.
    Reports the failure of Swansea's city council to purchase
    Thomas's home and the consequent attempt to find bidders in the
    U.S. and Europe.

3   DALTROFF, LUCY. "Where Dylan Lives On." <u>Sunday Times</u>
    (London), 23 May, p. 9.
    Reports on the official opening of the Boathouse as a
    museum.

4   DILWORTH, THOMAS. "Thomas' 'Poem on his birthday.'"
    <u>Explicator</u> 40 (Winter):5-6.
    Explicates the lines in the poem where the poet counts his
    blessings. The list of blessings "evokes" Thomas's humanity,
    link to the universe, and awareness of time.

5   "Hammer Over Dylan's Home." <u>Sunday Times</u> (London),
    10 October, p. 7.
    Reports on unsuccessful plans to turn Thomas's Swansea home
    into a museum.

6   HARDESTY, MARGARET ANNE. <u>That Momentary Peace, the Poem</u>.
    Washington, D.C.: University Press of America, 169 pp.
    Sees Thomas as a "mediator of a sacramental vision of
    life" and his poetry as "an attempt to establish the harmony and
    communion" between the material and the spiritual worlds. Placed
    against philosophical and literary traditions. Thomas is shown

to be a unique visionary who was primarily concerned with the
problem of "being."

7   HOFFMAN, RICHARD S. "Thomas' 'The Hunchback in the Park.'"
     Explicator 40 (Spring):49.
         Finds that the Garden of Eden legend recurs at the climax
     of the poem.

8   HOLLEY, LINDA TARTE. "Dylan Thomas' 'Fern Hill': The Break-
     ing of the Circles." Concerning Poetry 15 (Fall):59-67.
         Gives "Fern Hill" a close, metaphorical reading. The poem
     "expands" from a "simple-hearted praise" to embrace "so much that
     the vision transcends the linear harmony of microcosmic/
     macrocosmic analogy" and arrives at a "changed state of synthesis
     and 'illimitability.'"

9   HORSNELL, MICHAEL. "Willing for Dylan." Times (London),
     26 January, p. 10.
         Reports the planned participation of Richard Burton and
     others in a memorial concert on behalf of Thomas.

10   KIDDER, RUSHWORTH MOULTON. "Dylan Thomas: Singing Flashes of
     Light." Christian Science Monitor, 10 March, pp. 20-21.
         Declares that, although kept out of sight for most of his
     life, Thomas pursued a "brooding search for an adequate theol-
     ogy." As his career continued, a "curious thing happens: the
     ambiguity recedes, the music strengthens, and his subject turns
     more explicitly to Deity."

11   "Museum Plan for Poet's Home." Times (London), 29 October,
     p. 3.
         Reports the purchase of Thomas's Swansea home by an anony-
     mous buyer who planned to turn it into a museum.

12   NOSAKA, MASASHI. "On Dualism of Consciousness in Dylan
     Thomas." Language and Culture 1:1-22.
         Analyzes the complexity of Thomas's "double" awareness.

13   PFISTER, MANFRED. "Die Villanelle in der englischen moderne
     Joyce, Empson, Dylan Thomas." Archiv für das Studium der
     neueren Sprachen und Literaturen 219:296-312.
         Surveys the tradition of the villanelle in English litera-
     ture, specifically in the writing of Joyce, Empson, and Thomas.
     Discovers an "existential ritual" in "Do not go gentle into that
     good night."

14   ROSENBERG, RUTH. "Thomas' 'Over Sir John's hill.'"
     Explicator 41 (Fall):50.
         Discovers that the source of the refrain in the poem where
     the hawk calls for its victim is a Mother Goose nursery rhyme.

15   SAMSTAG, TONY. "A Big Day for Dylan and St. David." Times
      (London), 2 March, p. 3.
         Reports on the well-attended ceremony celebrating the in-
      clusion of Thomas, the "patron saint of dissolution," in the
      Poets' Corner of Westminster Abbey.

                                    1983

1   ANDREA, MARIANNE. "The Many Faces of Poetry." Queen's
      Quarterly 90 (Winter):1134-44.
         Tries to define poetry, that "most elusive" of art forms.
      Uses a section of Thomas's "Poem in October" to illustrate
      poetry's tendency to employ "charged" language.

2   CROUCH, MARCUS. Review of Dylan Thomas: The Collected
      Stories. School Librarian 31 (December):400.
         Gives the collection only a mildly favorable review notice
      since much of what is contained goes to show just how great an
      artistic gulf exists between Thomas's mature and prentice work.

3   HAMILTON, IAN. "The Artist as a Young Bard." Sunday Times
      (London), 12 June, p. 44.
         Reviews The Collected Stories, emphasizing the fact that
      early on Thomas was just as ambitious for his prose as his
      poetry. His best stories are autobiographical pieces that reveal
      him as an "alienated dreamer" who is at the same time "crafty,
      self-deluding and entirely mockable."

4   HARRIS, JOHN. "Big Daddy Meets the Nogood Boyos: Caradoc,
      Dewi Emrys and Dylan." Poetry Wales 18:43-47.
         Describes the occasions when Thomas visited Caradoc Evans.

5   INGOLDBY, GRACE. "Young Dogs." New Statesman 105 (24 June):
      25.
         Reviews The Collected Stories, concluding that it provides
      a "cubist portrait" that "corrects, alters and simultaneously
      complicates" the picture of the "chameleon" writer. Reading the
      stories in sequence reveals him discovering his "prose-writing
      muscles, flexing them with genius and sadly, eventually, using
      them to throw his weight about a bit."

6   LARRUELLE, DANIÈLE; PIERRON, AGNÈS; ROCHE, DENIS; and ROSS,
      ETHEL. "A propos de Dylan Thomas." Cahiers de la Compagnie
      Madeleine Renaud-Jean Louis Barrault 105:104 pp.
         Celebrates Thomas from a French point-of-view in a special
      issue. The various writers look at Thomas's correspondence with
      Lawrence Durrell, recall vivid memories, consider his character
      make-up, focus on his relation to the amateur theater, look at
      his special quality as a controversial poet, and provide a chron-
      ology and selected bibliography.

7   LEVI, PETER. "Gruesome." Spectator 251 (9 July):22-23.
      Reviews The Collected Stories, finding the earliest samples
"gruesomely pretentious" and the later ones "sad and full of
self-pity." Thomas never developed as a prose writer.

8   O'DONOGHUE, BERNARD. "Gabbing." Poetry Review 73 (Septem-
      ber):74-75.
      Reviews The Collected Stories and finds that reading the
early stories in particular is a "dispiriting experience." They
illustrate the reputation for "misty vaticism" that Celtic literature has generally had. Thomas was "maddened by the image of
the visionary Celtic poet that the literary world told him he
was and that he constantly yearned to be." He lay waste much of
his great talent due to his ambition to reach the "higher
Celticity."

9   ORR, PETER. Review of Dylan Thomas: The Collected Stories.
      British Book News, November, pp. 710-11.
      Praises the collection, concluding it to be the work of an
"immensely gifted prose writer." The finest stories come from
childhood and youth. At his best, Thomas is "acutely observant"
and is "aware of the humour and pathos" of human existence.

10   Review of Dylan Thomas: The Collected Stories. Contemporary
      Review 243 (October):216.
      Posits that the collection is the "surest guide" to
Thomas's development and inspiration.

11   ROBERTS, LYNETTE. "Lynette Roberts: Parts of an Autobiog-
      raphy." Poetry Wales 19:30-50.
      Includes descriptions of several visits Lynette Roberts
made with Dylan and Caitlin Thomas.

12   ROGERS, BYRON. "Portrait of a Friend by Gwen Watkins." Times
      (London), 22 September, p. 9.
      Reviews a memoir by the widow of Vernon Watkins in which
she remembers Thomas. While her husband thought his fellow poet
was a genius, she found him rather "boring."

13   ROSENTHALL, M.L., and GALL, SALLY M. The Modern Poetic
      Sequence: The Genius of Modern Poetry. New York: Oxford
      University Press, pp. 478-80 passim.
      Comments on Thomas's sonnet sequence. "Like so much of
his other writing, it fuses Rabelaisian exuberance, obsession
with the physiology of sex and procreation, Joycean word-play,
and mesmerization by the death-bound journey of individual
lives."

14   SALMON, ARTHUR EDWARD. Poets of the Apocalypse. Boston:
      Twayne Publishers, p. 2, passim.
      Touches on Thomas's connection with the New Apocalypse
movement.

15   SINCLAIR, ANDREW. "A Passionate Sensibility." Times
     (London), 23 June, p. 13.
          Reviews The Collected Stories, noting that the primary
     value of this volume is its sequential arrangement. Discovers
     that the "overwrought quality of the early works . . . gives way
     to the control and rich humour of the later works." The arrange-
     ment reveals the growth and refinement of a "passionate sensi-
     bility."

16   VAN PEER, W. "Poetic Style and Reader Response: An Exercise
     in Empirical Studies." Journal of Literary Semantics 12
     (October):3-18.
          Investigates, with the aid of computer, the kind of liter-
     ary effect certain stylistic devices have on the minds of the
     readers of three selected poems by Emily Dickinson, E.E. Cummings,
     and Thomas ("Was there a time . . .").

17   WEICK, GEORGE P. "Thomas' 'When once the twilight locks no
     longer.'" Explicator 41 (Summer):53-55.
          Explicates the poem as one that moves from "the twilight of
     infancy's murky semi-consciousness," to a loss in imagination,
     then a "fascination" with dying, to a final reawakening into the
     "world of light."

                                  1984

1   CROUCH, MARCUS. Review of A Visit to Grandpa's and Other
     Stories. School Librarian 32 (December):359.
          Recommends the stories especially for reading aloud.

2   JONES, TIM. "Portrait of the Artist in Bronze." Times
     (London), 22 March, p. 4.
          Reports the unveiling in Swansea of a statue of Thomas
     "sitting in a meditative mood." The inscription is taken from
     "Fern Hill."

3   MORRIS, FRANCES. "The Man Who Loved and Haunted Himself."
     Times Literary Supplement, 2 March, p. 227.
          Reviews The Collected Stories, finding that in them Thomas
     is always searching for a "self that eludes him." The earliest
     creations tend to be "strained, inward, vaguely charnel and
     obscene"; in the next phase comic reminiscence dominates;
     finally, the stories become "public, sentimental and detached."

4   PHILIP, NEIL. Review of A Visit to Grandpa's and Other
     Stories. Times Educational Supplement, 19 October, p. 25.
          Praises Thomas's "lyrical evocations" of the early years
     even if the "heady allure" of the rhetoric can suggest a "manu-
     factured quality." An adolescent is especially bound to be
     charmed by the stories concerned with growing up.

5   PIEILLER, EVELYNE. "Au format de poche." Quinzaine litté-
    raire 408:27.
       Notes the emotional nature of Portrait of the Artist.

6   "Poet's Chintzy Bohemia in Camden Town." Times (London),
    10 January, p. 3.
       Reports on the unveiling of a plaque commemorating the
    London house where Thomas lived a "gypsy existence."

7   Review of Dylan Thomas: The Collected Stories. Booklist 80
    (August):1601.
       Recommends the stories both for their striking narrative
    techniques and the "poetic impulse" that pervades them.

8   Review of Dylan Thomas: The Collected Stories. Publishers
    Weekly 226 (13 July):45.
       Discounts the "wellsprings of the lyric poet" marking the
    stories.

9   ROFFMAN, ROSALY De MAIOS. Review of Dylan Thomas: The Col-
    lected Stories. Library Journal 109 (August):1469-70.
       Gives the collection a complimentary notice. Thomas gives
    life to his landscape "by making unexpected connections between
    the geography of nature and the emotions."

10 SEYMORE, JOHN. "When Dylan Meant Thomas." Times Educational
    Supplement, 13 January, p. 25.
       Reviews The Collected Stories. The forty selections,
    "lined up like schoolchildren by age," are provided with Walford
    Davies's "useful" sources and dates notations and Leslie Norris's
    foreword.

11 WATTS, ANN CHALMERS. "Pearl, Inexpressibility, and Poems of
    Human Loss." PMLA 99 (January):35-36.
       Uses "A Refusal to Mourn the Death, by Fire, of a Child in
    London" as an example of a dramatic struggle to express grief
    "against what mere tongues can say."

12 WELCH, DENNIS M. "Antithetical Thinking in Science and Liter-
    ature." Centennial Review 28 (Winter):1-22.
       Uses Thomas as an example of a poet who challenged "anti-
    thetical thinking" by means of his verbal, cognitive, and aes-
    thetic abilities.

                                1985

1   ACKERMAN, JOHN. "Poets as Friends." Poetry Wales 20:59-65.
       Using Gwen Watkins's Portrait of a Friend as a springboard,
    looks at the poetic friendship between Thomas and Vernon Watkins.

2   "Devil Rides Out." Times (London), 29 June, p. 38.
     Summarizes the history of how The Doctor and the Devils
finally was made into the film that the director, Freddie
Francis, denies is a horror movie.

3   "Dylan Thomas Screenplay: Saved from the Grave." Greenville
     (S.C.) News and Piedmont, 10 March, p. 2E.
     Notes that The Doctor and the Devils, Thomas's "very lit-
erary" screenplay originally written for Rank Films, was in
production after previous failed attempts.

4   HOFMANN, MICHAEL. "A History of Inflation." New Statesman
     110 (29 November):34.
     Reviews Paul Ferris's edition of The Collected Letters of
Dylan Thomas. Calls it a "depressing book, full of waste and
(enforced) deceit." Objects especially to the "fawning" letters
in which Thomas is begging for money.

5   KAUFFMANN, STANLEY. "Fall Roundup." New Republic 193
     (18 November):29–30.
     Reviews the film version of The Doctor and the Devils. The
revision of Thomas's script is found wanting. "The clumsily pre-
dicted difficulties are freighted with platitudes of good and
evil."

6   KEEFE, JOAN TRODDEN. "The Graves of Connemara: Ireland's
     Máirtín Ó Cadhain." World Literature Today 59 (Summer):
     363–73.
     Compares Under Milk Wood with Churchyard Clay. Thomas's
work "makes full imaginative use" of the radio medium.

7   KIEFER, BARBARA. Review of A Child's Christmas in Wales.
     Language Arts 62 (December):888.
     Welcomes Holiday House's publication of the Christmas
classic and applauds Trina Schart Hyman's "fresh" illustrations.

8   MAUD, RALPH N. Review of Dylan Thomas: The Collected Stories.
     Choice 22 (May):1337.
     Recommends this amalgamation of material appearing in pre-
vious books primarily for libraries. The foreword by Leslie
Norris should be appreciated by the general reading public.

9   PARK, JAMES. "'Doctor and Devils' Rolls in U.K. 30 Years
     after Script Finished." Variety 318, no. 2:23.
     Recounts the journey of The Doctor and the Devils to the
start of filming decades after the script was first written for
Rank Organization. The final version changes some of the original
structure but keeps most of the language.

10   Review of Dylan Thomas: The Collected Stories. Wilson
     Quarterly 9 (Spring):150–51.
     Offers the collection as proof of Thomas's great gift for
spinning tales. Gives special praise to the early "haunting,
somber fantasies," surreal stories concerned with weird and
deadly events.

11   Review of <u>The Collected Letters of Dylan Thomas</u>. <u>Economist</u>
     297 (7 December):101-2.
         Describes the essence of what is revealed in Paul Ferris's
     edition of Thomas letters. He "lived fast and died young before
     it became fashionable."

12   Review of <u>The Outing</u>. <u>Contemporary Review</u> 247 (November):280.
         Welcomes J.M. Dent's publication of this "delightful" tale
     which is illustrated by Paul Cox.

13   TIGHE, CARL. "Kitsch Sinks Drama." <u>Drama</u> 155 (First
     Quarter):44-45.
         Reviews the New Vic's production of <u>Under Milk Wood</u>, find-
     ing it a serious mistake to place "this superb" creation on the
     stage, especially if its "Welshness" is paraded like a banner.

14   WHITTINGTON-EGAN, RICHARD. "Dylan Thomas: Collected
     Letters." <u>Contemporary Review</u> 247 (November):278-79.
         Reviews Paul Ferris's edition of <u>The Collected Letters of</u>
     <u>Dylan Thomas</u>. The letters "demonstrate irrefutably" Thomas's
     "poet's eye and ear." Ferris's editing work illuminates
     "without intrusion."

Index

Index

Index

212